Samantha Irby

wow, no thank you.

〜〜〜〜〜〜〜

Samantha Irby is a writer whose
work you can find on the Internet.

www.bitchesgottaeat.com
www.bitchesgottaeat.substack.com

wow, no thank you.

wow, no thank you.

ESSAYS

VINTAGE BOOKS

A Division of Penguin Random House LLC

New York

A VINTAGE BOOKS ORIGINAL, MARCH 2020

Copyright © 2020 by Samantha Irby

All rights reserved. Published in the United States by
Vintage Books, a division of Penguin Random House LLC,
New York, and distributed in Canada by Penguin Random
House Canada Limited, Toronto.

Vintage and colophon are registered trademarks of
Penguin Random House LLC.

"country crock" first published, in different form, in
Nasty Women: Feminism, Resistance, and Revolution in Trump's America
(Macmillan Publishing Group, 2017), and "hysterical!" first published,
in slightly different form, in *Gay Mag* on April 10, 2018.

The Cataloging-in-Publication Data is available
at the Library of Congress.

Vintage Books Trade Paperback ISBN: 978-0-525-56348-8
eBook ISBN: 978-0-525-56349-5

Book design by Anna B. Knighton

www.vintagebooks.com

Printed in the United States of America
10 9 8 7 6 5 4 3 2 1

This book is dedicated to Wellbutrin.

CONTENTS

wow, no thank you.

into the gross

I live for a glamorous lifestyle blog featuring some gorgeous ingenue with piles of secret wealth that she never divulges to the unsuspecting slobs on the other side of the screen. How does she afford three-hundred-dollar eye cream if her job is listed as "freelance editor," and why is it tossed so casually on her nightstand like she wouldn't cry if she lost it? I want to admire her floating through a bright and clean apartment in photos so beautiful and overexposed that it hurts your ugly regular-person eyes to look at them as she describes the minutiae of her daily routines, but all the cat dander clouding my eyes makes it difficult. "Maybe I should try alkaline water," I murmur to myself, as I squint through the unidentifiable goo dried on my phone screen, making a mental note to look up what "adaptogens" are after I search for the cheapest gratitude journal on Amazon. "Wow, she got that skin just from vitamins??" I sigh, taking a sip of a warm Crush grape soda I opened either three hours or three days ago. I subscribe to so many of these blogs and newsletters, I can't even tell them apart. Partly, I'm curious about the stuff people buy (oh, I am not curious I am actually obsessed and, if I pee at your house, I will make note of the hand soap you use and immediately copy you if it's fancier than mine, but in an admiring way not a *Single White Female* way, I promise). But mostly it's just straight-up awe, because I love STUFF so fucking much, and I want to know how people get to be so pretty and chic.

I buy a lot of face washes from targeted Instagram ads, but no one gives a shit about what I use probably because I have chin whiskers? Plus, if a hip photographer with cool shoes came to my home, the cats would definitely bite her and we don't have a single glamorous white wall to use as a backdrop. Even if we did, would anyone be interested in pictures of my stacks of discounted K-Beauty face masks from Big Lots? Um no!!! Still, being featured on a stylish lifestyle blog is my biggest secret dream, and because I am too disgusting to ever be asked in real life, I want to tell you how mine would go:

I like to wake up naturally, gripped by a heart-pounding panic as the sun slices through my eyelids at noon, when it is perfectly aligned with my bedroom windows. I wince against the sun's garish rays, a sick feeling spreading through me. It dawns on me that I have already wasted an entire day. AGAIN. I grimace loudly as I slide off the bed and feel around blindly with my toes for the orthopedic flip-flops I keep close enough to find without my glasses on. Sure, I probably could shuffle to the bathroom gripping every flat surface I come into contact with along the way, but who are we kidding? I desperately need the arch support. I have to pee since I've been horizontal for several hours, and all the fluid on my legs has pooled backward (upward? what is physiology?) into my bladder. Then I grope through all the bottles in the medicine cabinet until I find the one that feels like Aleve. I get the liquid-gel capsules because they look more science-y and futuristic, and after fumbling with the arthritis cap, I get one lodged in my esophagus despite the fact that I have dislocated my neck desperately lapping at lukewarm faucet water as it slips through my cupped fingers to wash it down. It crosses my mind that I should just stagger back to my room and get in bed and try again tomorrow but—guilt! So I return to the toilet instead (my Kegel muscles no longer hold urine in like they used to) and will myself to just turn the shower on. *Turn it on, just turn it on, you can do it, turn it on.* I risk shattering my phone in the sink trying to queue up a podcast, probably *Who? Weekly* or *The Read*, which I listen to because they're both very popular and entertaining, but also, if I turn the volume all the way up, it helps to drown out the noise of my washing. I consider doing a single one of the approximately ninety-six beauty treatments littering the vanity and erupting out of the plastic shoeboxes I hide them from my wife in, but I already drank a tablespoon of water, so what else is there even to do?

In the shower, I use a big block of Irish Spring and because I am black, I was raised to always use a washcloth no matter what, so I do. I also scrub my scalp vigorously with anti-dandruff shampoo, which is a thing beautiful people never have to use. (Just once, I want to read one of these profiles where a slender, shiny-toothed model is like, "Hey, bitch, I have psoriasis!" while aggressively slathering T/Gel onto her roots.) I don't shave my armpits or legs, but somehow I still take an inordinately long time to get clean. After my shower, I use Neutrogena body oil, because you can get a giant bottle super cheap at Target and it smells like rich people. My towel smells like mildew, but I ignore it!

Yoga, meditation, and calming morning rituals are for people who actually wake up in the morning, so instead I skip all that and launch into my day, gathering everything I brought up to bed last night when I was pretending I might work instead of watching TV. I load it all into the pink Baggu I schlep with me from room to room, because, listen, I am not walking back up these stairs until nighttime. I wear the same thing pretty much every day: a tucked-in T-shirt, high-waisted sloth pants, and a Madewell sweatshirt. Despite my having what is obviously an impossibly flashy and lavish life-style, I regret to inform you that Madewell is not a sponsor.

Breakfast was over four hours ago, so I start with lunch. I once read one of these profiles where the woman featured talked about alkalizing her body at the start of the day with lemon water, and I am being 100 percent sincere when I say that sentences like that fucking mystify me. What does that mean? How did she learn those words?? I go to the doctor every other day and never has one of them told me about alkalization. Alkalining? Alkalinization? THE NEED TO BE ALKALIZED. I'm in awe of people who talk like that with a straight face, and let me tell you: the shit stuck. So now I start my morning (I mean, afternoon) by drink-ing some room-temperature water from the pitcher on the counter with a few slices of Meyer lemon from those little bags of them you can get at Trader Joe's. It has done abso-lutely nothing for me, from what I can tell, but later on, when I eat an entire jalapeño-and-pepperoni pizza and feel bad about it, I can think to myself, "Bitch, remember when you alkalized?!" and feel clean.

We live up the street from a middle school, and children are already on their way home, for fuck's sake, so I don't feel bad having six Diet Cokes in a row. I'll finish my water, but, like, I don't ever want to be *too* hydrated. All these magazines tell you how you should really be drinking your weight in water every day, and all these movie stars would have you believe their skin glows because of that water bottle they're carrying around, and I believe them, but also, why doesn't anyone ever talk about how much peeing you will have to do? I no longer have a pelvic floor, Jennifer Aniston. I cannot just be gulping down smartwater with reckless abandon!

After consuming all the liquids I'm going to for the entire day, I settle down to work, which I'm really going to do as soon as I put on a little cream highlighter and blush that no one else is ever going to see. My work: I occasionally write jokes on the Internet for free because I am the last person on Earth who still has a blog. Sometimes I have freelance projects, but there's nothing right now. No one is going to pay me to write another book about nothing for at least the next two years. Unfortunately, I don't have anything new or exciting to say online and absolutely zero paying scams, so my heart sinks as it dawns on me that I have gotten up and gotten dressed just to read what other people are saying on Twitter. This is the glamorous life of a writer!

After feeling like a boring failure for a while, I pivot to watching TV. If I don't want to feel like a total scumbag, I'll watch something on the iPad, which I can quickly disguise as work if, oh, I don't know, the mailman glances through the blinds while delivering my many boxes from Amazon Prime. Now would be a great time to snack on some quick-pickled beans or fermented slaw, but I am a regular person, so I dig through the pantry to find half a bag of sourdough pretzels I remember leaving in there a week ago and a jar of creamy Jif. Some people would warn you that that's just eating one type of sugar smeared on top of another kind, and I would agree with them. I could really go for a fresh cold-pressed juice, but I don't live in Brooklyn, so I settle for the next best thing: another Diet Coke.

Okay, so here's the part in the profile where the model meets up with an equally attractive non-model friend someplace cool. The reader is flooded with envy because she doesn't have (1) friends or (2) cool places to go, and the models are always like, "Oh, tra-la-la, I walked seventeen blocks in these heels I'm posing in to meet up with my girl Monica at a vinyl-only music shop to listen to some vintage hard bop records, and then we walked twenty-three more blocks to get affogatos at this hidden gem that you can only enter through a portal, and after that we went to SoulCycle." I'm winded just reading that. My afternoons are always like, "searched through all my jacket pockets to find a half-melted lip balm before catching the cat eating its own vomit off the kitchen rug," but since you're here taking my picture, I am going to light this fancy candle from Diptyque, pretend it doesn't make me sneeze, and scroll through shit on my phone while trying to look pensive.

My evening routine is pretty simple. My lady comes home from work and we'll opt for something light for dinner, maybe some sous vide chicken and fresh steamed vegetables from the market, followed by one glass of wine and a single square of 70 percent dark chocolate, consumed while fully clothed on a white couch in front of a tastefully sized television playing a chic foreign film. Wow, I'm sorry, let me try that again.

My lady comes home and grimaces silently at the pile of mail I've left unopened on the table, simultaneously shrugging out of her coat while uncorking a bottle of white wine from Walgreens with her teeth. She gets into her pajamas, and I scramble to boil water for pasta and throw whatever is in the vegetable crisper into a pan to make sauce. Then we eat in our sweatshirts in front of whatever soap opera is on while yelling at the cats to stop jumping up onto the stove. This lasts for approximately forty-five minutes before she is asleep, curled around her wineglass in the corner of the couch, and I try to finish her food as quietly as possible and change the channel to wrestling.

At night, there are many soothing rituals I could perform. I could put on a pot of tea or light some calming incense or put on a collagen mask or rub some moisturizing cream into my hands, but you know what? I don't live like that! I put all my stuff back in my Baggu, and I drag it upstairs. Then I clean the tank of my sleep machine with vinegar and take all my pills so I hopefully don't die during the night, and then I pretend I'm going to read but instead I put the news on our BEDROOM TELEVISION SET and worry about the state of the world.

At eleven thirty or so, I remember that despite not having left the house all day, I'm still wearing a bunch of old makeup, so I get out of bed and use one of those time-saving cleansing wipes you have to use three of to clean my face while I brush my teeth, which, honestly, I wouldn't have done if I didn't also have to pee. There's a bunch of little oil droppers on my bedside table that would look really cute in a still life if they weren't next to toppled bottles of potassium supplements and industrial-strength callous creams, but I sort through them and extract one rosehip oil (for my face) and one oregano oil (for under my tongue). I use the rosehip so my skin continues to glow with the health and vitality of a newborn, despite my salt intake, and the oregano is a holdover from when I had thrush that I just keep taking because I haven't had thrush again since then, and, also, why the fuck not? I roll some compression hose onto my legs to remind myself that I am sexy, and change into pajamas that look exactly like the clothes I wore all day, which are folded atop the hamper because I will be wearing those same things again tomorrow.

I watch Brian Williams and some reruns of Rachel Maddow and Chris Hayes, and pretend I understand what is happening in the world. Then I set the sleep timer before burrowing beneath this T.J.Maxx comforter that has been surprisingly durable, and I drift off to dream of adaptogens and other beneficial herbs. Which I will never take.

girls gone mild

My lady and I were out getting hammered at the local watering hole on a weeknight and feeling like cool olds, when the waiter asked if it was "moms' night out," while offering to explain to us what whiskey is. And now I'm a corpse—please bury me in my L.L.Bean comfort fleece.

ME: "Excuse me, I have tattoos, *Jeff*."

HIM: "Oh my goodness, ma'am, I'm so sorry, I just saw the fluid collecting at your ankles and assumed—"

What the fuck is happening to my life? What vibe am I giving off? Yes, I am wearing soft, pull-on, straight-leg Gloria Vanderbilts, but I also have cool glasses and a motherfucking hand tattoo. Couldn't it just be middle school art teachers' happy hour, Jeff?! I should write a girls' night out movie. But a realistic one, featuring people my age who have neck pain and no cartilage in their knees and spend the entire movie trying to calculate how to split a check and figure out the tip across four different cards. Or two women with questionable credit try to rent a car on their way to a wellness retreat neither of them can afford and the teenager behind the Enterprise counter asks them to show nine different forms of identification. A group of friends goes on a wild Caribbean cruise, and "when things get spicy, they get heartburn." (That's the poster.)

I used to party a lot. The only reason I stopped is because I got too old to do it right. Also I moved to a town where the most popular bar has a mechanical bull. I spent two months on the road once when I was nearing the end of my thirties, lugging around a bright orange suitcase full of disposable underwear plus a bunch of impractical shit I thought I was going to need to wear to become a different person, and I tried to party again. Here's how that went.

8:30 a.m.: pry eyes open at the sound of the alarm.
That's right, preparation for Girls' Night Out starts in the morning at this age.

When I was a kid, I could work a full eleven-hour shift on four hours of sleep, change my shoes and put mascara on in the back of a moving cab, and go from drinks to dinner to the club without a second thought. When I turned twenty-one, my roommate in Chicago was this old queen who worked a corporate job and partied five out of six nights and almost never went to bed. Every other night he was at clubs like Manhole (RIP) or Berlin dancing with his shirt off, his waxed chest glistening as he worked his hips to the *unce-unce-unce* of a European house beat. Then he'd cruise home at four in the morning, brew a pot of coffee, and have a suit on by seven. When I told him I was finally going to be of legal drinking age, he arranged a weeklong celebration: a group of his friends and I were going to hit a different club in Boystown every night for a solid week. The first night, on my birthday proper, was at a gay bar called Roscoe's, which I clearly remember because I was wearing fuchsia bell-bottoms and a sheer shirt, and how the fuck could I ever forget that? My birthday is the day before Valentine's Day, and Chicago is always a freezing, slushy mess. At some point in the wee hours, I misplaced my shoes (read: took them off because they were hurting me, and fucked around and forgot where I put them) and left the bar after dancing all night in bare feet and, as my mother would say, with my chest all exposed. I woke up the next morning and went to work with a fever. I went to the Jackhammer later that night, and I went to Sidetrack the night after that, and then the night after *that* I died and now my ghost is writing this.

9:00 a.m.: lie very still and contemplate getting up.

I can't just wake and pop right out of bed like someone in a commercial for antidepressants. I have to summon the will. In the minutes after I groan myself awake, I lie there taking a mental inventory of all my various aches and pains: *Oh, my lower back is sore, must've slept funny during the night. . . . Wow, the fingers on my left hand are numb, clearly I forgot to wear my carpal tunnel brace to sleep . . . If I don't move a single muscle, how long can I get away with not peeing?* Also for the past few years I have been having very vivid near-nightmares every single night, and I like to use my lying-down morning time to reflect on them and try to figure out if the one I just woke up from is proof that I've finally lost it. Here's an example of a dream I had on February 2, 2018, which I immediately wrote down so I could tell my Internet therapist about it:

> I agreed to house-sit former attorney general Eric Holder's giant, rambunctious Bernese mountain dog? At the beginning of the dream I have this horrifying feeling in the pit of my stomach because it dawns on me that I was supposed to start taking care of the dog days ago and not only has he been all alone in the house, where he's likely been shitting all over everything and knocked over the refrigerator trying to get at some food, but this fucking dog has been left alone in Eric Fucking Holder's house and I'm probably going to get sued and definitely going to lose when I do. Inexplicably, Amy Poehler (is she even friends with Mr. Holder?) was at the house (RANSACKED) when I got there and was in the kitchen (COVERED IN TRASH) talking on the phone and writing down all the damages my negligence had caused, while the dog chewed on a designer shoe in the corner of the room. I never met the attorney general—he never came home, at least not while I was there—but Amy ended her conversation and was very pleasant to me despite standing in the middle of canine wreckage that was absolutely my fault.

I'm not sure how this dream ended—the endings are always hazy—but I remember waking up and thinking, "WHAT THE FUCK IS MY PROBLEM?"

10:30 a.m.: consider showering.

I don't know if this is middle age or what, but if I'm going to go to a thing, I like to bathe right before the thing happens so anyone I might encounter will know that I am a clean and virtuous person who cares about presenting her best self to the world. I am not that person, but if you ran into me at a party, I could probably convince you otherwise. But I cannot muster the strength to shower two times in one day, unless there has been an incontinence emergency, and even then I'm only washing from the waist down. So on event days I face this conundrum: shower in the morning and try not to ruin it by being a gross asshole, or be disgusting all day then shower right before the event.

I decide to skip the morning shower and instead drink a bunch of lemon water to wash down a handful of Advil and the assorted giant vitamins I've decided to start taking this year instead of going to the doctor.

11 a.m.: should i eat?

So here is the thing about carting around a bowel disease when you actually have to leave your home and do things out in the world: you're always thinking, "What if I have to poop?" I'm not shy. My favorite thing to do in a public restroom, other than cruise for closeted gay politicians with whom to have loud anal sex, is to get comfortable in the stall with my butt directly on the seat and poop like a person who understands that this is a normal function of my human body. I don't love to go number two during a night out on the town because: (1) guaranteed it's going to be a mess, and (2) the bathroom at the club is probably not the most relaxing place to completely unclench your sphincter and get out a healthy, fiber-fortified stool. I'm not saying I *haven't* had explosive diarrhea while holding up my ill-fitting sequined skirt with both hands, party clutch full of valet stubs and coat check tickets clenched between my teeth, while a line of drunk party animals whine collectively because there's only one stall, but those were definitely emergencies. Which brings us back to my original dilemma: What is there to eat in this place that won't cause me agony in the middle of the dance floor? I select a banana from the stash of emergency food I got at the airport and hastily shoved into my purse at the cab stand.

12:15 p.m.: quickly cycle through all five kübler-ross stages of impending-social-engagement dismay.

1. Denial: "Did I really tell homegirl I would meet her for dinner and drinks tonight, or is this a dream?"
2. Anger: "WHY THE FUCK DID I AGREE TO THIS I HATE GOING PLACES AND DOING THINGS WHY WOULD THEY EVEN INVITE ME?"
3. Bargaining: "If I go to this restaurant tonight, and I tell some jokes and act real sweet, I will keep this friendship intact, plus I won't have to make up a transparent lie or sneak around trying not to like shit on Instagram, and also I don't ever have to leave my crib ever again."
4. Depression: "Is there anything worse in life than someone wanting to hang out with me? Especially in

a fancy bar that serves 'handcrafted' cocktails? Maybe I can throw myself off the organic rooftop urban garden and end this miserable charade for good."

5. Acceptance: "Fine then, I'ma just watch four episodes of *SVU* and eat saltines with my shoes on until it's time to call a Lyft."

12:30 p.m.: in the old days, i would do something to my eyebrows and nails.

I used to like to go out to get wasted with my friends and dance to house music, but also I was aggressively hunting for people to mate with. The year 2002 was a less cynical time, and the possibility of glancing up from my nine-dollar Stoli Razberi and 7UP with a lime to find myself locking eyes with my future soul mate while a Crystal Waters deep house remix pulsed in the background felt (at least to me, a very naive person) like a real thing that could happen. To prepare, in case it did, I would walk down the block to the nail shop after work and get a polish change (two coats professionally applied to my natural, bitten-down nails for half the price of a regular manicure, a dirtbag life hack) and an eyebrow wax.

Would anyone notice my scuffed red polish and brows stripped thin enough to slice deli meat in a strobe-lit disco? Definitely not. But what if someone fell in love with me on the dance floor and invited me back to the apartment they shared with nine roommates to drunkenly hump me before passing out at dawn? I needed them to know that I was worthy of their attention, and clearly the only way to do that was to pay someone to push back my ragged cuticles! Nowadays, who even cares? I don't think my wife even notices that I *have* nails. Instead, I use this time to make a plan for the evening, i.e., imagine, in excruciating detail, all the things that could go wrong.

12:40 p.m.: start making the plan.

Remember when you could be roused from a night being spent on the couch in your pajamas, curled around a pint of Chubby Hubby, and goaded into joining your friends at the bar even though you'd already taken off your bra? Yeah, I can't either, but I know those days existed. I have the liver damage to prove it. Now when I go out I have to start gearing up for that shit at least three days in advance, and if I'm actually going to go through with it, it has to include both an ironclad reservation and a reliable seating arrangement. Showing up at a restaurant and hoping for the best is a young person's game. If I'm going out, I need to know that there is a table with my name on it and a comfortable seat pulled up to it. I'm too old to hover anxiously near the door, sweating under my coat in my good outside clothes, watching people who actually planned ahead be ushered to their awaiting tables and served the foods I am dying to eat.

I'm not that organized, though, so I spend a long time scrolling through OpenTable to try to find a reservation for 7 p.m. at a place that has more than a few high-tops left and won't attempt to put us outside. It's slim pickings.

1:00 p.m.: get the text chain going.

I'm going out tonight with three people who all get along, and I don't mean that they can endure each other for two hours without scratching one another's eyes out. I mean they have relationships that are established enough that I don't have to spend the whole time babysitting them or pointing out the things they have in common. In the past, I would have been just fine being the common thread in a random group of people and spending my entire night bouncing from person to person screaming, "You like pasta, right? So does Melissa! Talk to her about it!" or "Emily has a weird boy-friend, too! Discuss!" and trying to make a group of virtual strangers feel comfortable while low-key ruining my own good time. It's exhausting, and inevitably one person hates another person, and then you have to defend the bad person to the good person, while internally questioning both of these stupid friendships, and *why the fuck am I doing this again?* Now I just ask the group chat if they want to go out.

3:30 p.m.: either a coffee or a nap.
It's the aging club kid's Sophie's choice: drink a giant watery espresso and risk further aggravating my irritated colon, or lie down for a refreshing ten-minute disco nap and wake up at seven the next morning. Both have their advantages. Cof-fee is cheap and readily available; or, if I overshoot my nap, I won't have to go out and party! It's usually around this time in the afternoon that I start rethinking my later commit-ments, no matter what the fuck they are. An eight o'clock movie on Tuesday night sounded plausible last Thursday, but now it's Tuesday afternoon. I just had a lot of soup deliv-ered while squinting at the laptop in my office, and now I don't think I'm going to be able to make that movie, okay? Going out on Saturday night sounded great on Wednesday,

but now Saturday is here and I'm in my cozy clothes and I've got Joni Mitchell's *Court and Spark* playing on this phone I've propped in a glass because I couldn't connect to the Bluetooth speaker and it's gonna be really hard to put shoes on, dawg. It's extremely hard to motivate myself to get to a place where I'm required to pay a twenty-dollar cover to get hip-checked by linebackers in church shoes all night, especially when I could just get back in my warm bed and NOT DO THAT. I decide on a coffee, because housekeeping is outside my room and I will literally die of shame if I am just lazily lying around in the afternoon half-sleeping while people are at work vacuuming, plus there is a Starbucks in the lobby of this hotel. Convenience is the number one driver of everything I do.

5:00 p.m.: it's put-up-or-shut-up time.

This is the absolute latest I can cancel without pissing off my friends. An hour ago would have been preferable, but it's really unlikely that anyone has already started prepping with two hours to go. The crime isn't bailing on the night. The crime is bailing on the night after hair has been shampooed and meticulously styled and Spanx have been squeezed into. If I've put on a real bra and you pick up the phone to tell me some shit about a headache, I'll meet you at the club with some Excedrin, bitch.

5:15 p.m.: the slog begins.

I've just spent an hour regularly checking my phone in the hopes that someone else would cancel, but they haven't, so I guess it's time to wash. First, I'm going to take a few Imodium in case my intestinal tract decides to get cute. Which it definitely will, either because or in spite of the fact that all I've consumed in preparation for this evening is a banana and a Luna Bar and three glasses of water (for health). And I'm not actually watching this movie, just putting it on so I have some comforting background noise. (Okay, fine, I'm watching it a little, but it's not going to make me late, I swear.) Now would be a good time to clear out my junk e-mails since my laptop is open anyway, but somehow I resist. I should also probably eat some dry toast in the shower so that my drinks have something soft to cushion their landing, then do my hair on the toilet, because the way my bladder works now is that I could just keep peeing forever if I wanted to. I'm perimenopausal and constantly dribbling. I definitely should pull out my best dark pants.

5:45 p.m.: "will anyone notice . . . ?"

. . . that these shoes are FitFlops and I didn't paint my toes? . . . that I messed up my eyeliner? . . . that these pants don't really fit right? . . . if I wear underwear that goes all the way up to my chin? . . . that I've stopped aggressively exfoliating? . . . that I didn't spend enough time with a comb? . . . that on the left side, my lipstick extends a centimeter above my top lip? . . . that there's an eensy-weensy, teeny little piece of tape on these glasses? . . . that this ill-fitting bralette is giving me quadra-boob? . . . my hair, which isn't curling right? . . . that I really did use tweezers, I swear? . . . that I recently switched to natural deodorant?

6:00 p.m.: panic city.

This is usually when I start worrying that some combination of lateness and extreme anxiety is going to ruin the evening for me, and tonight is no different. I'm sitting on the side of the bed and I've already unsuccessfully tried on:

a sequined top (why on Earth did I buy that?)
a cold-shoulder sweater that obviously snuck into my fucking closet
boots with a conservative heel (wtf)
jeggings (um, I do not believe in clothes I have to peel *on*—this is a violation)
lace (itchy)
something called "tapered peg leg trousers" (just use your imagination)

Not only do I have to throw all these clothes in the garbage before I leave, but I also have to seriously evaluate who the fuck I thought I was buying these clothes for, since obviously it wasn't me. I like to wear nightgowns from Lands' End. Why are there zippered pants in this suitcase? Who okayed the stabby underwire bra? No time for an existential crisis like the present, and honestly, when better to slide down a self-esteem spiral than when a cab is outside with the meter running and I'm about to embark on a full evening of casual judgment from inebriated strangers? It's obviously the perfect time to rip the lid off Pandora's box and launch a deep investigation into Why I Buy So Much Aspirational Clothing, right? I know my friends are currently putting on one final swipe of mascara while getting ready to walk out the door, but instead of getting my shit together, I'm trying to exorcise the demon inside me that purchased a fitted satin skirt.

6:10 p.m.: this is fine.

I've been sleeping in these high-waisted, black yoga pants and a scoop-neck T-shirt that has gone loose around the collar since my book tour stop in Omaha, so why not keep the party going and wear them out? I mean, who's going to know. Okay, let's be nakedly honest: I am wearing actual pajamas, not just real clothes I've fallen asleep in. I'm talking a nondescript pile of gauzy black fabrics that came from the sleepwear section at Kohl's, worn outside of my house, where other people can see them. And not just to the grocery store—I mean I've worn them in meetings. During interviews. Onstage. These days, disgusting cozy clothes are my main sartorial vibe.

One Saturday night, in my early twenties, I was sitting alone on the floor in my room watching rom-coms on my combination television and VCR in the apartment I shared with my old roommate Joseph, who by that time was already knee-deep in his evening's festivities, I'm sure, when our house phone rang. It was never for me, but I answered it anyway, and it was a girl whose friendship I maintained mostly because we liked to go dancing at the same Chicago clubs. And by "dance" I mean "drink a lot and sway." I couldn't tell you whether she liked horror movies or what kind of cell phone she had or if she was a vegetarian, but I knew that bitch liked a Grey Goose L'Orange with soda, no ice. It was after eleven when I brushed the crumbs off my sweatpants to get up and answer the phone, and if then was now, I would have had a hearty laugh at her proposition that I leave my warm apartment in the dead of night to meet her downtown in a dark warehouse with no chairs, but once upon a time I was fun, so I struggled into a tight pair of *magenta polyester bell-bottoms* and *a shiny silver shirt* (imagine this, I dare you), then took the bus (!) downtown, where I met her outside a club called Ontourage, spelled with an O because it was on Ontario Street. That's the only thing you need to know to formulate an accurate mental picture of exactly what that place was like. Dudes with fresh fades wearing sunglasses at midnight accompanied gorgeous half-naked women on stilts past the bouncer, who was collecting twenty-dollar covers, and I was there dressed like I was about to shimmy down the *Soul Train* line. I paid the cover with a collection of crumpled bills I dug out of the couch cushions (I am not and have never been cute enough to have the charge dismissed) and was ushered into the cavernous club, where I made a beeline for the bar. I jammed myself between several men in silk, collared shirts (this place had a dress code, because it was all class, you see) and ordered a gin and tonic, which a young man wearing many chains over his T-shirt slithered over and paid for, unprompted. An hour later, he had purchased several more and per the terms of our unspoken nightlife contract was allowed to surreptitiously grind against my outer thigh in a far corner of the dance floor next to a speaker, while drunkenly slurring, "Let me see that ass," into the side of my neck to the tune of "U Know What's Up." My neurotransmitters and synapses dulled by watered-down Tanqueray, I took him literally (omg) and proceeded to remove my pants in the middle of a fucking disco. I know that the mental image this creates is one in which I effortlessly slip a pair of silky trousers down my unstubbled legs and gracefully step out of them in one smooth motion, but nah—sweat and humidity (and possibly urine?) had given my pants an adhesive quality that required my tugging them over my thighs inch by constricting inch. At no point did anyone in close proximity grab my arm and ask just what the fuck I was doing, and my new boyfriend was clearly thrilled at the return he was getting on his investment (my stark white underpants glowing fluorescent under the neon lights). So when I was asked by security to leave the premises, I did so in a pair of Just My Size Cool Comfort™ briefs, with my soaking-wet glue pants balled up in my hand.

But tonight, the waist of my loose-fitting yoga pants is so high that I can tuck my nipples into it, which I am doing.

6:55 p.m.: i'm not that late.

If my Lyft doesn't get lost, and there's no traffic, and we hit all the green lights, and no pedestrian steps off the curb while texting right in front of this 2007 Camry, and we go sixty miles per hour on city streets, and I can figure out how to bend the space-time continuum, I will be only twenty-seven minutes late.

8:30 p.m.: i swore i was just gonna eat rice.

So far I have ordered: two cocktails (one on purpose, and the other I had to get to replace that one, because I didn't want to tell anyone that I don't really know what Lillet is, and when the drink came, I hated it and immediately replaced it with a wine, which, if we're being honest, I didn't really like, either); water—*that we had to pay for*—so I wouldn't have to dry swallow a naproxen; a bread basket, which is fine, I guess, except it's fucking health bread with seeds and that's definitely going to be a problem on the way out; some baked-cheese business with herbs on top that is impossible to eat while looking sexy, thank God these hoes are my friends; a deconstructed designer salad that came piled high with shaved fennel and preserved lemon and asparagus ribbons, and yes, it was gross, but I want the people who love me to think I care about myself; and a fancy vegan dessert donut, which, come on, just why.

9:30 p.m.: in the backseat of the cab dissolving three imodium under my tongue just in case.
Wow, remember when I used to be cool!

10:20 p.m.: i know the door guy!
Remember that opening scene in *The Social Network* where Mark Zuckerberg was trying to shame Rooney Mara for getting their underage asses into a Harvard bar by snarking, "the reason we're able to sit here and drink right now is because you used to sleep with the door guy!" as if she was supposed to apologize for that shit?! Or, I don't know, feel ashamed? Let me tell you about a little dream I have called "I Fucked All the Door Guys." In that magical fantasy world,

I never have to stand in an interminable line outside the Promontory while shifting my weight from foot to foot and puffing air into my mittened palms to try to stay warm, or shout "LOOK AT MY NECK" when I get stiff-armed and carded in the doorway at Hopleaf because that grunting ogre barring the entry of regular peasants FUCKED ME ONE TIME, and, sure, he was disappointed, but now he's not going to make me catch hypothermia. I never tried to sneak into bars when I was an underage child because I never managed to find a fake ID featuring the photo of an unzipped body bag, but I have stood outside on a Thursday night in February in Chicago, huddled with other pigeons pecking around beneath an underperforming heat lamp, and that is an overrated experience. Anyway, that's why I suggested my friends and I go to a place where I know a guy. We got out of the car, and I nodded at the imposing mountain of outerwear piled on a broken stool outside the door. He grunted and got up to wave us past the line, and I heard some little racist say, "Who the fuck is that bitch, Oprah?" and I yelled, "YES, BEFORE THE MEAT WAGON."

10:30 p.m.: are there really not any chairs?

We split up: one of my ladies makes a beeline for the crowd surrounding the bar, the one who drank the most of that expensive filtered water goes to find a bathroom, and I start circling the room trying to stake out a seat because I have arthritis in my knees. I knew we should've skipped dinner and gotten here before it got dark to snag ourselves a table. Now we have to spend the next hour or two hours or six days hovering anxiously near a table crowded with People Who Look Like They Might Get Up. It may surprise you to know that the seats being occupied by your newly single dad and his middle-management pals are the least likely to become available, despite the fact that they look like they should've been in bed three beers ago; those boneheads are gonna be here all fucking night, risking it all (all = a duplex in Aurora with a bored wife and uninterested kids) for a bottle-service waitress with low standards. Better odds are to post up near the table of people screaming in one another's faces the loudest and having the most visible fun, because there's likely some cooler place with some hotter people that they have to get to so they'll be leaving this one *we* found on our way in any minute now.

I know better. This is as good as it's gonna get, because it's at the only place I'm gonna go. Sure, the newest Bears draft pick is at this more exclusive spot I saw on a person's Instagram, but even if I wanted to go there I would have to chase the bartender down to close my tab, get my coat out of coat check, feel bad because I don't have paper money to tip the coat check attendant, be COLD and OUT-SIDE again, then take my chances getting in somewhere else, only to circle another corner booth like a desperate vulture waiting for a seat that hopefully nobody barfed in. We're staying.

10:42 p.m.: oh shit.
Those assholes finally left!!!!!!
　　knocks half-empty vodka soda glasses onto the floor before sprawling across table

11:05 p.m.: this music is too loud.
I'M SORRY, WHAT????

11:06 p.m.: i mean.
WAIT, WHAT DID YOU SAY??

11:07 p.m.: i just.
WHO? DID I SEE WHO????? I CAN'T.

11:08 p.m.: bitch, what?
WHISKEY. WHISKEY! YES, JUST GET ME ANY KIND THEY HAVE, IT DOESN'T—

11:15 p.m.: was i ever this young and tolerant?
I ordered a whiskey because you can take the tiniest, most imperceptible sip in front of your friends to prove you aren't a party pooper and then set that shit down somewhere when they aren't looking and switch to water for the rest of the goddamn night without these bitches hassling you. "Yeah, I'm partying! I'm having fun! I mean, sure, I'm drinking this eight-dollar Aquafina now, but remember when I had that Jameson?" If you get a High Life, you have to drink the whole damn thing, and even then people will be nudging the next two into your hands before you can catch your breath. The dope shit about being forty at the club is that you and your friends are old enough to

have credit cards to open tabs with, but the thing that sucks about that is your body can no longer handle the after-effects of those seemingly unlimited drinks! I love to hand my credit-building, secured Indigo MasterCard to a man with a mustache and a leather bar apron and wave in the general direction of the four people I came with. That is an incredibly powerful feeling. But if I have more than half a beer and two wines, girl, I gotta go sit down somewhere. This is why I love a lounge, because you can sink into a plush banquette in the corner and not move your sloshing stomach around.

11:35 p.m.: oh my goddddd, are you roxane gay??!!??!?!!!?!?!!??!
Yes, I am, sweetie. Get on in here and let's take this selfie!!

12:15 a.m.: it's officially the next day.
This is an accomplishment. I was never really a get-home-at-sunrise kind of guy; the minute the sky turns to slate, which is darker than dawn but lighter than dusk and right before the sun starts coming up and you can see how horribly your lipstick aged throughout the night any time your horrifying visage flashes across a reflective surface, despair sets in. And what's left of the day feels like it's already lost. What can I reasonably expect to accomplish if I'm going to bed at 7 a.m.? But, for a fleeting moment, hitting midnight is a great fucking feeling: I'm not at home in bed in a sweatshirt, under the covers with a package of Oreos, but it's also not so late that I feel like I'm going to die.

12:55 a.m.: i'm ready to go.

At this point in the evening, the liquor fairy alights gently upon my shoulder and coos sweetly in my ear, "BITCH, YOU CAN'T AFFORD TO PARTY LIKE THIS," and the gears in my brain slowly grind into motion, trying to recall exactly how many drinks I've had, and how much those drinks cost apiece, and whether or not anyone would notice if I tried to squeeze myself out of the tiny bathroom window and hitchhike home. I don't feel stupid until I'm locked in a bathroom stall doing drunk calculus on a paper towel to determine if I can pay both my bar tab and my card payment that month. It was cute to throw that flimsy piece of plastic with 67% APR at the bartender two hours ago, but now I can't find my friends and I know they've been running up my bill all night. What if I actually get my cell phone shut off because these bitches are too stuck up for well liquor?

"Three vodkas divided by the light bill times the minimum payment plus cab fare back to my hotel—shit, I gotta go!!"

12:56 a.m.: oh, hey, there's that baked cheese from earlier.

Seriously, what is my problem? And thank God I'm already in the bathroom.

1:10 a.m.: watching people flirt makes me nervous.

Another side effect of getting older is caring about things. I get emotionally invested right from the jump in whether or not a real love connection is being made, and my skin is crawling with anxiety over whether or not I'm about to suffer vicariously through an awkward rejection. This dude has tried to get this woman's attention three different times after she's gotten distracted by someone cuter, and I can't tell from here if he's just dumb or a predator, but he clearly thinks they had something and could have something again if she would only turn her face back in his direction and wow my heart is breaking for him. My shoulders have crept up to my earlobes, and there's a knot of fear (or fennel salad!) in my stomach. Why doesn't he just leave and swipe an app? She is having a very animated discussion with that new guy, and I'm so sorry, but I am going to have a full panic attack in this place if he reaches out to tap her on the shoulder again, I can feel it. Everyone thinks I'm going to eventually die of a heart attack, but joke's on y'all—it's definitely going to be of secondhand embarrassment.

1:15 a.m.: she left with that guy.
And now I have to sit here and commit the rejected dude's face to memory in case I have to describe it to police later. Why am I here?!

2:47 a.m.: what the—
I feel the fangs break through my gums and a sharp prickle as hair sprouts from behind my ears and the backs of my hands. I cross my hands under the table and nod as my one friend gives me her "bitch, are you okay?" eyes, and the

other flags down the waitress (is she actually our waitress?) with the universal club signal for "one of us is either going to vomit or fall asleep," and we begin the process of collecting all our things so we can go. Where's the charger cord for my spare battery? Whose lip gloss is this? Why is my left shoe in the farthest corner underneath this table? My vision sharpens, and I can smell every bead of sweat in the room: I am up five hours, forty-seven minutes, and nineteen seconds past my bedtime, and that is a dangerous place for me to be, awake at rat o'clock, in uncomfortable shoes and itchy eye makeup. I hear the seams of my shirt ripping as my chest broadens, tufts of coarse hair forcing their way out of the collar of my shirt. I bolt from my seat as I feel my claws split my shoes open. My flank is totally about to burst through my threadbare pants. People throw themselves out of my way as I launch myself at the coatroom, nosing through the hanging fabric until I locate my jacket (no, it won't comfortably fit over my lycan form, but that shit was expensive so I'm taking it). I yank it free with my teeth, then rip the door to the club off its hinges and stalk through River North swatting junior partners and finance bros out of my path with my massive paws. I pause briefly to consider eating a stray dog, but honestly, it's skinny and I don't feel like chasing it, so I keep running until I reach my hotel. Up on my hind legs to fool the dozing doorman, then I'm back in my room where I can—muzzle retracting and haunches reverting to their gelatinous state—lie prone on the shower floor as hot water rains down on me and I eat those Sun Chips I bought this morning at Union Station.

3:30 a.m.: how embarrassing would it be to order a
bowl of room-service oatmeal right now?
GOOD NIGHT.

Maybe I should try my gnarled old hand at horror instead?
I'm Awake after Ten on a Weeknight ★shivers★
Margaret Brought a New Person to Book Club ★shudders★
Vacation Constipation! ★chills★

hung up!

I once starred in a horror movie called *I Was Caught Waiting, Alone, in a Public Place, without My Fucking Cellular Phone.* I didn't have a book or a magazine or a newspaper to distract me from the clanking glasses and hushed conversations in a hotel coffee shop, but even if I had, none of those things could hold a candle to my beloved mobile cellular radio system. My iPhone is my constant companion in this dull and irritating world.

Man, I love my phone. I love its faintly cracked screen and lightly buttered handfeel, its dodgy Bluetooth connectivity and sliver of available storage space. I wish I could pretend it has been some torrid, complicated courtship between us, or that after much cat and mouse, the two of us succumbed to our mutual attraction and decided to settle down and make an honest go of it, but I can't. I remain in breathless pursuit, hustling to keep her both updated and paid for, connecting it to the fastest Wi-Fi speeds available, wooing her with exorbitantly priced protective cases and as many off-brand charging cords as there are outlets in my home. Yet my phone barely acknowledges that I'm alive—and that only makes me want her even more.

I was late to the technology game. I'm staring down the barrel of my fortieth year, and I bought my computer six or seven years ago. I didn't get my first iPhone until they'd been around for years, partially because I thought, "Who needs that? I prefer to live in the real world!" Mostly, I was skeptical because the idea of walking around with a five-hundred-dollar computer in my pocket seemed ridiculous and dangerous to me. And the idea that I could somehow scrape together the money to purchase said pocket computer while also maintaining a roof over my head (read: partying all the time and paying for basic cable) was hilarious and unrealistic. I was the last dinosaur at the club sending multi-tap texts on an analog Nokia E51 with no camera.

When I finally upgraded to a smartphone several years after unsolicited selfies had taken hold of the nation, my exhausted thumbs cracked and bleeding from a decade of repeatedly jamming down the 2 key to make a letter C, I didn't get what all the fuss was about. Okay, sure, this glowing rectangle in my bag can tell me the weather anywhere in the world at this exact moment, but who cares? But, wait, it could also figure out precisely what wrong street I'm turning down and steer me back in the right direction? And it can count how many steps I took today while saving for me all the passwords I can never remember? Please excuse me while I build a shrine to the new most important thing in my life!

I've read (on my phone) that we, as a nation, as a species, have a problem with cell phones. [Insert facts about the harms of cell phone usage that I am never going to research because I do not enjoy feeling like an underachiever.] But do we really? Is there actually a problem with rescuing our brains from the doldrums of sitting at a red light or from the malaise caused by having even a single second to sit alone with one's terrible thoughts? I don't have children; therefore I don't have any opinions on whether electronic devices are a bad influence on the mental growth and development of a child. If you tell me they are, then I believe you. I'm sure there's scientific evidence to prove it. And I'm positive there are doctors and licensed professionals who would attest to the deleterious effect modern technology has on the brains and interpersonal skills of adults, but hear me out. Maybe it's worth it.

A terrible thing happened to me when I went to dinner with the kind of pretentious know-it-alls whose idea of fun is to condescend to you about wine and make fun of you for pronouncing "Niçoise" incorrectly. One of these smug assholes boldly suggested that we all put our phones facedown in the center of the table for the entirety of the meal and the needlessly lingering discussion afterward. They did it. Grudgingly, I did it, too. I placed my phone facedown next to a twee mason jar with a plant in it and ordered an Aperol spritz and a focaccia to start, which is a dangerous choice because I can never tell from the menu description whether I'll receive a piece of pre-meal snack-bread or if the waiter is going to wheel out a whole fucking pizza. When a modest board with a perfectly reasonable slab of rosemary-crusted bread was placed in front of me, the first thing I thought was "I wish I knew what everyone else on Earth was doing at this exact moment. I wonder if there is a device nearby that could tell me."

We talked during dinner because my companions wanted to connect to one another. Everyone talked and talked and talked, but it was the kind of talking where you know every single person at the table is low-key wondering what they're missing on Twitter. The only thing I'd done that had been more excruciating was the meditation I tried to take up but had to stop because I kept falling asleep. Now, okay, I didn't die during dinner. But I also didn't know what time it was or if anyone had texted me. I'm not really a post-a-picture-of-my-fancy-meal kind of person, but I could tell that other people wanted to. The air in that extremely Instagrammable restaurant was heavy with missed opportunity. Do you know what we talked about while cringing internally as the carafe of tap water we actually had to pay for came perilously close to splashing on our helpless devices every time it was passed? TV shows, which you can watch on a phone. Books, which, if your eyes haven't already burned through the back of your skull from being on your phone all the time, you can read on it. Murder podcasts, which are specifically designed to be listened to on a phone in the shower or during a nightmare commute. Okay, fine, maybe you listen to podcasts on your computer while you're working, but can't we admit that your laptop is little more than a giant, foldable phone?

It's annoying when someone bumps into you on the street because they're looking down at a screen instead of paying attention to where they are going. I have had a handful of close calls in which I accidentally almost pinned a pedestrian under my front tires because they'd stepped into the street without glancing up from a phone. I bristle when the peaceful darkness of a movie theater is interrupted by a rude cell phone light, or worse, when a *Parks and Recreation* ringtone blasts through a tense, quiet moment from inside the pocket of a whimsical cherry-printed dress. I saw Dave Chappelle do a stand-up set one night in Nashville, and there were signs posted everywhere yelling at us in bold font that phones and cameras weren't allowed in the theater. We would be ejected by security if we tried to record any part of the evening's festivities, and I did a silent but enthusiastic cheer as a handful of people were escorted out as they tried to Snapchat parts of the act. Just be present, Gabe! Laugh along with the rest of us! You paid sixty-plus dollars for the ticket to this once-in-a-lifetime experience!

It's bonkers to pay money to go to a Broadway show on opening night and sit in the front row and text. I get it. But if I have to go sit in the lobby or on the toilet, I would like to get a couple rounds of *Words with Friends* in. It's only fair.

I deleted my Facebook account. I mean I really deleted it, "scorched-earth, can't ever reactivate it, good-bye to all my 2012 photos" deleted it, "whoops, I forgot to get your phone number before I bailed and Facebook was the only connective tissue between us, guess I'm never going to talk to you again?" deleted it. Having intimate-seeming connections to people I don't actually know was starting to weird me out. Sure, there's value in community, but I was sick of seeing fake-news links and thinking, "Wait, how do I know this dingbat again?" But I kind of loved some of those dingbats! And I really loved being able to scroll through their lives and see everything they've been doing that they're comfortable sharing with an audience of virtual strangers without having to, you know, ever talk to them! Do you ever think about how incredible it is that you can pop on your aunt Tracy's page while in the waiting room at your doctor's office like, "Great, her dog is still alive! Wow, she got a new car! That haircut is pretty cute. . . . Man, my cousins are a fucking mess. Damn, I see she's still into conspiracy theories. Oh no, my strep test is positive?" That's the magic of your pocket computer. You can find out everything you need to know without subjecting your full attention to your college crush's bad jokes and awful personality. When is the last time an actual human interaction made you laugh more than a meme did?

Sometimes connecting with other people online sucks, like when some dummy you barely remember is assaulting you with posts about beauty products that you can purchase only if they sell them to you from out of a suitcase in your living room, or when people won't stop trolling you with their truly terrible takes. This makes my case for cell phones > real human interaction even stronger, because you can just block people and pretend they died. You know, without going to jail for murdering them. One time, in an incredibly brave act of self-care, I blocked a dude because he posted the grossest-looking photo of food he was eating, two seconds after I had blocked another dude who was trying to sell me his mixtape in the year of our Lord 2018. Wow, sir, no fucking thank you! I could go on and on about a fifth-grade locker partner adding me to various LuLaRoe legging groups or spamming my Instagram with links for "Free iPhones!" but listen, you know who I'm talking about. And you shouldn't feel bad for even a second for blocking that hoe and throwing her a funeral in your heart.

Every time someone's Internet presence feels like a personal attack on my life, I first try to have compassionate thoughts like, "What if something terrible is happening in her world?" because there's still a very slim chance that hell is real and I'd like to have a plausible defense of my actions on Earth should there be some sort of way to argue my way out of damnation. But then I think, "Well, if she was actually suffering, there's no way she'd be spamming me links to all these pyramid schemes," and my guilt evaporates just long enough for me to click that block button so I can move on with my day. I'm a patient person and hesitant to alienate anyone who might have fifteen dollars lying around to buy my books, but it dawned on me the other day that, for me, the Internet has to be a meticulously curated digital space in which your uncle's vaguely racist tweets have no place.

I hate fighting. I'm sensitive and, frankly, not good at it. If the consequence of bickering online means I've got to spend the afternoon feeling bad because a kid I don't remember from high school called me a "fat-ass Kelly Price" over a *Reductress* article, please murder me. And if my tweets get on your goddamn nerves: BLOCK ME FIRST. Kill me with your powerful brain! There are too many places in real life where blocking is not a viable option to tolerate someone ruining your secret lives online. You can't block the coworker who won't stop fucking talking while loitering nearby as you're just trying to put half-and-half in your breakroom coffee, but you can block that friend of a friend who says shit like, "I'm not prejudiced, I don't care if a person is purple or green or blue." LMAO, blue people???? SHUT THE FUCK UP. You can't delete the neighbor whose eyesore of a car is parked halfway across your driveway and whose cat keeps shitting on your deck, but you can delete your cousin who earnestly believes that rap music is reverse racism and vehemently comments as much on every Kendrick Lamar video you share. There's no mute button for the woman at the grocery store who won't stop asking you where the shampoo is, even though you're pushing your own cart while wearing both sunglasses and a coat. But you know who you *can* mute? Everyone you hate on the Internet! Yes, everyone is annoying and also Extremely Online, the state of the public discourse is robust as ever, and the incredible thing about it is if you aren't into it you can just log right off. Imagine if real life had an off switch!

Apple put this new Screen Time feature on the iPhone that's supposed to, I don't know, shame me into putting down the drug they won't stop peddling to me. Every time I get that notice, I take it as a challenge to spend *even more time* messing around on my phone. Only one hour and thirty-seven minutes of Social Networking yesterday, you say? Let me put down this informative book I was reading and try to top that.

So here's to love and loving your portable handheld telecommunication device. Stay inside where it's temperature-controlled and there are no bugs and spend some time celebrating your beloved today. Make a delicious home-made casserole (look up the recipe on your phone), dip out to pick up a fancy bottle of wine (request a Lyft from your phone), sit next to a cozy fire (YouTube a fireplace video on your phone), sing along to your favorite jams (find it on Spotify on your phone), listen to your favorite book (open Audible on your phone), watch some cheesy movies (did you know you can get Netflix on your phone?!), send an update to the family members you haven't seen in a while (use e-mail from your phone), order some Indian takeout (Grubhub dot com on your phone), text your homegirl some juicy gossip from your phone, and since you're playing around on it anyway, why not do a little shopping on your phone? Is it holiday time? If so, maybe you could stop being a huge grinch for a change and just buy everyone in your circle the one thing we've been conditioned to constantly want: A NEW PHONE.

late-1900s time capsule

I keep every CD I've ever bought, since high school, in black Case Logic binders hidden in the closet in the sunroom of this house I didn't grow up in and don't have a real attachment to. Also in that same closet there's the evergrowing, tangled wad of plastic bags intended for reuse that will most certainly outlive me, a couple cans of bug spray that are all clogged and nonfunctional, the seltzer cans I keep meaning to return for cash, a gooey tube of superglue, several non-matching batteries rolling around the bottom of a deteriorating plastic cup, backup gardening gloves—I mean, why do we even have these?—and an original and heavily scratched copy of Sneaker Pimps' *Becoming X* purchased from a Blockbuster Music in downtown Evanston in 1996.

The closer I creep toward the precipice of forty, the more time I spend listening to the same songs I listened to in high school and combing through surprisingly vivid memories of my time there, which is wild, because I did not actually have a good time being young! Why can't I bear to part with the copy of Sheryl Crow's 1996 self-titled album *Sheryl*

Crow that I last listened to in a battered Sony Discman I got as a hand-me-down from a friend? "Home" has lyrics I could neither understand nor relate to at the time of its release, because they're about a grown-ass woman and her disappointing relationship with some useless bonehead she's desperate to cheat on. But when I was sixteen, I used to put it on repeat as the melancholy soundtrack for my brooding walk to school.

Mixtapes were the love language of my youth. If you got one from me, that shit was as serious as a marriage proposal. Maybe because they were so time-consuming to make? I had a painstaking process I went through before I put a mix together. First of all, I would figure out what mood I was trying to create: How cool did I want the recipient to think I was? Is this a person who would understand my deep and abiding love for They Might Be Giants? Would they see through my artificial cool and realize that 50 percent of the songs I'd chosen had come from the *Pulp Fiction* soundtrack?

The second thing to consider: What was the goal? What kind of overwhelming pressure was I placing on a meager 1.43 ounces of plastic film and magnetic tape? Was I trying to convince someone that I was worthy of their love and/ or friendship? Or did I just want them to know that I, too, spent a lot of time hanging out at the indie record store after school digging through all the used CDs in the alternative section hoping to find something interesting that was also less than seven dollars? Or, failing those two, was I trying to make them jealous of my wide-ranging interests? (Why, yes, I *do* enjoy both Phish and Nina Simone!) And, most important, should I use a ninety-minute tape or a sixty-minute one? (Oh, I know, I know: GIRL, WHAT THE FUCK IS A TAPE?!)

Here is my '90s mixtape for you. Please love me.

A SIDE

"World Falls," Indigo Girls (live version)
What do you mean, you're "surprised I ended up with a lady"?

"Black," Pearl Jam
I first heard Pearl Jam in the seventh grade, when this kid I didn't know very well was brandishing a copy of *Ten* on cassette in our language arts class. I asked to borrow it and took it home and held a tape recorder up to the speaker in our living room for an hour to record it. (This, sweet babies, is my version of "in my day, we used to have to walk up a hill to get to school with plastic bags for shoes!" Please kill me.) I then listened to that recording for months and months and months while brooding. Being very *complicated* and *deep*, I was enamored with this idea that love was difficult and stressful, and that torrid relationships fraught with passion and rage were exciting. This was, of course, before I knew how tiring life can be for an adult. Oh my goodness, "my bitter hands cradle broken glass / of what was everything"? Yes, please! "All the love gone bad turned my world to black"? Swoon city. Eddie was the perfect embodiment of Brokenhearted Sensitive Grunge Man; I lived for him then, and I still do. I would totally listen to him howl about his electric bill.

"Elsewhere," Sarah McLachlan

Freshman year of high school, I failed gym class. Oh, I know. It's easy to think you know why, and guess what, you're right! I appear to be as athletic as a boiled chicken sandwich under a heat lamp in the cafeteria. That's something I understood about myself, which is why I spent an entire semester sitting on the sidelines of every gym activity pretending to be suffering from debilitating menstrual cramps rather than pissing off my classmates while trying to play kickball. Listen, I don't need to trip over my own feet trying to dive for a volleyball that's inevitably going to bust me in the face, and you don't need to waste all your budding testosterone yelling at me for making us lose; it's a win for everyone to have me sit out! So I failed a semester due to lack of participation, which is perfectly reasonable. I also failed a semester of history that year, and math, which was less so. My mom was dying! But I also literally never did any work. In a fit of optimism, I signed up for summer school to try to make up some of the classes I'd failed, and the only available gym class was first thing in the morning. In the fucking summer. Unbeknownst to me, it was full of super seniors who should have graduated already but didn't have all their credits completed, so I was out there trying to play catcher behind grown men with full beards swinging their bats harder than Barry fucking Bonds. These were gentlemen who smoked cigarettes in the outfield and ran full speed into you when you tried to tag them out, so after a week of crouching with my arms over my head while crying, I would get off the bus at school in my gym shorts and walk to the McDonald's a few blocks away, grateful that it was still early enough in the day to get a one-dollar sausage biscuit, while listening to this incredibly soothing song. I failed gym again that summer. Senior year, I had to take two gym classes so they would let me graduate. I got very good at badminton.

"I Miss You," Aaron Hall
"I'll Do Anything/I'm Sorry," Ginuwine
"Beauty," Dru Hill
"Hey Now," Carl Thomas
There is a specific breed of crying-ass, begging-ass, I'm-sorry-ass, you're-so-beautiful-ass '90s R&B songs that at first blush sound like they are intended for sensuous lovemaking, but if you actually stop and listen to the lyrics, it's like, "Hold up, wait, you cheated on me with *who*?" *Or* it's six real minutes of a dude in either a torn-off shirt or an oversize cashmere turtleneck (sorry, there's no in between!) crooning super hard and laying it on real thick about how beautiful you are and that is 100 percent the type of R&B song that got me through my elderly teens.

"Softer, Softest," Hole
I was obsessed with Hole mostly because I was obsessed with *Sassy* magazine, and Courtney Love was, like, queen of the alternative girls, and I very much wanted to be an alternative girl, down to the steel-toed Doc Martens I saved my babysitting money to buy and then wore every single day because I could not afford multiple pairs of shoes. Picture me, lumbering through the halls of my high school between classes trying not to be noticed, wearing your grandfather's cardigan and shoes literally the size of cinder blocks, humming "your milk turns to cry" under my breath. There was a certain type of girl in the '90s that I dreamed of channel-

ing, chief among them Veronica Sawyer and Vickie Miner and Daria Morgendorffer. They all seemed like the kind of girls Hole made music for. So I listened to Hole a lot, even though 99 percent of the lyrics were confusing as fuck to me back then. Who am I kidding? They still are! I'm putting this track at the beginning of the mix, so you know that I'm sweet but also kind of scary, which I hear some people find sexy. (I am actually not the least bit scary, which is why I let Courtney Love scream on my behalf.)

"Mad Lucas," The Breeders

I still fuck with the Breeders, heavy. *Last Splash* came out and one of my rich friends—you know, the kind whose parents could afford a dual-cassette-deck boombox—dubbed me a copy of it. I was like, "HOLY SHIT, WHAT THE FUCK AM I LISTENING TO?" I don't know, I was kind of a square, so in hindsight I probably said, "This sounds neat!" But you get it. It's a little surf rock, a tiny bit alt-country, sometimes straight-up grunge, and it was like magic to my ears. I know everyone loves "Cannonball," and believe me, I do, too. But if I'm going to make you a tape, I'm going to make you a tape that has a truly bonkers surf-rock slow jam that you probably could bone to on it.

"I'll Back You Up," Dave Matthews Band

Once upon a time, I lived in a crack house. It wasn't so much a crack house as it was a rooming house that a lot of people who enjoyed smoking crack cocaine lived in, but "crack house" rolls off the tongue better, so I'll just call it that. It was a decent-looking house on a well-kept street in a nice part of town, and if you looked at it from the outside, you'd have no idea that behind those imitation wood blinds operated a literal den of iniquity, and you know what? It was fine! I had a bed and I could afford it! Which is honestly a low bar, but what do you really care when you're twenty-two? One day, I came home to find that someone had broken the lock to my room, and, haha, joke's on them, because unless you want a bunch of cried-on journals and a keytar, you're going to be incredibly disappointed with my belongings. I pushed open the splintered door and found a crackhead in my room sitting on the floor, riffling through a bunch of grunge CDs. I don't know what the appropriate response should have been (screaming, maybe? outrage?), but I just burst out laughing. A genuine, hearty, throat-opening laugh. I couldn't believe it. Of all the rotten underwear and poorly rolled, half-smoked joints littering my floor, this young man was really going to take, what, a couple Ben Folds records? He jumped up as soon as he noticed me, clutching *Under the Table and Dreaming*, the Dave Matthews Band masterpiece. (YES, MASTERPIECE.) I put my hand out to take it back, humiliated for us both, and when he tried to scoot past me with the cracked jewel case tucked under his shirt, I grabbed at him, and we had an embarrassing tug of war, which of course I won. Come on, "Satellite" is a jam. Anyway, this song isn't on that record, but it's the best. Give me some whispery, warbling male vocals, some gorgeous falsetto, some plaintive guitar plinking and plucking. Honestly, what's not to like? If you hate Dave Matthews, that shit is on you. *wink*

"Wake Up," Alanis Morissette

There was an article going around in early 2019, written by a woman around my age about how she was listening to

Jagged Little Pill, Alanis's first album, which is fucking canon for angsty '90s teens, and now that she's an adult, her husband made her realize that the album sucks. First of all, why you would ask a man anything is beyond me. Also, accepting his assessment of an album meant for hyperemotional girls twenty years after it came out is bullshit. Why does he care? Was "Hand in My Pocket" even written for him?! I really love some emotional singing, and I also love copious amounts of rock harmonica, so basically this album is perfect.

"Tear in Your Hand," Tori Amos

SPEAKING OF EMOTIONAL SINGING. Seriously, is there anyone better to dramatically weep to? I skipped school one day sophomore year to go to the new girl's apartment—the most stressful day of my life, to be honest, because I thought you could get arrested for ditching, so every time a car door shut outside I braced myself for jackboots and a battering ram. Her dad was divorced and too permissive, so we spent the entire day listening to *Little Earthquakes* while she told me all her illicit sex stuff. I had only had one sex thing happen up to that point and it wasn't even that exciting, so I just sat quietly with big, shocked eyes and tried to pretend that I knew what "blow job" meant. Tori's music always made me nervous because I didn't understand a lot of what she was talking about, but I knew it all sounded like it was about masturbating or fucking, and that was embarrassing. I wasn't raised in a sex-positive way! I mean, my mom didn't say "dirty pillows" or anything, but she wasn't, like, *teaching me about clitoral stimulation* or whatever. All Tori's songs are either about Jesus or getting banged, and I was so mortified every time I heard one, even if I couldn't articulate exactly why. "Me and a Gun" is about her own experience being raped, right? And "Leather" is definitely about fucking. "Precious Things" is about making someone come! I wasn't even sure what that meant, but I knew it had to do with private parts and that if I got caught singing that shit, I was going to be in trouble. Anyway, "Tear in Your Hand" is about a girl who gets broken up with (definitely can relate) and then spends an entire song telling the dude who left her that he made a huge mistake (DEFINITELY CAN RELATE). Me and the new girl ate so many bags of chips and sang our hearts out, truant officer (are those real) be damned! I got front row seats to see Tori a few years ago at the Chicago Theatre, and a sobbing woman broke my toe (she stomped on it while wearing what I can only assume was a chunky-soled Steve Madden clog) as she ran screaming for the stage when Tori sang this during the encore. I wasn't even mad. I get it!!

"Soma," Smashing Pumpkins
"Spin the Bottle," The Juliana Hatfield Three
I listened to Q101 a lot in high school, because it was the "alternative station." And, because I didn't have any disposable income, my musical tastes relied pretty heavily on whatever the middle-aged programmers thought kids with shaved heads and eyeliner should be listening to. In 1993, it was Smashing Pumpkins. I have heard the song "Today" easily one hundred thousand times, and I know "Soma" is a weird choice, but what can I say? I like sad and soothing shit. I come for the angst, but I stay for the drear. I got *Siamese Dream* at a record store called Second Hand Tunes where you could get used tapes for three bucks. I picked up the

Juliana Hatfield Three's *Become What You Are* the same day, mostly because I was obsessed with *Reality Bites* (and with the idea that my very own brooding, misanthropic urban cowboy was out there with some obscure novel jammed into his jeans pocket, just waiting for me to save him), but they didn't have a copy of the soundtrack, so getting her record was the next best thing. Yes, asshole, I mostly wanted that soundtrack for Lisa Loeb's song "Stay (I Missed You)," but it doesn't take away from how good "Spin the Bottle" is, and honestly, it doesn't even matter, because I could listen to either over and over in the hope that I would go to sleep one night and magically wake up in a complicated situationship with Troy Dyer.

"Waltzing Back," The Cranberries

Sometimes I get super tender when I think about how dumb and naive my child self was, and I wish I could go back and hug her while also reminding her to tuck in her shirt. I often think about how I was really into grunge especially because it seemed accessible to me, a person on welfare, because the whole premise was that you could dress like a grandpa who looks like shit and everyone would think you were cool and "alternative" instead of just dirty. I saved up a bunch of odds-and-ends money until I had enough to get a few things from the Salvation Army, because while I was fully grunge in my heart, on the outside I was dressed like a woman setting up for a church luncheon, as most of the available offerings for fat women at clothing stores were of the choir-rehearsal-on-Wednesday-night variety. I studied my copies of *Sassy* and decided that I needed some threadbare cardigans and at least one buffalo-plaid flannel shirt. I walked to the Salvation

Army one day after school with the Cranberries blasting through the foamy headphones of my Walkman. I discovered there that even if you thumb through every rack of clothing until your eyes water and your throat closes from the dust, and the lady at the register jokingly threatens to physically remove you from the premises because it's time for her to go home and start dinner, unless you are looking for a shapeless sack to attend a christening in, there will be no suitable cool clothes that fit you.

"Breakdown," Mariah Carey ft. Bone Thugs-n-Harmony
Easily in the top five Best Breakup Songs of All Time.

There was this Chicagoland chain in the late '90s called Dr. Wax that had three locations, one of which was smack in the middle of downtown Evanston, within spitting distance of both a two-story Barnes & Noble (remember when they were also trying to be a record store?) and a Borders (pour out some of your overpriced coffee from the ~café~ in honor of that revolutionary scan-the-barcode-on-a-CD-and-listen-to-thirty-seconds-of-each-song feature). Dr. Wax was this indie record store that was dusty, covered in posters, crammed with crates full of vinyl and a diverse offering of new and used CDs, and manned by semi-hostile music nerds who scoffed openly at your bad taste when you approached the counter with your tacky Top 40 albums. It was as if your friend's parents had let them open a very specific record store in their cluttered basement. I remember when *High Fidelity* first came out and I saw it in the theater. I was like, HOLY SHIT, I KNOW THESE FUCKING GUYS.

I used to hang out at the Dr. Wax on Berwyn, under the train, and just listen to the dudes behind the counter arguing with each other about groups I'd never heard of, then parroting their opinions and presenting them as my own to my dumb-ass friends who definitely didn't care. I hung out there often enough that they started recommending new things for me to listen to (Massive Attack, Stereolab, OutKast) to expand my limited horizons, and I got comfortable enough to share my embarrassing requests with them ("Could you guys order the new Harry Connick Jr. for me, please?") while they tried to not make fun of me.

If you'd asked me what my dream job was back then, "disgruntled music store employee" would have been at the top of the list. Nothing was more glamorous to me than the idea of tearing open boxes of new releases before anyone else got to hear them, or having the power to subject an entire store full of patrons who were trying to just stop by and get the new Kenny Lattimore on the way home from work to my very eclectic music tastes. All I ever wanted—shit, all I *still* ever want—is a cool-T-shirt-appropriate job where I can eat snacks and sit around talking shit with my friends all day while hiding all the good CDs behind the counter for myself. I wouldn't even care what corny music you came in to buy as long as *you* don't care that I am softly crying to Patti Smith's *Gone Again* as it plays in perpetuity.

The last mixtape I got wasn't even a tape; it was a CD from a dude I was dating who didn't bother to do anything cool, like decorate the dull side with some abstract doodlings or write all the track names on the insert so I could stare at his handwriting in a totally not-creepy way while I was alone in my apartment waiting for him to call me. The night he gave it to me, I went to Cara's house and she poured Absolut into pint glasses full of limes, and we sat on her couch parsing every single track choice. This is what passes for an acceptable Saturday night activity for two women who were definitely thirty-plus years old at the time. The mix kicked off with the song "You" by Raheem DeVaughn, and I remember Cara turning to me with this grave look on her face and saying, "Oh, girl, this is true love." It ended up not being shit. But at least I was provided a soundtrack to grieve to.

B SIDE

"Explain It to Me," Liz Phair

You don't get to be from the Chicago suburbs circa 1993 and not be a fan of Liz Phair. I'm sorry, I don't make the rules, I just abide by them. You could plug in almost any song from either *Exile in Guyville* or *Whip-Smart* (ahem, "Shane" is the best track on that album, in my opinion, even though people will argue that "Supernova" is, because they are morons), and I will know enough of the words from memory to be impressive, if you have low standards for things that impress you. I don't know shit about the Stones, so I definitely don't understand the correlation between this album and their *Exile on Main Street*, because, honestly? I don't have to! It's clear at this point that I live for a downtempo jam, and this is one of her best. I still have my well-loved, scratched-up *Exile* CD, and it skips when she sings "piece it together / it's like weather," which reminds me every single time that I don't really understand what the lyrics to this song mean.

"Undenied," Portishead

I did not understand Portishead when they first came out. Everybody loved that "Sour Times" video, but I didn't feel like I was cool enough to understand it. I'm still not cool enough for a lot of things; for example, I have not made more than one attempt to suffer through *Breaking Bad*. During my one miserable year in college, I was sustained mostly by soap operas, ice-cream sandwiches, and a copy of *Braveheart* on VHS, but also the occasional care packages sent by my friends. That year, my only joy came from Delia's catalogs and boxes of CDs my friends in cooler college towns sent me. My friend Jon sent me new music every week and one week he sent me, at the behest of his girlfriend, a jewel case wrapped in paper with a bunch of stamps taped to it, and inside, miraculously unharmed, was the second Portishead record. I will listen to anything that has been recommended by exotic women who don't shower or wear bras, so I spent a week not going to class and weeping silently as Beth Gibbons sang directly to my pain. I was taking Prozac, really leaning in to being a clinically depressed person, and a moody trip-hop beat was the perfect soundtrack for my moping.

"Mixed Bizness," Beck

Beck—yes, that Beck!—made a banging R&B album in the late '90s, and if I was going to make you a mix, I would definitely want you to know that I know that.

"Swan Dive," Ani DiFranco

I got my first-ever tattoo as an homage to Ani DiFranco. She was on the cover of *Spin* magazine (remember that?!)

in August 1997, in a black leather bustier with a shock of teal and seafoam-green hair sprouting from the top of her head and a thorny, vine-looking thing inked a couple inches below her clavicle. I, an already devoted fan who'd meticulously written out the lyrics to "Not a Pretty Girl" in my journal years before, painstakingly removed the cover with a razor and affixed it to the cork board over my bed in my college dorm room. While I was home for spring break, my friend Ylang and I, realizing that we were both certified eighteen-year-old ADULTS, decided to go get tattoos. Actually, she decided to get her belly button pierced at a tattoo parlor, and since that wasn't exactly my thing, I decided that while I waited I was going to get something exciting and dangerous tattooed on my body. I'm pretty sure I had less than fifty bucks in my pocket because I rarely ever have more than that, even now, and I looked at all the flash on the walls and was really surprised at how expensive tattoos were? Like, even the small, boring ones were hundreds of dollars! I had a check in my pocket from the government that was probably allocated for textbooks, but instead of that, I deposited it into an ATM down the street from the tattoo shop and said a silent prayer to the money gods so that they would do that magic thing where some of your money is available right away. Voilà! I was able to withdraw two hundred dollars! I did it quickly, before the machine could change its mind, and picked a tribal design off the wall because there was no way in hell that wasn't going to be in fashion twenty years later! When the artist asked where I wanted it, I panicked and said, "Where Ani has hers!" and he looked at me like I was nuts, because, seriously, who the fuck is Ani to this fifty-year-old biker tattoo artist with a beard to his navel. I pointed to my breastplate and he asked me to unbutton my shirt the same way you'd ask for a glass of water, which I was somehow too stupid to have anticipated. Then he shaved my sternum with a bar of soap and a cheap disposable razor, while I lay back in a chair completely horrified by my hairy chest. He had to basically lay on top of me to get the tattoo where I wanted it, and I clenched my teeth while taking shallow sips of air in an attempt not to rattle him. I went back to school proudly sporting a healing, oozing wound in the dead center of my chest. I received a care package my friend Anna sent with some SARK books and Ani's new CD inside, and I listened to "Swan Dive" on a loop while tenderly applying A+D ointment to my peeling sub-neck area for a week.

"Makin' Happy," Crystal Waters

I love house music. I live for a house remix. I have dated *counts fingers* six-ish deep house DJs (some of them would argue about my generous use of the word "dated," hence the *-ish*). There is no clear picture of my musical history that doesn't include *some* kind of club bops. You can't grow up Chicago-adjacent and not have a deep appreciation for house music. It's against the rules. I wasn't old enough to really party, but my sister would give me tapes of all the good shit (Dajae singing "Brighter Days," and Cajmere's "The Percolator,") and then I would get whatever I could from Saturday late-night mixes on the radio. I was obsessed with Crystal Waters' "Gypsy Woman (She's Homeless)," just like everybody else when it came out. I got the cassingle (A side: radio edit, club mix; B side: seven-plus-minute Basement Boys mix, instrumental), and wore that shit OUT. Then I saved up and bought her full album, which in the old days was a fucking *commitment*. Nine dollars for an entire album was an *investment*. This was pre–Columbia House for me, which meant that I had to be really careful when purchasing an entire album, because it's not like I was going to get a bunch of new ones anytime soon if it sucked. So I had to be sure it was worth it. I went to Rose Records (there's a futon store there now, RIP) with my mom and got *Surprise* and knew that I was going to be listening to it for weeks, which I dutifully did. "Makin' Happy" is a fucking jam, which I probably only discovered because every time she caught me in front of the TV, my mom was like, "I know you're not watching a SHOW after you begged me for that TAPE!" and chased me out of the living room and into the warm embrace of my busted Aiwa boombox, but that's fine.

"Ecstasy," PJ Harvey

Rid of Me changed something in me. Yes, I tend toward the hyperbolic, but Polly Jean thrashing on her guitar while caterwauling about sex in this super-raw way seriously cracked something open inside my most shame-filled places. There was a time when the most glamorous thing to my tiny brain was the prospect of having someone worthy of the title "lover," someone sweaty and elusive who would make me feel things that warranted a song being written in their honor, and PJ is mostly to blame for that. I listened to a lot of the Beatles' later work and other shit that made me feel like I wanted to be on drugs, but PJ and Tori made me long for someone to put their tongue in my mouth while I had many very deep thoughts about it. Imagine being that stupid. Remind me to tell you about the time I thought I was going to be a spoken-word poet and at my first open mic said "rim shot" without realizing that it could be interpreted as referring to butt stuff. The entire audience laughed hysterically at my Feelings Poem. It dawned on me too late why it was funny, and then, because I am a humorless toddler, I stopped reciting the poem and tried to explain to the crowd that I meant it in the music way, and then they started snapping to get me to leave the stage, but I didn't know that was a thing, so I talked for four more excruciating minutes until I died.

"On the Bound," Fiona Apple

Umm, Fiona has exactly zero bad songs. I could totally make a case for just strapping you down and forcing you to listen to *Tidal* over and over until you're inconsolable, but as much as I love that album, *When the Pawn . . .* is the one that, for me, has the most necessary and heartbreaking shit on it. I do not knock on Fiona's door when I'm trying to have an upbeat good time; I am coming to her with the shattered pieces of my heart in my hands, setting the pointy shards at her feet, and lying very still until she stomps on them with her words. The urgency with which she growls "you're all I need" is so visceral and great, and I have never spoken to anything that wasn't shaped like a burrito with such fervor in my life.

"Brown Skin Lady," Black Star

When I first started listening to rap music, I was deeply invested in West Coast rappers, mostly because the music was so aggressive that it made me feel tough by association, and also because I looked like a young Ice Cube. He, DJ

Quik, and Too $hort ("What's my favorite word? Bitch!") provided the bulk of the soundtrack to my aggro tweens. I used to walk around rapping "I hope you know I'd rather be dope than use it" to myself, but what do those words mean to an eleven-year-old girl in the rough part of the suburbs? No one had offered me dope. And I myself was most certainly not the other kind of dope. I always felt like a voyeur listening to NWA, or anything else that referenced crack cocaine and guns, but then De La Soul came along, and I was like, "Ooh! Okay! They're rapping about roller skates!" I wore hemp necklaces and a velvet choker almost every single day: backpack hip-hop was made for me, especially because that peace-and-love shit really resonated and, deep down, I was terrified of doing crime. "Brown Skin Lady" is maybe the first time I'd ever heard anyone earnestly and unabashedly rapping about a beautiful woman and not feeling good enough to approach her, and I am a sucker for that kind of naked vulnerability. Also, I think this ushered in my "smooth jazz with vegetarian dudes spitting rhymes over it" phase, and I haven't left it.

"It's Oh So Quiet," Björk
The video for this is maybe the most impactful thing I watched during my years as a sensitive teen. Okay, fine, this and *My So-Called Life*. They both still hold up.

"The Love I Never Had," Mary J. Blige
I felt a kinship with Mary from the second I saw the "Real Love" video on the Box, and I immediately begged my mom to find a baseball jersey in my size, although at that

point I definitely had not experienced the soul-crushing romantic pain that you could feel ripping through her vocal cords as she sang. But I aspired to! I grew up in an Al Green/Anita Baker/Teena Marie/Isley Brothers house, so I knew of heartbreak. I was steeped in unrequited desire, lost love, and romance gone bad. I performed Betty Wright's "After the Pain," a song about an abusive relationship, at my second-grade talent show. I've been riding with Mary from the jump, and *Mary* is her finest work. "All That I Can Say"? "Your Child"? "Let No Man Put Asunder"? The duet with Aretha Franklin, "Don't Waste Your Time"?! ALL EXTREMELY GOOD. But "The Love I Never Had" is a real "scream-sing your sorrows in the car on the highway" kind of jam, and that is the true measure of a quality song.

"You Got Me," The Roots (the live version from The Roots Come Alive, duh!)

Okay, so this was a tough one, because junior year, Tim Herman made me a tape of *Do You Want More?!!!??!* and I completely destroyed that thing rewinding "Mellow My Man" over and over and over again. But as much as I love that album and as much as it feels pedestrian to put a group's most popular song on a mix (everyone knows that you're only a true fan if you appreciate the deep cuts), I'm going to be basic and choose this one because I have a really good story that goes with it. After I dropped out of college and was wandering around aimlessly because all my friends had gone back to school, I started going to tons of shows because they were cheap and I was eighteen and I felt like ~interesting~ people Did Stuff At Night. At the very least, it gave me something to write about in the e-mails I sent from my freshly minted EarthLink dot net address. De La Soul and the Roots did a show at House of Blues, and I missed getting tickets because this was the old days, remember, when you had to stand in line all day and pay for a physical ticket to go to a show. But then, due to demand, they added a late show, the idea of which is against my religion, but I loved them so much that I copped a ticket anyway. Then I spent all afternoon the day of the show lying down before driving my Escort downtown at 10 p.m. and parking illegally next to Harry Caray's because there's nowhere to put your car down there that doesn't cost a minimum of sixty bucks. Anyway, I'm at the show, alone, wearing an orange vest that I thought looked cool, packed like a sardine with all these dudes with sparse mustaches wearing backpacks and fitted caps. The Roots did their set and started "You Got Me," which is a kind of sad love song that features Erykah Badu on the original. Of course, she was too famous to just tour with these dudes to accompany them on one song, so instead they brought out this relatively unknown singer named Jill Scott to sing her part, and I was blown THE FUCK AWAY by her voice. Just standing there, covered in other people's sweat, breathing in their clouds of Cool Water cologne, dumbstruck by this woman and her incredible voice. It was one of the best nights of my life, despite the hefty parking ticket and having to drive home 75 percent asleep at 2 a.m. (Also, I would include a Jill Scott song or five on this mixtape, for sure, but *Who Is Jill Scott* didn't come out until 2000, and I'm trying to stick to the rules here.)

"No Surprises," Radiohead

I don't know what I was doing before *OK Computer* found its way into my life. Every single song is the best song I've ever heard. Well, maybe this one is the *best* best.

Flip the tape over. Play it again.

love and marriage

I got married, and now I am an expert on marriage and relationships. Here are the answers you so desperately need to your desperate questions.

My wife and I are dear friends with a younger couple. They both have busy careers and text and e-mail incessantly for work. Recently the four of us dined out at a wonderful country inn, and they texted throughout the meal. I care very much about my relationship with them and do not wish to offend them, but this behavior bothered me. How can I nicely ask them to put their smartphones away?

Everything is boring. You're boring. There's a 95 percent chance your wife is pretty boring, and going to a "wonderful country inn" is probably, definitely Totally Fucking Boring. I'm boring, too! This is something that I have had to come to terms with as I am now staring middle age right in its sensible orthopedic inserts. I have to get over myself and let go of young-person shit that is irritating to me. If I'm too old for it, I don't give a shit about it. And that's not to say that it shouldn't exist, which is an old person thing I *really* don't understand. Jesus God, the stuff kids are into is literally too exhausting to get pissed off about. WHO CARES. Let them do whatever they want. My lady and I aren't friends with any young couples because I don't want to have to learn what the fuck "no cap" means. I want to eat my sensibly balanced meals and spend my days listening to jangly guitar music that came out in the years before I graduated high school.

There are two types of awful old people. There are (1) the silently awful who grind their rear molars into stumps and pray for sudden death as some teenager tries to record them for their story and (2) the "put your phone away, young lady, and pretend to be interested in this *New York Times* article about charter schools I am misquoting" awful. My favorite thing is to spend my old-person money on expensive electronics for the babies in my life, because I will actually die if I have to figure out interesting things to say to a Gen Z-er that might make them think I'm not as cool as my tattoos (how do I say "tattoo" in a cool way? "Ink"? "Body art"?!) would lead them to believe. And they most certainly don't care about listening to all my ancient leisure activities. What the fuck do I even talk about all day, 1099s and full-coverage underpants? LIKE, FOR REAL, WHO EVEN CARES? JUST POINT ME TOWARD THE SUN AND WATER ME OCCASIONALLY.

I can't tell you about the first time I thought I was in love (yes, I can, it was Wil Wheaton on *Star Trek: The Next Generation*, and it was devastating), but I can tell you each and every time some adult tried to bully me into a conversation about low interest rates or whatever seniors with rain-indicating knees and hip problems talk about, while I plucked out my eyelashes one by one in despair. I don't want to sit at the kids' table, because, truth be told, I can't sit with my legs at a ninety-degree angle for more than forty-five minutes, but if they sit at mine, I need to know that these dudes are for sure texting the entire time while pretending they care about that foreign film I saw at eleven thirty Sunday morning. Whether I like it or not, and despite my having neither a mortgage nor a dedicated gynecologist, as the bitch with the SEP-IRA, I am *absolutely* going to be stuck paying for that wonderful country meal.

I have been living with a man for more than a year. We get along perfectly, and he says he loves me. The problem is he will not make a commitment to get married. I do everything a wife would do to make a comfortable home for us. I am approaching middle age, and I want the security of marriage. Should I wait for him, hoping he will change his mind, or should I move on and find someone who would like to make a commitment?

What does "get along perfectly" mean if there's a big glaring blockade like "I want to get married and he doesn't" in the way? Why do people willfully ignore these giant logs scattered across their roads to domesticated bliss? Oh, I know, sex. But seriously, though, why??

I feel like just reframing how you see your relationship would shift your entire perspective. What if you just said,

"He says he loves me but the problem is he won't commit and I need that"? Then you're done, right? You can easily walk away! I have been accused of being cold and unromantic, but this isn't that, I promise. I have often listened to the words a person I was in love with said to me and ignored what they actually meant, to instead project onto them what I wanted it to mean. That shit will keep you in a weird emotional death spiral for the rest of your relationship until you shake yourself out of it, and you don't deserve that. I know that self-delusion can feel protective, but, ultimately, you're going to do what we all do at some point: cycle through all that old shit he said, and all those red flags you ignored, while chuckling softly at your naïvety. You believed you could change a person who was telling you exactly what they didn't want, and now the reality is setting in that you can't. Don't feel dumb; it happens to the best of us.

There are dozens of anecdotes to illustrate this in my own interpersonal-relationship canon, but the first is always the worst: my first real relationship, at twenty-one, was with a man ten years older. We met at a house party where he was, OF FUCKING COURSE, the DJ. I didn't know anyone except the friend who'd brought me along, and I hovered in the kitchen like a creep, watching other people have fun. To this day, this is my preferred approach to partying. Anyway, later in the evening, the DJ came over and pointed out that I didn't look like I was having a good time, and in a panic to prove him wrong I drank a tumbler of gin in one gulp and went home with him. (Other stuff happened also, but you get my point.) The next morning, when he dropped me off, he said, very spe-ci-fi-cal-ly, "This was fun. I'll call you. I don't want to get into anything serious," and pulled off in a haze of SUV exhaust before I could even close the passenger-side door all the way. I proceeded to spend an entire calendar year convinced I was in a boyfriend-girlfriend relationship with a not-serious person, who then did everything he could to prove that he was *even less serious* about me than he'd initially warned.

I couldn't be mad at anyone but myself when it finally dawned on me what an idiot I was being. (Okay, yes, I was bitter and I blamed him, too, but this is not the time to deconstruct my immaturity.) My problem was that I had hoped that I could do enough stuff to convince him I was worth his undivided attention. I mean, I wasn't doing "wife stuff" like you are, but I *was* making him cool mix CDs and lathering myself in the finest Bath & Body Works scented lotions before he came over for sex. So, yeah, pick up what he's putting down. He's probably not your future husband, and that's okay.

Also, what does "a wife do"? You know what my wife does? Asks me three times in a row if I've e-mailed the HVAC company yet, and moves my shoes to places where I can't find them and then calls that "cleaning." If that's what you're doing, I understand his hesitation. I'm kidding, I'm kidding. Anyway, he's not a bus—stop waiting for him. Catch the next one!

I am twenty-five and have been with my boyfriend on and off for five years. I love him very much. I often overthink things, and a constant frustration of mine is that he makes no romantic gestures at all. I worry that when we get married, over time I will grow bored or no

longer be attracted to him because he is so unromantic. Am I just overthinking this?

I wasn't in an actual romantic relationship until I was 137 years old, but doesn't the idea of being with someone you met when you were twenty weird y'all out? I was so stupid when I was twenty. On December 31, 1999, I was nineteen years old, and terrified (more than I feel comfortable admitting) that Y2K was going to kill us all before I had been kissed properly. My sister convinced me that rather than propping up our tits and going to a glamorous party, at the end of which someone would feel compelled to passionately kiss us, that we should *instead* put on our nicest long-sleeved cotton shirts and sensible close-toed shoes to spend New Year's Eve at church. I conceded that, sure, maybe the safest place to be when the Lord Almighty plunged us all into everlasting darkness was with a tambourine in my hand, surrounded by sinners who cheated God out of their tithes but clearly had a better shot at heaven than the drunks vomiting next to me on the train. I'm not saying that it wasn't surprisingly fun or that riding a wave of brimstone and gospel music into the apocalypse wasn't thrilling. I'm just saying that maybe the person hunched over in that pew, her eyes squeezed shut in an effort to seal out the impending rapture, that naive idiot screaming, "WE MADE IT! WE MADE IT!" when the clock struck midnight and literally nothing happened and not even one computer malfunctioned . . . I'm just saying that maybe the teenager who had unplugged the clocks at home and filled her cabinets with indestructible cans of kidney beans probably would not have made the wisest decision about with whom she should spend the remainder of her days.

"Over time I will grow bored"—yikes!—"or no longer be attracted to him"—yikes!!—"because he is so unromantic"—okay, come on, am I the only one who sees what's happening here? What the fuck, and also, BITCH, YIKES. Before I got married I made a list of all the reasons I might have to eventually bail on the union, but it was full of stuff like "if her kid pulls a knife on me" and "if she reprograms my radio stations in the car." You know, hypothetical shit that probably wouldn't happen, but, if it did, we could probably work it out. I don't know why you'd attach your credit score to someone you can already imagine being bored and repulsed by, especially when you don't have to. And I don't understand why people won't just say "listen, babe, I am not going to get better once I legally saddle myself to you," because, for real, he won't. If he's not sending flowers now, there's no way you're going to get them after his years of listening to the slimy squelch of your DivaCup extraction. He should! But he won't! I know being in love fills us with a blinding false optimism, but listen to me: he will not change. I didn't! As a matter of fact, all my bad behavior is heightened, because where is this bitch I'm married to gonna go? She's stuck with me now.

My boyfriend and I have been together for over two years, but I've met his parents only a few times. As he has told me, they have deemed me unworthy due to my age (I'm four years older than he is) and my health (I had a case of sinusitis on one occasion). They do not want me in their house or at any of their social events—even at my boyfriend's birthday dinner. As a result, things are pretty awkward, even though my boyfriend has confronted them about it. What can I do to get them to accept me?

Acceptance is overrated! So are birthday dinners, good health, and, frankly, having parents. I killed mine while I was still a teen, because I knew that if I didn't, my adult life would be ceaselessly tormented by the insurmountable demands of my overbearing mom and dad, people who couldn't be bothered to teach me how to balance a checkbook but would nevertheless feel entitled to weigh in on my choice of career and life mate and Internet service provider. Neither of them lived long enough to suffer through the indignity of an introductory meal with someone I was sleeping with, and thank goodness for that. My parents have been dead for twenty-two years and even now my insides churn at the very thought of my father scowling at my wife over his leather-tough tri tip at the Sizzler like, "You're a what now? A teacher? Do you make any money doing that? Who's gonna pay for that rib eye?!" as I burn with white-hot shame while eating directly from the all-you-can-eat salad bar. FUCK THAT SHIT, YOU GOTTA DIE. *makes stabbing motions*

Back when I had feelings, my self-esteem was a toilet. It caused me actual physical pain to know that someone didn't like me. I mean, it still does, but I'm better insulated by drugs these days. A handy trick is to think long and hard about what the person who hates you would realistically add to your life if they were to actually be a part of it. Most people really do have absolutely nothing to offer you. Pull out the abacus and make a pros and cons list if you have to—I'll wait. If you require a push to get started, here's an example from a recent entry in my diary about some asshole I don't miss anymore:

> **pro:** once made me laugh at a dad joke
> **con:** EVERYTHING FUCKING ELSE LOL BYE BITCH

Okay, okay, now let's do yours:

> **pro:** made a son that you like
> **con:** weird about a four-year age difference between you and that son. I mean, come on, have they never seen any celebrities?
> **con:** obvs do not understand basic tenets of healthcare and infectious disease
> **con:** insist upon hosting "social events" in their home
> **con:** They suck. It's pretty obvious.

Once you make your list, frame it inside your heart and refer back to it every time you hear these dudes are having a backyard luau or whatever kind of garbage party regular people throw. Come on now, do you really want to sit on the edge of a hard-backed chair clutching some Costco Chardonnay while Bob and Janice regale you with stories about the Alaskan cruise they took last fall? No, you want to be blowing your nose on the sleeve of your sweatshirt and watching *Billions* while you and the cat share a bowl of ice cream. WIN, WIN.

It seems I will never meet my "Mr. Right." Every person I'm attracted to is either in a relationship or doesn't like me. When is it okay to just "settle"?

Honestly, you can settle whenever the hell you want. I think it's just a matter of deciding what you want and what's important to you, and if you find it, lasso that bull and drag him into the stable. But first you have to recognize that there being one right, perfect person is a fallacy sold to you by romantic comedies. Dismantle the lie that finding said person is an achievable goal for someone who is not a bland actress in one of those Netflix movies you keep scrolling past. I'm not mad at it—I love the lie—but I also understand that it's a fantasy.

Maybe this is the upside of being ugly, but when men throw shit at you and scream lewd shit at you from passing cars on the street when you're just trying to get to the bus stop after school, the idea of there being one in a bespoke suit descending from a carriage to escort you to a fancy party doesn't seem like a thing that could happen in real life. Oh, really, Prince Charming is going to find a glass slipper to awkwardly slide onto this elephantine size 11 foot? Hollywood won't sell me that dream! Television forced me to look at romantic relationships from a practical perspective; I would be like Mabel, waddling through the door after an endless shift at work to yell at my fatherless children, Raj and Dee, about whatever hijinks they'd gotten into while I was out cleaning houses or whatever. Or my fate would be Shirley, a closeted lesbian forced to wisecrack with disrespectful teens while making two dollars an hour.

"Settling" is a coarse way of saying "adjusting my expectations," and I think that gets a bad rap. Dude, I would rather settle than be "chronically unfulfilled due to my outsize desires." I don't mean that you should marry someone you hate just because they won't go away, but I do think it's worth examining what you actually want while being honest about what is important to you. Then it won't feel like such a compromise, you know? On top of that, it's totally unfair to make a flesh-and-bone person compete against an imaginary ideal that was imprinted on you when you were too young to understand what was happening. Shit, growing up I wanted to marry the Beast from *Beauty and the Beast*. A strong, virile creature who read tons of books and could fuck up a wolf? Yes please! Sign me up! I could've lain awake every night waiting for Mufasa to save me from a wildebeest stampede in a gorge, but do I climb into bed next to a fucking lion? No, bitch, because I am realistic. Instead, I married this person who makes her own kombucha and charges her crystals under the new moon. Girl, adapt!

Lately I have become perplexed at the vanity and immoral behavior now associated with the task of dating. I'm a single man living by myself, with no responsibilities but my own. I am looking for someone who will fit into my lifestyle. Unfortunately, I have encountered some roadblocks that keep me single. First: I am not looking for a ready-made family. Second: I'm not in a position to analyze her last relationship, which left emotional baggage. Third: I am definitely not looking for someone who isn't business- or life-oriented. What I want to find is someone who doesn't have a long history

of suitors or life issues that cause further relationship problems. How do I go about separating the disposables from the possibles?

CAN YOU GET ON A ROCKET TO MARS? First of all, don't knock a ready-made family. I joined one and you know what? It's fine! There's so much less for me to do, and that's comforting. Second, is this emotional exploration really being asked of you, a regular person who wrote to a housekeeping magazine for advice? Is this a thing, asking a single man you met on Tinder for deep Jungian analysis? Third, are there sentient, breathing women who are not life-oriented? What do those words mean? "Business" I understand, but if I am alive, am I not life-oriented? Also, my kingdom for a person on Earth over the age of five who does not have any "life issues." LIFE IS MY ISSUE, SIR.

Who cares about helping some asshole who refers to people as "disposables," but is this what it's like to date these days? I'm not asking from the snooty perch of the Smug Married. I am genuinely concerned that this is what women are encountering when they are trying to see a movie and get a pizza with three toddlers stacked in a trench coat masquerading as an adult human male. The thing about having this many stringent requirements is not that you aren't allowed to want what you want. Of course you are! You should have standards. You deserve to be happy! It's that, if I had this many stipulations, I would feel like I had to offer the exact same and then some in return. And I couldn't. I'm fucked up.

I imagine that if this is the standard I expect a person to meet before I'd consider dating them, I have to have a dope crib and an 850 credit score and a lifetime six-figure job with benefits and a clean bill of health and regular therapy sessions and a mom who loves me and all my chakras balanced and be very good at bringing a person other than myself to orgasm. I don't have even *one* of those things, which is why the job application to be my boss is incredibly short. It's basically: "Can I pick all the music and have 75 percent ownership of the remote?" And if you agree to tolerate me, I'm yours! I aspire to have the confidence of this perplexed single man. How does one build up nerve like this?

My husband has an extensive sexual history. He has had sex with more than eighty partners. All the encounters were from when he was in high school and in his early twenties. Most were one-night stands with female friends. When we met, he was honest, and I was understanding. He didn't keep in touch with any of those women (pre-Facebook). But now he's friends with several of them on Facebook, and while he doesn't "talk" to them, he comments and "likes" many of their posts. This makes me uncomfortable, because I don't feel that past sexual partners should be part of one's life once someone is married. I'm not jealous or insecure, I just think it's disrespectful. Am I controlling?

You know what feels like a lot of pressure to me? Being the sole object of one person's affections. Stay with me—I'm not about to surprise you by pretending to understand what being polyamorous actually means. I'm saying that I spent many, many agonizing years *desperate* for someone to pay attention to me, and now that there's a spotlight on everything I do, it's like, "Hey, babe, should we get you a girlfriend?" I'm not as interesting as I thought I was. I mean, is anyone? It's one thing to be cool and glamorous on date night once a week, but when you have to see a person Monday *and* Tuesday *and* Wednesday: I do not have enough party tricks for this.

Every time I glance over and my lady is texting someone, my brain screams, *THANK GOD, I HOPE THIS BITCH IS GOING OUT!!!!!* "Wow, sweetie, are you liking someone's Instagrams? Would you like to talk to that person while I try to do literally *anything* I can tell you about later?" I am flooded with relief every time I walk in the house and she's on the phone with someone I've never met. You know why? That takes the heat off my ass for five minutes. Listen, I'm not posturing as one of those ~cool girls~ who is supremely confident and doesn't get jealous. I just don't get jealous of my wife double-tapping some stud in cornrows and boxer briefs on her pocket computer. What's the harm? Is she going to leave me for her? Probably not—all her shirts and canned tomatoes live here!

Control is a wild concept. I think the one thing I've learned from my many exes—most of whom I do not follow on social media, because it's fine if they have a better life than mine, but I don't need to fucking see it—is that you just can't have it. Short of imprisoning someone, it's just not possible. There is no such thing as total control. And if you're a reasonable person, you probably don't even really want it. It's a lot of work being in charge of a whole other person and their Facebook likes.

One day, you should secretly add up all the minutes he spends online, surreptitiously favoriting pictures of women named Debra and Jackie as they pose in front of slot machines on the riverboat with Virginia Slims dangling off their lips, and imagine he's spending all that time focused on what you're doing instead. Watching you pick at your cuticles, and try on old pants, and giggle over dumb gossipy shit in the group chat, and eat peas out of the can, or whatever silly shit you like doing without an audience. Disconcerting, right? Let him have his likes! You've got episodes of *Basketball Wives* clogging up the DVR.

We've only been married for a couple years, and our love life is still pretty hot if you ask me, but why won't my wife have sex with me in the shower?

Probably because she values having intact front teeth. If life were a movie, you would return home after a grueling day at the office, sexily loosen your tie as you drop your briefcase in the mudroom, brush past the towering stack of overdue credit card bills on the kitchen counter, and take the stairs two at a time up to the master bedroom where your beloved sits weeping over a "hey just thinking about u" text from that one dude she really thought she was going to marry back in 2007. Ignoring her attempts to hide the phone, you kick a path through piles of soiled laundry to the bathroom you meant to bleach last weekend when your mother-in-law was in town, wait for the water to get hot and the pressure to build, then coax her into joining you in the shower with promises to carefully shave that stubbly bit of thigh-back that always gets missed when she bathes in contended solitude. You initiate clumsy, ham-handed slippery-fingered lovemaking that is over before it has really even begun, then immediately retreat to a separate corner of the house. You indulge in whatever SPORTS!!! happen to be on television for the remainder of the evening while she locks herself in the spare bedroom to text homeboy back.

Sadly, life is not a movie. Life is an impossibly long and unyielding march to the grave, peppered along the way with myriad disappointments and misfortunes. Living is a mistake and everyone is trash, which is why shower sex usually winds up with one or more of the naked parties shivering alone at the back of the shower, trying not to slip on a viscous glob of body wash, while the other gasps and sputters as shampoo burns her sensitive eyes. Your wife sounds pretty sensible. Just leave her alone already.

I am a morning person, and my newly retired partner is the opposite. At night in our bedroom, they read on their iPad for several hours while I try to sleep. I am in bed by 11 p.m. while my partner usually stays up till 1 or 2 a.m. If I wake up, they're on our couch in the bedroom with a glow of light from the iPad. We have been married twenty years and usually went to bed at the same time because of work, but now that they're retired, they like staying up reading, watching movies, or watching videos on YouTube. Bottom line: it bothers me that one person is doing an activity while the other sleeps or tries to sleep. What would be your advice?

I don't have a job. I mean, not *for real*. Sometimes people try to act like writing about my asshole on the Internet qualifies as work, but those people have obviously never worked as receptionists for veterinarians and been vomited on by a dog with parvo while trying to schedule dentistry for a cat. THAT SHIT IS WORK. Burning my knees with an over-heated laptop all evening after crawling out of bed at 3 p.m. is most certainly not!

That said, I love to go to sleep at 2 a.m. Which is weird, because I'm an extremely jumpy and anxious person, especially in the dark. As soon as night falls, a family of raccoons will skitter across the deck eating compost or a deer will ram its head repeatedly into the garage door, causing my heart to skip several beats as I brace myself for a horror-movie villain to come crashing through the glass door while my wife sleeps peacefully upstairs, blissfully unaware of the corpse she's unfortunately going to have to heave out of the way when she wakes up to get past the guy in the *Scream* mask hiding in the closet. But let me tell you what your partner won't: it's worth risking getting your head chopped off by Freddy Krueger to watch your makeup tutorials and/or read a couple chapters of your Book of the Month in blissful unadulterated silence.

When I lived alone, I would go to bed at 9 p.m., but now that there is a family in my home who won't stop talking to me, I can't really get anything done, or enjoy anything in my life, until all those people go the fuck to sleep. Respect a pair of headphones? Give a shit about a locked door?? No, ma'am, not in this house! If the sun is up, guaranteed there is someone beating a snare drum or sprawled in front of a blaring television or bleating, "Sam? Sam? Sam? Sam? Sam? Sam? Sam? Sam? Sam?" while standing right in front of me until I drag my eyes to wherever they want me to look. So when they sleep, I'm up. It's just me and the cats watching

R-rated violent, sexy shit without anybody asking where the scissors are or if lentils are okay for dinner. Sure! Cook whatever you want! I'm going to have my real dinner (Triscuits and pimento cheese from Zingerman's) at midnight.

I'm up writing this at 1 a.m. on a Thursday, with nothing but the drone of a couple fans and a white-noise machine whirring in the distance for company. Four hours ago I stood in the assembly line outside the bathroom waiting to double cleanse, pat some drops of antiaging serum into my cheeks, brush my teeth a little, dab on some moisturizer, and get into my PJs. As everyone completed the routine by settling into bed, I turned on the recorded episode of *Real Housewives of New York* they wouldn't allow me to watch uninterrupted when it aired a few hours ago.

You either have to let it go or quit your job. Or maybe get them a pair of fancy headphones so Wendy Williams reruns aren't filtering into your dreams. Now that that's out of the way, what is this I'm reading about a "bedroom couch"? What exactly is that, and how can I get one?

My husband of many years has an offensive eating habit. When finishing his meal, he takes the plate or bowl, puts it up to his mouth as one would a drinking glass, and shovels the remains into his mouth. As he does it, he makes little sucking movements with his lips like an animal lapping food from a bowl. I find it revolting, but how can I address it without offending him?

I do this. Everyone does this. How the fuck else are you supposed to get all the liquid part of the stew? Tell me how to finish my entire bowl of Corn Chex in under an hour without tipping the last of it from the bowl directly down my throat. If I have to eat room-temperature soup with you at four in the afternoon, I want to be able to eat all of it. You can't insist I try gazpacho, and then make me scoop out the last bit one-eighth of a teaspoon at a fucking time. Don't address it, you monster. Just let him eat his runny oatmeal and unsalted broth in peace.

are you familiar with my work?

You don't have to cry for me, but listen: trying to make new friends as an adult is the hardest thing I have ever attempted to do. Harder than multiple colonoscopies? Yes. Harder than listening to the dentist pry my tooth bone away from my jawbone while I lie there wide awake? Also yes!

When I moved to Kalamazoo from Chicago, I thought for sure that I was going to be happy being in the house and never going outside. And, for the most part, I am. I get to travel and work in fancy cities with mass transit and Ethiopian food, then come back and pay $1.87 for a gallon of gas for the car that I can park anywhere on my sprawling 2,000 acres of land that were practically free. Okay, I'm exaggerating, but I used to pay $850 a month for 350 square feet of living space, which is $2.43 per foot, and now I pay $2.39 a foot for 1,700 square feet. Yes, I probably fucked up the math, but my point is FUCK THE CITY.

But, how does one make friends without an office to go to? Or a club to participate in? Or various PTA meetings to grimace at each other through? Are you just supposed to walk up to an interesting-looking person on the street and ask them to be your friend? I don't know if this is some kind of reverse profiling, but I can usually glance at a person and know at first sight that we're probably going to get along. I don't have it down to a science (I'm not researching shit, dude), but here are some dead giveaways:

- interesting, alternative, "cool person" hair
- visible armpit hair
- hip glasses
- dumb tattoos, because people with serious tattoos are exhausting
- carrying a book, multiplied by a factor of ten if it happens to be one I wrote (I'm sorry—I am an egomaniac)
- fat
- mean
- has an old-ass cell phone
- eating something gross, with fervor
- feline

But even if you see a girl on the street who looks like she climbed right out of the most whimsical page in the plus-size section of ModCloth, eating a whole pizza with a well-loved copy of *Bastard Out of Carolina* tucked under her arm, what are you supposed to do? Can you just go up and introduce yourself and ask her to do a friend thing with you? "Um, excuse me, miss, would you like to sit around and vape sativa with me and eat Trader Joe's Cubano wraps while MSNBC plays on a continuous loop in the background?" Or, "Hey, stranger, would you like to skim the extensive collection of sad memes saved on my hard drive to see the kind of shit I will regularly be texting you at three in the morning?"

Have you ever considered what a friendship is, or what any of your current friendships are, and thought about how to present that to a prospective new friend? You know, like how you are going to eventually be sending them selfies of you trying on twelve similar-yet-slightly-different pairs of glasses in your ophthalmologist's waiting room while your garbage insurance is being processed? How do you convince a stranger to give you their real e-mail when you are definitely going to litter their gmail dot com with dumb nonsense. Scrolling through my phone to find recent examples of what I text my stupid-ass friends has yielded this treasure trove of idiocy:

jenny (12:09 a.m.): "AT ELEVEN AT NIGHT?? wow mom ★devil horns emoji★"

cara (2:22 a.m.): "lmao i mean great i hope they feel good, but you gotta be gross AND show tits"

megan (9:39 a.m.): "it's nothing, just capitalizing on the love being sent my way"

Michael (10:43 a.m.): "hey this is really important" ★posts link to a Twitter profile★

Jessie (1:11 p.m.): "we're thinking about adopting this orange cat from the shelter and his name is reginald but i want an orange cat named pumpkin so what do you think if i call him 'reginald pumpkin' aka 'little reggie pumps' that's a cool name right!"

john (1:12 p.m.): *mo'nique meme: "see when you do clownery, the clown comes back to bite"*

abbi (2:13 p.m.): "i just don't like that i can feel my organs working, you know? like my gallbladder burns and that makes me terrified that it is going to burst out of my body."

jenn (3:12 p.m.): "i am too humble and ashamed, i had guilt throwing out a face wash i hated"

helen (4:11 p.m.): "BEETS ARE DISGUSTING"

Fernando (4:17 p.m.): "do you think i could go to urgent care to get tested for stress shingles?"

keely (9:06 p.m.): "i'm glad it's finally spring, because i always thought i hated it as a season but i've actually missed the sun!! i even bought a sad lamp wtf"

A few years ago (before I moved to Michigan and joined my wife's community of backyard composters and travel-soccer chauffeurs), my lady and I went to her friend's costume wedding and—I know you already know this, but let me just say it for anyone who is new or still has a shred of hopefulness in their heart—I did not wear a costume. The last time I wore a Halloween costume was in the second-grade costume parade at Lincoln Elementary School in 1986 (go, dolphins), and the only costume I could come up with was "housewife," a concept I didn't fully understand but thought I could approximate with my mom's tattered old robe, a half-melted spatula, and the satin cap she slept in the nights after a fresh press 'n' curl. Because I was a Very Large Son, everyone just thought I had worn my shitty pajamas to school. I think I can speak for anyone who has ever been mistaken for their friend's mom, that any kind of childhood dress-up situation is precarious at best.

Anyway, my wife and I were at this wedding where I knew a few people well enough to say "Hi" but not well enough to say "Hi, _____," and as we're sitting in our assigned dinner seats I'm looking around the room, taking it all in, wondering who I can latch on to in the hopes of a semipermanent relationship once I officially moved to Kalamazoo. A dude named Ike came and sat next to me as we waited for the buffet to be set up, literally the only reason I braved a room full of people unironically dressed as Tolkien characters. He was wearing a Scientology uniform as his costume, and I immediately fell deeply in love. I talked to Ike for a while, writing his name in permanent marker on the Potential New Friends list in my mind.

After he abandoned me to go fill up his plate with communal vegan enchiladas from the hot bar, a cool-looking woman with shiny bangs and interesting glasses (PRO) carrying a tiny crying baby (CON) and wearing a Ruth Bader Ginsburg costume (NEUTRAL) came over to introduce herself to me. We got on like a house on fire. After a few minutes, my palms started to sweat in anticipation of what would surely be an awkward transition from a pleasant introductory conversation to the method by which I could secure her contact information to lock down a future friendship.

Is there an app for this? I wasn't the best fucking dater you ever saw, but by the end of my run I had certainly grasped the machinations of "let's turn this thing into the next thing": clandestine shared glance over the heads of the other people at the bar; awkwardly squeezing past other people's sweaty boners to reach each other; eight minutes of scream-talking the coolest things you can think of directly into each other's ears, standing close enough to get spittle on your neck; an arm caress, but super casual; *fake laughter*; *effusive praise you'll eventually come to regret*; "oh, hey, sorry, looks like my friends are done doing coke off the public toilet"; EXCHANGE OF PHONE NUMBERS. At ten the next morning, smoking a joint and listening to some Anita Baker and deciding whether you are too hungover to make it to brunch, you stare at your empty inbox and curse yourself for being so desperate and eager. That, I have mastered. I am the queen of "they probably input the digits wrong, I shoulda had *me* call *them*" when it comes to a deal I couldn't all-the-way seal. But with friends it's weirder. For instance, I have some treasured Instagram pals that I would maybe like to text rather than DM, because memorizing people's handles and organizing them all in my brain is difficult plus I assume everyone is like me and turns all their notifications off because all that popping up is stressful. On the flip side, some of these people live in faraway places like Omaha and Los Angeles, and it's not like I need their numbers for emergency purposes, just for my convenience. It's not important, but what if I wanted to call them? How in the fuck do people ever make non-romantic friends?

RBG sits down next to me at the table, and my lady is off being charming and laughing with her head tossed back, because these are the adulthood friends she's acquired through various Parent Teacher Associators and Slumber Party Coordinators, circles I don't have access to. Also, a lot of these peoples are Neighbors, a club I have no interest in joining! RBG's given name is actually Emily, and Emily is funny and smart and has a bubbly energy that is very appealing to me, and the more she talks, the more vivid my fantasy of us listening to somber podcasts in her minivan while driving to the petting zoo becomes. I can literally taste the nutmeg silt from the bottom of a pumpkin spice latte on my tongue when her husband (CON) comes over with a towering plate of food for her (PRO) and coaxes her away from my table. I start to say "hey, do you like tweeting?" or some other useless shit, but she's got that goddamn baby and this Jedi Knight is looming anxiously over us balancing a precarious platter of nachos, so I stammer out a "Nice talking to ya!" in my most nasal midwestern twang and go back to fucking around on my phone.

When I moved half a year later, rather than thinking about making new friends, I spent my first few days hiding from the surprising number of people who knocked on our door throughout the day. It's possible that they were coming over to offer me homemade bread or a hand-drawn map to all the local breweries or perhaps even their friendship, but I will never know, because I'm from Chicago and I don't believe in answering an unsolicited door knock. I took a couple weeks to get myself situated: I ordered fancy Internet deodorants from Aesop and had a desk shipped to me from CB2, stacked boxes of cozy Madewell cardigans in the front hall and ripped Ladurée macarons from their smoosh-proof packaging, all in an attempt to approximate my old life in a place where you can buy gym shoes at the grocery store. Which is hilarious for a person who had previously done 60 percent of her food shopping at gas stations and corner stores.

Fast forward to the next Halloween. I'm living in Kalamazoo. I'm still not wearing a fucking costume. My wife is corny, and to prove how much the evidence of our visit to an actual pumpkin patch is lined up on our porch. We live in a house, up the street from a school, in a neighborhood filled with children, and there are going to be trick-or-treaters. Since I hadn't bothered to meet anyone or answer the door I'd hidden behind while someone proffering a welcome casserole knocked on it, I'm going to have to sit on the steps with a bowl of premium miniature candy and assure all the little ghouls and goblins that I am indeed the witch that lives in this haunted cottage. When I was a kid, in 1984, I had this Care Bears book called *The Witch Down the Street* about a little bitch named Melissa who decides to leave a nasty note on the door of this harmless old cat lady she wrongly assumes is a witch until the Care Bears swoop in and show her the error of her ways, and the only thing running through my head as I emptied comically large bags of little Snickers into our novelty Halloween bowl was "I wonder how many of these kids think that about *me*?!"

Turns out? All of them. I don't know if they smelled my desperation and eagerness to please or if they could hear my cauldron bubbling in the backyard, but I spent the afternoon freezing half to death in arctic winds chasing third graders with single-serving bags of Sour Patch Kids as they ran screaming past my house. After several hours of creepily trying to coax kids whose costumes I had no reference for (what is a Minecraft?) to unload ten pounds of Skittles off me, I spotted a familiar pack of white people making their way down our hill and at the head was old Ruth Bader G from that wedding the year before: My Possible Friend Emily! I waved, despite my hesitation to appear enthusiastic in public. She and her family were convincingly dressed as the family from *Bob's Burgers*, the littlest one (now walking!) toddling around in a pink bunny hat. I poured mini boxes of Milk Duds into the kids' outstretched pillowcases and made small talk, trying to come up with a smooth segue into asking Emily if she was in the market for a new best friend.

"Ha-ha, it's cold out here, huh?" Omg, stop. "You guys look so cute. Do you have a cheeseburger in your pocket?" Holy shit, swallow your own tongue. "Tell me everything that has happened in the year since I last saw you." Samantha Irby, if you don't shut the actual fuck up!

A crowd gathered as I put on my best show to convince her telepathically to beg me to hang out sometime, flop sweating and awkwardly laughing way too much as children who had never met one another before swarmed around our knees, loudly chattering and comparing costumes. They were instant friends. HOW WAS THIS SO EASY FOR THEM? "Hey, Hendrix," I hissed under my breath at a child in a *Handmaid's Tale* bonnet hugging some sort of plush human dinosaur, "so did you just, like, ask for Clementine's phone number or did the moms have to get involved or what?"

Emily's kids were ready to go; the block was buzzing that the people with the pool in their yard were giving out full-size Twix and inventory was going fast. My palms grew slick from nerves as another wave of shouting kids threatened to trample us in the pursuit of sour Nerds. I could not let her get away again.

"It was great to see you!" she said, drifting toward the sidewalk. Why has age made me better at so few things? I thought getting older was supposed to make me wise and good at stuff? Should I ask her if she has trouble emptying her bladder all the way? Invite her to an early afternoon book discussion at the local library? HOW WOULD YOUR MOM DO THIS? "I'm gonna friend you on Facebook!" I blurted at the back of her red shirt and mom jeans feeling my bones weaken and my arteries calcifying as I aged forty years in one second. "We should get together! We could eat some black licorice and watch *God Friended Me*!"

We settled on lunch. Lunch is a good friendship-testing situation, because nighttime feels too much like a date and doing anything during the day makes it easier to pretend you have something urgent to get to if it fucking sucks. "Hate to eat and run, I have a meeting!" Bitch, you don't have a meeting. But no one can *prove* that you don't have a meeting, especially since it's noon. Also, pro tip: if you're friends with someone who has a kid, you better learn to love a daytime hang; otherwise you're going to find yourself sipping Juicy Juice and saying nonsense words like, "Girl, you are not gonna believe this, I found a fu— I mean, a *frigging* boo-boo on my hoo-ha," while a six-year-old who should've taken his little bad-frigging-ass to bed two hours ago screams, "WHAT?!" and throws peas at your face.

I picked a sushi spot even though I don't love sushi, because the restaurant is really sunny and cute, and I wanted to make a good impression. Which, in hindsight, is fucking misleading, because I am 100 percent the kind of friend who wants you to pick me up so we can go to the drive thru and gossip over Big Macs in the McDonald's parking lot. All my real friends are like, "Sushi? *Table* service? In *daylight*? I once had to watch you eat a hot dog on the bus!"

I don't dress up anymore, ever, for any reason, so I'm sure I just wore a dumb T-shirt and high-waisted pants, but I put on some blush because it's a quick and handy way to make you look like you care about yourself, even when you don't. Never leave home without something you can blindly rub on to your cheeks in a public bathroom stall. I keep a grimy, dusty NARS multipurpose stick in the bottom of my bag just in case I run into someone who knows me and might ask, "Damn, are you sick?" all loud and shit in the middle of the mall.

Emily showed up to the empty restaurant, and I heaved a huge sigh of relief. I mean, that's the biggest hurdle, right? Just getting someone to put on pants for you? I don't remember what she ordered, but I do remember that I was brave enough to order edamame with sriracha salt to start, and by "brave" I mean "foolish," because it was way too hot for me and I had to fake that I actually enjoy eating flavored foods. She was talking to me about her life, and I was thinking about how to excuse myself to the bathroom and fake my own death. Sriracha salt?? We talked and ordered rolls and laughed and ordered tempura and laughed even harder, and I resisted drooling over the dessert menu, and then the meal drew to a natural close and our waiter, a young man I don't think was even old enough to serve us alcohol, hovered nearby with the check. I pulled out my debit card and waved him over. It had been my invitation, plus I really wanted Emily to like me and I don't believe I can win anyone over with charm alone, so I was going to pay. That is another benefit of asking someone to lunch: THAT SHIT IS CHEAP. The waiter took my card and vanished.

I had checked my bank account before I even left the house, because I don't fucking play that. Chase Bank is not gonna be embarrassing *me* out here in these streets. So when it took several seconds longer for the waiter to return, I assumed there had been a glitch with the machine, or he'd had to stop and fill someone's water and got lost on his way back to our table. The clock ticked excruciatingly slowly. Emily was on the booth side of the table and I had my back to the restaurant, so I didn't notice when the waiter silently appeared behind me with the black check holder. He held it open and looked at its contents for half a beat too long, and I felt my insides liquify. My brain panicked. "How is he going to say it? Is he going to announce to the entire place that I don't have forty-seven dollars or is he going to let me have my dignity?" He looked at me, really studied me, and my heart clawed its way up to my throat. Oh my god, were the police already on their way? I stole a look at Emily, unable to tell if she was the type of person who had broke friends and would be cool with this. "Will she spot me a few bucks or just abandon me here to pay for our meal by washing miso cups and sushi mats?"

He set the check down next to my elbow, and I tried to be chill and just, you know, casually glance over at it to see if anything was circled in red marker or if my card was cut into shards like you sometimes see in the movies. "Excuse me," he began timidly, "but are you from Chicago?" I relaxed immediately. Of course! He's a fan! Honestly, I don't even know why I got all worked up—I'm over here crawling around the floor looking for a Xanax and this dude is hiding out trying to think of an unobtrusive way to ask for my autograph! Emily perked up when he asked where I was from. Her eyes danced, as if to say, "Am I actually eating lunch with a celebrity?" I nodded and smiled back. "Yes, regular-person-who-is-lucky-I'm-considering-being-your-new-friend, you are."

I am nothing if not totally gracious. "I am!" I gushed, hoping that he hadn't remembered me from anything embarrassing. "Are you familiar with my work?"

The oxygen was instantly sucked out of the fucking room. You could hear a mouse fart. The waiter's face, while sweet, looked confused. I registered it immediately and searched the table for something to cut my throat with. Of course, this young, cool person with pink hair and hand tattoos wasn't familiar with the self-indulgent ramblings of a middle-aged depressed lady with chronic diarrhea! Why am I even still alive?

Okay, let's assess: my card worked, that's good; I've humiliated myself in front of my new friend and haven't yet figured a way out of it and both of them are still looking at me, and that is very, very bad. And I hear you—how could a person who still has a blog on Al Gore's Internet in the year of our Lord 2020 possibly delude herself into thinking that she is notorious enough to be recognized in a mid-priced sushi chain in Kalamazoo, Michigan? Back home in Chicago, where it is busy and overpopulated and I am not one of six blacks, it happens to me all the time, so why not here?

"Um . . . no?" he replied sheepishly. We blinked at each

other for a solid three seconds, which is an incredibly long time in shame city. He nudged the book with my card in it. "I'm not exactly sure, but isn't that the Chicago skyline on your debit card?"

SON OF A FUCKING BITCH. I should've opened an account at fucking Wells Fargo, goddammit. I *knew* this stupid card was going to ruin my life today. Emily, my brand-new ex-friend, stifled a laugh behind her hand and averted her eyes. My face filled up with blood. "Yep, you're right, son, that is the Chicago skyline." I sighed, dejected. Our waiter valiantly attempted to save my ego. "What is your work?" he asked earnestly, trying to give me a hand up out of the grave I'd dug for myself. Imagine my answering this without crying. I would rather eat my own shoes than explain to this teenager what blogs are with soy sauce dripped all down my shirt.

"Are you familiar with my work?" What kind of fucking asshole says shit that way? It echoed off the walls of my brain, mocking me. Dude, I don't even talk like that. I meet people all the time who breathlessly come up to me like "HI, I LOVE YOUR STUFF" and I play it cool ("Oh my gosh, thank you so much! You're the sweetest!"), and then they shout *"BAD FEMINIST* REALLY CHANGED MY LIFE" right before their husband uses his phone to capture the exact moment my heart breaks in half like Ralph's in the "I Choo-Choo-Choose You" episode of *The Simpsons.* But at least in those moments, as I gratefully lap up the dregs of effusive praise intended for Roxane Gay—who, by the way, does not look like me at all—the person talking to me has at least an idea of what it is I do. Am I smart enough to write sharp cultural criticism? No! Am I fat and typing words on

a computer? Absolutely, yes, and I would love to accept that glass of wine you are mistakenly sending to my table because you enjoyed my talk in Australia so much!

Why couldn't I just have said nothing, or played dumb and waited for him to point to the Sears Tower on my card? Why didn't I just say "Evanston, technically," and wait for him to ask what the Hancock Building looks like? Am I ever going to stop writing the horror movie I have been starring in since the day I was born?

Today, Emily and I share an office. It's above a coffee shop that doubles as a moped warehouse, and even though I pay rent, I still have to pay full price for an oat milk latte, which, if I were to go there and pretend to work every day, could cost me twenty-five-plus dollars a week. The office is a big, airy space with shiny hardwood floors and gigantic windows that we've filled with plants and crystals and candles. I ordered another CB2 desk (an office one, for my office, rather than my at-home one, which is for piling shit on and forgetting it) and bought a fancy stapler even though I never, ever need to staple anything, and they look right at home next to Emily's draft table and rolling cart crammed full of oil pastels and gouache materials. She writes and illustrates gorgeous children's books about little glasses-wearing babies who explore the ocean and learn about weather, and I do a lot of anxiety-snacking while writing about my prickly labia and feeling self-conscious about the music I choose for us to work to. We have a strong, solid relationship.

We talk a lot about how beautiful Meghan Markle is and what podcasts we listen to, even though talking about talking is dumb, but we have fun. I know that her littlest kid is in kindergarten now and doesn't wear the bunny ears anymore.

She probably knows me well enough to tell you what to get me for my birthday, and she's been in my house enough times to tell you where we hide the best snacks. I like working next to her every day. We drink a lot of carbonated water and take a lot of CBD tinctures that don't work. I somehow survived the awkwardness of that early attempt at courtship and we've settled nicely into the very comfortable next stage of friendship, also known as "do you want this old lipstick that looks weird on me/can I borrow five dollars until the end of the week."

A few months ago I was entering my debit number into an unsafe website to buy some trash I definitely didn't need and noticed that my card was on the verge of expiration, and with a pang of despair in the center of my chest that humiliating sushi date came flooding back to mock me. There was no way I'd be issued a Chicago card to my adopted Michigan address, right? Would my umbilical banking cord finally be severed? The day the new one showed up in the mail, I almost threw the envelope away because it looked like something from a bill collector, and I peeled the flap open slowly, braced for the reveal of my Built Ford Tough card or whatever it is they have here. Blessed be, they sent me another Chicago card, made of a dipped Italian beef and a lock of Rod Blagojevich's hair. I immediately texted Emily to see if she wanted to meet me for lunch, my treat.

hysterical!

I got my period for the first time, without warning, when I was in the fifth grade. Which, in hindsight, feels incredibly early? How old are you in the fifth grade—nine? Ten? What did I even know in the spring of 1990? Could I accurately identify the president? Had I ever been outside the state of Illinois? Did I know what a penis was? Or the journey, exactly, it had to embark upon to fertilize an egg?

I knew not to take pills from shady dudes on skateboards, because I had a crush on one of the D.A.R.E. cops, so I paid attention to every word that was coming out of his handsome mouth, even though deep in my soul I knew my yearning to be socially accepted would make me take any white powder or "marijuana cigarette" anyone cooler than me offered. But did I know where the uterus was located and whether there was one in my body? I knew why hair turned gray because I watched this informational cartoon about follicles, but I couldn't tell you where South Dakota is on a map. And I knew all the words to "U Can't Touch This" because I had *Please Hammer Don't Hurt 'Em* on

cassette and had lain across my mom's bed for an hour playing and rewinding that song as I tried to write the lyrics on
the steno pad she kept next to her phone, but I couldn't
draw you a fallopian tube if my life depended on it. Also,
why do people who don't conduct any important business
whatsoever keep paper by the goddamn phone? Who of any
importance was calling my mother in 1990? Also, is he saying "fresh new kicks and pants" or "French new sticks and
pans"?! WHAT IS AN INTERNET?

The day the flood came, none of the other villagers surrounded me with offerings, no women keening at the blood
moon circled an altar of red candles, and no symbolic doves
were released as I submerged myself in a salt bath. I was on
a cold toilet gawking at the smear of rust-colored blood in
the crotch of my threadbare Hanes Her Way, trying to recall
exactly what Mrs. Kantner had said to do when discuss-
ing puberty in the two-week introductory health segment
wedged into our fifth-grade social studies class.

Having requested a full hysterectomy mere months after
squeezing me out into the world (no, I didn't take that decision personally, nope, not at all, I am very well-adjusted!),
my mom didn't have any menstrual products in the house,
so I had to sit on the toilet leaking unstrained beef soup into
the bowl while she rummaged through the junk drawer to
find a kitchen towel that she didn't mind being sacrificed for
the cause, before folding it into my underpants to tide me
over while she went to the corner store whose specialty was
scratch-off lottery tickets and cartons of rancid orange juice
with the long-past expiration dates rubbed off—definitely
not a place with a wide variety of products to serve a young
woman's menstrual needs. You walk into a Walgreens right

now and there are: thirty-seven kinds of maxi pads of varying strength and thickness and recyclability, curved or
winged or otherwise; tampons for both work and play, with
applicator and without; medical-grade silicone shot glasses
that you're expected to wedge up against your cervix while
also somehow not turning a public bathroom stall into that
blood elevator from *The Shining*. My mom returned home
with a plastic bag of generic sanitary napkins that she had
clearly dragged out from the back of a bottom shelf, her
fingerprints still visible in the inch-thick dust on the top of
the box.

I took having my period very seriously, which for a ten-
year-old meant never changing my pads at school or alluding
to its existence in any way. I missed the sanitary-pads-with-
belts era, thank goodness, and Always had just come out
with their revolutionary Dri-Weave technology, the limits
of which I tested. Our school bathrooms had low toilets
and a big communal garbage bin in the corner next to the
sinks; there was no way you were going to catch me casually
tossing my Stayfree Surefit covered in blood next to where
Jessica R. was standing on a stepstool dutifully washing non-
toxic watercolor paints from her hands. Can you imagine
Katie C. and Jenny H. gossiping about their latest Garbage
Pail Kids acquisitions over the drinking fountain and here
comes an actual ovulating womanchild grumbling about
lower back pain while cracking Midol between her teeth
like grape Nerds? No way, dude, I was just going to punt that
kickball as hard as I could (read: mope sullenly at the edge
of the kickball field waiting for the bell to ring) and pretend
that my organs weren't wringing themselves out inside me,
valiantly resisting the urge to kick my shoes off my swollen

feet and nurse a cup of black coffee in the teacher's lounge with Mr. Harris.

I'm pretty sure my mom was annoyed at having to deal with this from a child so young, but listen, I'm not the one who brought home milk pumped with hormones. My period was so weird and irregular, it wasn't like I was constantly disrupting her soap operas demanding chocolate and heartfelt conversation. Like every other poor kid with sick or addicted parents, I knew that I needed to make myself small, that my problems should remain my problems only. If a young woman came to me now and was like, "Yo, my period is a problem!" I'd remind her that officially I have a twelfth-grade education and probably say some stupid shit about the beauty of a working body or whatever pseudo-parental, positive thing I could come up with on the fly, but navigating my early womanhood with a person who wasn't equipped to deal with it was fucking bonkers. It wasn't like she explained breast sensitivity or took me to the doctor to get it noted in any sort of chart. For a while I tracked that shit on a pocket calendar that had come with a free my first period kit that I had sent away for, but after a while I forgot what all the dots and hash marks were supposed to mean and scrapped the project altogether. Every subsequent month, or six weeks, or eight weeks, after I'd forgotten to be on the lookout or to figure out my body's cues for my period's impending arrival, in the middle of a math test it would throw a surprise pool party all across the crotch of my Goodwill lavender corduroys.

My period has remained this way for decades: hostile, elusive, disrespectful of the lengths to which I'd had to go to line up the adult human sex it was interrupting. I never get a sore-boobs warning or cautionary twinge of back pain, and I cry at dog-food commercials regardless of the state of my hormones, so I'm never prepared with a tampon or a maxi pad or a beach towel whenever my fucking life gets ruined for a week (or several).

I flew to Austin in November 2017 for the Texas Book Festival. I'm not really a Texas kind of guy, but I have friends down there who'd lied and said that the fall "isn't that hot," and, like a fool, I believed them and agreed to participate. I took a commuter plane from my tiny regional airport to Detroit; we pulled into gate A78 and according to the app on my phone my connecting flight was leaving out of gate B437. I mean, not really—there aren't actually over four hundred gates in the Delta terminal at the Detroit Metro Airport—but that's what it felt like after skip-walking two-plus miles across the entire airport in ten minutes with a sweaty backpack full of trashy magazines jostling against my back.

I know I would feel guilty riding on a trolley through the airport because technically my legs work, but after having been on two book tours? Man, I fucking get it. All I want forever is a man in a little vest to get me from one flight to the next on the back of one of those carts football players who break their legs in the middle of the third quarter get to ride off the field.

I'm not a scientist or whatever, but I knew something in my body had shaken loose somewhere between the miles of subterranean moving walkways and the Zingerman's kiosk near the gate that charged me fifteen dollars for an undressed turkey sandwich. I landed in Texas and felt as good as one can on pavement that is literally vibrating from warmth in a place where you can see heat waves in the air. I got to my hotel and turned the thermostat as cold as it would go and waited for my sweat to turn into icicles.

The next morning, groggy and vaguely sticky, the lingering perfume of an ill-advised oily vegan eggroll I'd gotten off a food truck the night before clinging to my tongue (because in Austin, I'm apparently the kind of person who eats food on the damn sidewalk), I woke up in a congealed pool of blood so deep you'd need galoshes to wade through it. This is the kind of corporeal surprise that, no matter how many gerbil-size clots I've passed in filthy bar bathrooms or navy-blue towels I've laid across unsuspecting Uber rear seats, I don't know that I ever would have been prepared for. Sure, I got the pamphlet in gym class about what to do when your flower first blooms and your neat and tidy menarche leaves one perfectly round droplet of blood in your underpants to let you know you are becoming a woman, but, yeah, Mr. Pabich never had us run any period drills illuminating the proper course of action one must take at thirty-seven years old when faced with crisp hotel sheets unexpectedly drenched in cervical mucus and endometrial tissue. I must have been asleep the day they taught adult womanhood at lady school, and as I glanced down at my dino print pajamas (see?!), at the slick, cold dampness up my back and across my stomach, I thought, "Maybe I am dead and this is hell."

No one ever taught me the protocol for what to do when you turn a Queen Deluxe room at the Intercontinental into a fucking crime scene, so I shoved a blindingly white hand towel into my underwear, googled "destroyed four-star hotel room with menstrual blood," and scrolled through a Reddit thread populated by very helpful anonymous strangers who all had relatively sound advice on how to deal with such a dilemma. I found a very reassuring subthread in which hotel workers detailed the various states of horror in which they'd discovered celebrity rooms, so I channeled Bruno Mars or whomever while stripping the bed and rolling the sheets into a uterine-lining burrito because Renee872 posted "if house-keeping sees balled-up bed linens, they know to just shove them right into the bag and send it straight to the laundry."

I feel like other people have legitimate nightmares of being eaten alive by ants or losing their child in a shopping mall, but all my nightmare scenarios are very specific embar-rassments that could happen only to me. I didn't know that "hotel employees catching me trying to dispose of a sheet full of bodily fluids" was one of them, but now it definitely is. What would I say if someone had ignored the DO NOT DIS-TURB, THERE IS A SURGERY HAPPENING sign on the door-knob and let themselves in as I was gingerly peeling the fitted sheet from the mattress, still clad in my only pair of pajamas, because for the first time in my miserable life, I packed my weekend bag like a breezy, casual person who doesn't feel the need to bring duplicates of clothes in case something accidentally gets ruined?

What must that be like? Having the confidence to just throw a couple T-shirts and a toothbrush in a backpack, then actually go someplace far away from your house where all the stuff you need is? Without your car, which has a trunk full of all the backup stuff you might require?! Remember that scene in *A Few Good Men* where my Single Good Man Tom Cruise is cataloguing all the things left hanging in San-tiago's closet? And the inventory is, like, three khaki shirts, three khaki pants, two navy jackets, four pairs of brown boots . . . etc.? That's how I pack. Except my clothes aren't neatly folded in the bag. They are all breathlessly flung in the general direction of the suitcase while I loudly panic about whether or not I will need nine bras or seventeen bras for a weekend trip to South Haven, which is an hour away from where all my socks live. "Okay, I'm taking my black glasses and a pair of prescription sunglasses and I'll bring my pink glasses in case I break my black glasses" is a conversation I have had in my head, with myself, as I contemplated a week-long trip to the woods I was going on in the hopes of making a dent in this book you're reading now. I brought three pairs of regular outside pants and two pajama bottoms and a pair of inside pants that can double as outside pants if the building I was staying at caught fire or I had to make a snack run, all to sit in my boy Fernando's subterranean Airbnb in the dark in front of this computer. Imagine the time and mental energy I could save if I were not this person.

I have with me five T-shirts and two dresses and a light-weight sweater and a heavier sweater just in case the air conditioner is strong, or I go out to see a movie. (I mean who knows what the night might bring because I'd rather put on more clothes than turn off that sweet, sweet refrigerated air.) But I tried to pretend to be a different, more easygoing person in Texas, a person who doesn't travel with just-in-case jammies, so I was forced to try to conceal my crime while wearing the evidence of it splattered down my front and up my back because I just don't enjoy doing things while naked!

They don't make those bed linens easy to remove, and I appreciate that. No one wants to wake up with their body touching the clammy sickness of an actual mattress. I could hear vacuuming down the hall but couldn't gauge how close it was or how much time I had to get the bed stripped and rinse myself off and get fresh clothes on before they arrived, and I would feel compelled to apologize for being a disaster to people who would probably just wish I'd shut the fuck up and leave. I yanked up the corners of the sheet and brought them together in the middle, then folded them again, then rolled them into an internally oozing blood tube, which I set on the floor near the door. I took a shower, soiling two washcloths and a towel and murdering that embossed rug-made-out-of-towel-material in the process, then I found the (modest) wad of emergency cash I keep in the bottom of my backpack when I'm traveling—because I *definitely* want to be killed taking too long getting the money out when an impatient robber rightfully pegs me as a naive tourist—and dug up three twenties and left them on the bed with a note that read *I apologize for my body. It is a toilet.*

My last period began on December 15, 2017, and ended on February 12, 2018. I only know this because that Texas episode scared the shit out of me, and since terror is my only motivation, I bought the kind of planner high school kids pretend to write their assignments in and marked a red dot on every day a torrent of blood rained down from my uterus, helpless as I stained every flat surface in my home. It wasn't the first time this kind of thing had happened to me, but it was certainly the worst and most extreme case; I couldn't live my life like a normal person, let alone live the exciting life of a woman in a Kotex ad! I don't rock climb or play tennis in tiny pastel shorts! I'm not sitting in a kayak or riding a fucking city scooter!

I got blood on the cart at Target while trying to decide between universal remotes. I left a rusty smudge on a light-blue chair at the DMV and tried to clean it off inconspicuously with an eyeglass wipe. A neighborhood kid asked if I spilled juice on my pants while trying to sell me shitty Cub Scouts popcorn. I went to see *The Shape of Water* and left *The Shape of Sloughed-Off Endometrial Cells* behind in my seat.

I wanted to scrape my insides out with a serving spoon, because I spent two consecutive months marinating in my own insides. I started taking the pill to try to stanch the flow, but the side effects were comically terrible, and the cruelest part of the whole thing was that it didn't even fucking work. I spent most days prostrate atop an unyielding crimson tide. Birth control begat acid reflux begat two esophageal ulcers begat vaginal and oral thrush, and by the way, I never stopped bleeding, not even for a second. There were weeks at a time when I had to take Diflucan to kill the yeast in my vagina, while rubbing on Nystatin cream to kill it in my armpits and droppering fiery oil of oregano (I was so itchy and delirious from near-constant blood loss that, yes, I resorted to natural remedies out of sheer desperation) onto the mucus membrane under my tongue to kill the yeast living and multiplying *on* my tongue, and I guess what I'm actually saying is that, sure, I move this body around every day but I'm not actually in charge of it, and I have no idea and no control over anything that happens within it. Why are people so terrified of the impending rule of our robot overlords when we have no idea where our pancreases are? I have spent years held hostage by the whims of a small, pear-shaped sex organ located somewhere between my butt and where pee comes out, that I can't see and have never had plans to even make use of. Why does no one talk about how weird it is to be so beholden to the dispositions of our intestines and our throats?

The doctors didn't know what was going on, either. I mean, dude knows more than I do, for sure, but I had three transvaginal ultrasounds and a battery of bloodwork and diagnostic tests, and, every single time, he shrugged like, "Welp, I dunno! I guess you're just a heavy bleeder!" while my uterus sloshed around sounding like a dishwasher and I could feel liquid seeping through four layers of protective padding onto that embarrassingly crinkly paper spread across the exam table. It seemed like he was cool with the idea that maybe I would just eat raw steaks for every meal in an effort to keep my iron up while waiting it out, until I finally just asked him if we could take a blowtorch to the entire apparatus and, after making sure for the millionth time that I really don't want to have a baby despite my apathy and rapidly advancing age, he was like, "Wait, but are you actually sure?"

Here is a list of things I would rather do than carry a human to term in my battered uterus, which I imagine at this point looked like one of those purplish beefsteak tomatoes that has rotted and been left in the compost bin under the sink for weeks:

- take a soupy diarrhea shit in the middle of the floor in a public place, then eat it
- listen to a man's jokes
- let city rats crawl on me and stick their rotting teeth in my eyeballs
- take a five-hour Amtrak ride without headphones in the summer with broken a/c

- post all the pictures of my nine greasy chins I've accidentally taken with my front-facing camera
- let a million bees sting me, one at a time, while watching my body swell like an infected water balloon
- remove a Cuterebra from a fractious dog
- tweet something politically spicy, then engage with every robot who responds
- ask a young person to explicitly describe their favorite meme to me using only words
- work as a bill collector for a predatory lending agency
- let a grown man named Chip try to sell me a car
- eat soft cheese, then play toilet roulette while running a bunch of errands on the bus
- ask a new mom to give me her stance on vaccines
- put money in my mouth after watching three cars run over it in the rain
- print my last hundred Google searches and hand them out to strangers
- try to get an unregistered firearm through TSA at a busy airport
- clean a public bathroom with no gloves on, with my tongue!
- have a wildly uncomfortable menstrual cycle for approximately 6,570 days, the eighteen years that I would be legally mandated to be responsible for my child

Here's the thing: if I had walked into the doctor's office on that bright sunny morning, brimming with joy while excitedly rubbing my hand over my belly, thrilled to share the news that I was going to have a baby and asking for a blood test to confirm its staking a claim on my uterus, that dude would have shit his pants and sat me down for a Very Serious Conversation about why embarking on the journey of motherhood at my advanced age and in my current state of advanced corporeal decay was a Very Bad Idea. I'm an expert in going to the doctor, man. The only thing they ever want to hear from me is "I've lost weight" or "Do you think you could tell me how to lose weight?" It's probably against some code of conduct to admit it, but he knew and I knew and he knew that I knew that if I'd said, "You know what sounds like a fun party we could throw? A high-risk geriatric pregnancy," he would have been on a conference call with both Mister Blue Cross *and* Mister Blue Shield, calculating whether or not they could afford to pay out the lawsuit my family would undoubtedly file after he threw me down several flights of stairs.

The last thing he wanted to hear is that this sick, old asshole was going to ruin his pre-retirement months by forcing him to coach me through a difficult pregnancy. Why not just yank this gooey, unpredictable blood bag out of my body so I can get on with living the rest of my godforsaken life? I'm sure there were practical reasons for denying my request, but who cares about menopause or fluctuating hormones or postsurgical complications? Twenty-eight years of a contentious relationship with my uterus had been long enough to come to terms with the fact that neither of us was going to change and maybe a conscious uncoupling would do us both a world of good. We still loved each other, of course, but the time had come for us to part amicably and maintain mutual respect.

Just kidding—I wanted the doctor to hit me in the head

with a brick and cut this traveling uterine circus out of my body, then toss it in the trash and keep it moving. But he couldn't do that, the insurance was like "lmao sorry" despite it begging to be jumpshot into the nearest biohazard receptacle, so we did the next best thing: a whole bunch of snipping and scraping that took all goddamn day and for which I had to be anesthetized and after which I had to wear a diaper for a while, which I hoped was to catch my uterus in case they accidentally dislodged it and it fell out but joke's on me it was only for DISCHARGE.

THE BALLAD OF MY ABLATION

1. **No food.** I had to fast the night before, which is fine, whatever, I love Sprite, but I had to very specifically clean all my parts while practically starving. The stress of this just made me want to fucking eat. I often think about what a gross monster I am, but never in as much detail as when confronted by the thorough methods I need to use to go about cleaning myself per a doctor's instructions, methods I definitely do not employ on a daily basis. Am I just disgusting?

2. **Paperwork.** At the hospital, they hand you all these forms and papers to sign prior to surgery and, come on now, I'm not reading that shit. It's early in the morning, and the only thing on my tongue is the memory of a pizza I ate two days ago. I'm not wasting my time with this contract. Besides, what am I going to do if I have a dispute? Get a lawyer on the

phone?! Can you *even imagine* being the person who holds up the Outpatient Surgery Conga Line trying to argue about clause A in subparagraph twelve on the hospital liability form while the tired and over-worked desk lady sighs exasperatedly at you? Yeah, right! I signed fourteen pieces of paper that probably said "grants permission to harvest any useful organs" and you know what? Fine! They can have a kidney if it means I don't have to actually read about them taking my kidney.

3. **Apparently, there was a fire drill in the surgical unit while I was waiting for the anesthesiologist.** So I was alone in this little holding pen after the nurse came in, put in the IV, gave me a sedative, made sure I was dressed properly and had the little surgery bonnet on, just staring at the pain chart on the wall because it's not like they let you read or mess around on your phone, when I heard this loud warning siren blaring in the hall outside the room. My first thought? ACTIVE SHOOTER. I'm a dramatic little bitch. The lights started flashing right before a deafening alarm sounded, and then a disembodied hand reached inside my cracked door and silently pulled it shut. Maybe it was the Ativan talking, but my brain was like: "Oh my god, they obviously don't want the gunman to know I'm in here." I kept looking down at my ashy hands and feet—because you're not even allowed to use lotion after all that fucking bathing—wondering if I could fight off a dude trying to shoot up a hospital in southwest Michigan.

4. **My boring, studious wife came in the anteroom and was actually asking my doctor serious questions while I was just trying to pal around.** I like to joke and be fun. I don't want to wreck a chill vibe with questions about "recovery time" and "success rates."

5. **If this is what death feels like, sign me up.** One nurse put microwaved blankets on me, then another nurse pushed my bed through the halls to the surgery suite. And because my brain is a nightmare, I kept thinking, "Is this bed too heavy for her to push? Is this the heaviest bed she's ever pushed? Is she going to need help to take that sharp right corner? Maybe I should just get up and push her in the bed instead," and thank goodness I signed that DNR because what is the point of living like this? Anyway, we made it to surgery. I made awkward small talk with a roomful of people who were about to see and move and manipulate my big, naked, unshaven body that probably wasn't as clean as they would've hoped as I lay there unconscious; then I had to move to a flat bed with a hole in it for all my fluids to drain through and wait for McDreamy to gaze down at me with his kind eyes, the lights creating a halo around his tousled brown hair, and tell me to count backward as I drifted peacefully to sleep. In reality, a faceless man in a green paper cap with a mask obscuring his features said, "You're going to feel some heat in your IV." I did. And then my brain exploded into a bunch of needles, and everything went black.

6. **Hysteroscopy.** The doctor dilates the cervix, inserts a hysteroscope (that's going to be the name of my submarine when I start my own navy) through the vagina into the cervix, then adds a liquid solution into the uterus and shines a light through the hysteroscope to look at the uterus and fallopian tubes. Honestly, I'm not sure what this is for, because clearly I have those things, as they are the cause of my unending torment. I guess he needed to make sure.

7. **D&C.** Also known as dilation and curettage, it's a minor procedure where the doctor takes a suction device or scraping tool and clears out the lining of the uterus. I was 100 percent asleep during this, but I'm sure the doctor did a great job.

8. **Endometrial Ablation.** I can't remember the exact kind I had. Sometimes they use microwaves (?) or they use hot water (??), but am I really a scientist? I told you I didn't read the paperwork! Plus, did you know that when they try to explain complicated surgical shit to you after your brain has been chemically asleep for an hour, the information doesn't always stick? Also, you don't care about the specifics. All you really need to know is that the doctor burned the lining of my uterus to a crisp, and I haven't had a menstrual period since. No longer having to carry around a diaper bag every time I go to Trader Joe's or the movie theater is priceless.

It's been three blissful, period-free years since I had a charcoal grill shoved into my vagina. I'm looking forward to living the rest of my life like I'm in a tampon commercial: recklessly wearing white linen pants, jumping into a crystal-clear cerulean pool while a camera zooms in on my spotless mons pubis as I balance at the edge of the diving board, soaking up puddles of blue food coloring with a plug of absorbent cotton, laughing wistfully with other emotionally balanced women over salad. My breezy new life is filled with earnest conversations atop light-colored couches, complicated yoga positions with my legs spread across a baby-pink mat, and carefree swimming in shark-infested bodies of water.

lesbian bed death

Sure, sex is fun, but have you ever accurately predicted when your period was going to start?

Sure, sex is fun, but have you ever been properly fitted for an orthopedic shoe?

Sure, sex is fun, but have you ever pooped on a reliable schedule?

Sure, sex is fun, but have you ever cried inconsolably at one of those ASPCA commercials?

Sure, sex is fun, but have you ever enjoyed eating a Brussels sprout?

Sure, sex is fun, but have you ever shared an electronic calendar with another human adult?

Sure, sex is fun, but have you ever pretentiously carried an NPR tote bag?

Sure, sex is fun, but have you ever changed out of one cozy shirt into an even cozier shirt?

Sure, sex is fun, but have you ever gotten your inbox down to zero?

Sure, sex is fun, but have you ever had a preferred tea?

Sure, sex is fun, but have you ever sat through an entire concert?

Sure, sex is fun, but have you ever found a really good hand cream?

Sure, sex is fun, but have you ever declined an invitation to a boat party?

Sure, sex is fun, but have you ever been to an Eileen Fisher outlet?

Sure, sex is fun, but have you ever listened to two perimeno-pausal women murmur indecipherably, handing each other sections of the newspaper while reading over the tops of their glasses?

Sure, sex is fun, but have you ever fought for a majority share of the electric blanket on the TV couch?

Sure, sex is fun, but have you ever clapped your hands with delight at the opening of a brick-and-mortar Bath & Body Works?

Sure, sex is fun, but have you ever watched PBS?

Sure, sex is fun, but have you ever gotten up early on a Sunday morning to beat everyone to the car wash?

Sure, sex is fun, but have you ever lain really still in bed after your alarm has gone off three times trying not to move because you don't want your pets to know you're awake?

Sure, sex is fun, but have you ever spent an entire afternoon looking for a misplaced library book only to realize you returned it two days ago?

Sure, sex is fun, but have you ever accidentally tried to put on your partner's bra in the dark?

Sure, sex is fun, but have you ever not invited one-half of a gay couple to ladies' night just to set some shit off?

Sure, sex is fun, but have you ever been to the wine store at 4 p.m.?

Sure, sex is fun, but have you ever eaten dinner in a restaurant at 4 p.m.?

Sure, sex is fun, but have you ever texted while driving and not crashed your car?

Sure, sex is fun, but have you ever googled a popular meme?

Sure, sex is fun, but have you ever spent several days meticulously menu-planning your book-club brunch?

Sure, sex is fun, but have you ever taken off your bra at the end of a particularly grueling day?

Sure, sex is fun, but have you ever argued about whether generic Advil is as strong as the real thing?

Sure, sex is fun, but have you ever "winterized" your car?

Sure, sex is fun, but have you ever accumulated nineteen different personal water containers between two people?

Sure, sex is fun, but have you ever debated takeout options for thirty-seven minutes?

Sure, sex is fun, but have you ever lit four different kinds of incense at the same time?

Sure, sex is fun, but have you ever passionately defended the purchase of an overpriced hand soap?

Sure, sex is fun, but have you ever owned more than two cats?

Sure, sex is fun, but have you ever had a favorite contestant on *Top Chef*?

Sure, sex is fun, but have you ever timed a pharmacy pickup just right?

Sure, sex is fun, but have you ever slept in a bed with both a mattress pad and a dust ruffle?

Sure, sex is fun, but have you ever brought two cardigans to the movie theater?

Sure, sex is fun, but have you ever set a reminder that *Survivor* is coming on?

Sure, sex is fun, but have you ever tried to control your hormones with tinctures?

Sure, sex is fun, but have you ever gone wild in a candle store?

Sure, sex is fun, but have you ever declined an invitation to a white party?

Sure, sex is fun, but have you ever cleaned a dirty saucepan after soaking it overnight?

Sure, sex is fun, but have you ever earnestly watched the news?

Sure, sex is fun, but have you ever been on a first-name basis with the guy at the plant store?

Sure, sex is fun, but have you ever filled out a comment card?

Sure, sex is fun, but have you ever sincerely inquired: "When are we going to go back to Pier One?"

Sure, sex is fun, but have you ever met your state representative?

Sure, sex is fun, but have you ever been to a lecture that wasn't for a class?

Sure, sex is fun, but have you ever wept openly while listening to Tori Amos?

Sure, sex is fun, but have you ever gotten your oil changed the day that sticker on the windshield says you should?

Sure, sex is fun, but have you ever charged your crystals under a full moon?

Sure, sex is fun, but have you ever folded your clothes on the same day you washed them?

Sure, sex is fun, but have you ever ordered Blue Apron with a discount code you got from a podcast?

Sure, sex is fun, but have you ever written a to-do list by hand?

Sure, sex is fun, but have you ever read a travel guide for a city you're never going to have enough money to visit?

Sure, sex is fun, but have you ever declined an invitation to a holiday party?

Sure, sex is fun, but have you ever watched a television program then read no fewer than six think pieces about it to make sure you understood what you just watched?

Sure, sex is fun, but have you ever picked up when you could have paid three dollars for delivery?

Sure, sex is fun, but have you ever taken a trip to Target just to get your steps in?

Sure, sex is fun, but have you ever eaten soup as a meal?

Sure, sex is fun, but have you ever written a letter to the editor?

Sure, sex is fun, but have you ever had toilet paper brand loyalty?

Sure, sex is fun, but have you ever made the text font on your phone bigger?

Sure, sex is fun, but have you ever sneezed really hard?

Sure, sex is fun, but have you ever had flowers bloom on a plant you thought you'd killed?

Sure, sex is fun, but have you ever actually finished the book your book club was reading?

Sure, sex is fun, but have you ever successfully hidden a tub of ice cream from your wife?

Sure, sex is fun, but have you ever been to Big Lots?

Sure, sex is fun, but have you ever had to stop drinking coffee before 2 p.m. because you won't be able to get to sleep later?

Sure, sex is fun, but have you ever put your bills on autopay?

Sure, sex is fun, but have you ever used a broom outside?

Sure, sex is fun, but have you ever sent an e-mail from your iPad with the signature "sent from my iPad"?

Sure, sex is fun, but have you ever eaten a weirdly misshapen tomato you somehow grew in the rancid patch of land on the other side of your garage?

Sure, sex is fun, but have you ever declined an invitation to a housewarming party?

Sure, sex is fun, but have you ever been through the Panera drive-thru?

Sure, sex is fun, but have you ever set a regular bedtime?

Sure, sex is fun, but have you ever voted for a contestant on *The Voice*?

Sure, sex is fun, but have you ever sorted your jackets by season?

Sure, sex is fun, but have you ever peed your pants a little while laughing?

Sure, sex is fun, but have you ever slept with a wedge pillow under your swollen calves and ankles?

Sure, sex is fun, but have you ever kicked a chunk of frozen gray snow off your wheel well?

Sure, sex is fun, but have you ever paid full price for replacement charger cords from the Apple store?

Sure, sex is fun, but have you ever cashed in a rebate?

Sure, sex is fun, but have you ever bookmarked a lasagna recipe?

Sure, sex is fun, but have you ever tried Lasix?

Sure, sex is fun, but have you ever been in McDonald's so early you couldn't get fries?

Sure, sex is fun, but have you ever watched a bunch of syndicated CBS comedies in a row?

Sure, sex is fun, but have you ever burst into flames while casually scrolling through Instagram and stumbling across your wife wearing some shit you know is yours?

Sure, sex is fun, but have you ever finally broken down and gone to see a dermatologist?

Sure, sex is fun, but have you ever talked to your cat like he was a real person?

Sure, sex is fun, but have you ever subscribed to a magazine that has more words than pictures?

Sure, sex is fun, but have you ever eaten the leftovers before everyone else wakes up?

Sure, sex is fun, but have you ever deeply related to a nihilist meme?

Sure, sex is fun, but have you ever done low-impact high-intensity interval training along with a YouTube video when no one else could see you?

Sure, sex is fun, but have you ever had a scalp massage?

Sure, sex is fun, but have you ever been to Trader Joe's right after a restock?

Sure, sex is fun, but have you ever given a crying baby back to its parent?

Sure, sex is fun, but have you ever unboxed a bunch of shit you don't need from Amazon, broken down the box, and gotten all that unnecessary plastic that came with it into the dumpster before your wife got home from work?

Sure, sex is fun, but have you ever tried noise-canceling headphones?

Sure, sex is fun, but have you ever split a water bill?

Sure, sex is fun, but have you ever rubbed CBD oil on an achy knee joint?

Sure, sex is fun, but have you ever cheerfully woken up at 7 a.m. after going to bed at a reasonable hour the night before?

Sure, sex is fun, but have you ever read a romance novel?

Sure, sex is fun, but have you ever ordered vitamins from a subscription service that delivers them to your house every month whether you've remembered to take them or not?

Sure, sex is fun, but have you ever cared very deeply for someone you never want to have sex with?

Sure, sex is fun, but have you ever watched birds eat from a feeder you filled and hung for them?

Sure, sex is fun, but have you ever been to couples therapy?

Sure, sex is fun, but have you ever watched *The West Wing* from beginning to end?

Sure, sex is fun, but have you ever paid real money to read articles on the Internet?

Sure, sex is fun, but have you ever worn a T-shirt with words on it, then spent the entire day awkwardly waiting for people to finish reading your breasts?

Sure, sex is fun, but have you ever cut a toxic bitch right out of your life?

Sure, sex is fun, but have you ever spent more than twelve dollars on one plate?

Sure, sex is fun, but have you ever explained your very specific food allergy to a waiter who doesn't give a fuck?

Sure, sex is fun, but have you ever tried Dijon mustard?

Sure, sex is fun, but have you ever bent down to ask a dog its name?

Sure, sex is fun, but have you ever listened to *Oprah's Super-Soul Conversations*?

Sure, sex is fun, but have you ever bonded with the one other person on this planet who likes black licorice as much as you do?

Sure, sex is fun, but have you ever thrown out your high school yearbooks?

Sure, sex is fun, but have you ever used a really absorbent towel?

Sure, sex is fun, but have you ever eaten jalapeño Doritos?

Sure, sex is fun, but have you ever responded to a celebrity tweet?

Sure, sex is fun, but have you ever filled out the paperwork at a new doctor's office and remembered all your current diseases and medications on the first try?

Sure, sex is fun, but have you ever had exact change?

Sure, sex is fun, but have you ever watched videos of Barack Obama surprising people?

Sure, sex is fun, but have you ever chosen to look at pictures of your twenty-year high school reunion on Facebook rather than attend it?

Sure, sex is fun, but have you ever gotten your phone to pair with a Bluetooth speaker?

Sure, sex is fun, but have you ever taken a cab when everyone else decided to walk?

Sure, sex is fun, but have you ever pulled your underwear all the way up to your sternum?

Sure, sex is fun, but have you ever put on new glasses for the first time?

Sure, sex is fun, but have you ever pretended to be on the phone when someone you don't like was trying to talk to you?

Sure, sex is fun, but have you ever called your wife by the wrong name?

Sure, sex is fun, but have you ever taken more than the recommended dosage of Aleve?

Sure, sex is fun, but have you ever played dead at work?

Sure, sex is fun, but have you ever declined an invitation to a bachelorette party?

Sure, sex is fun, but have you ever cut your own hair?

Sure, sex is fun, but have you ever Shazamed a song in public?

Sure, sex is fun, but have you ever tried to convince a young person to care about a single thing that is meaningful to you?

Sure, sex is fun, but have you ever dug through the skincare bins at Marshalls trying to find the fancy shit you love on clearance?

Sure, sex is fun, but have you ever intentionally gotten a stupid tattoo?

Sure, sex is fun, but have you ever organized your sock drawer?

Sure, sex is fun, but have you ever swiftly avoided answering a phone call that unexpectedly came through while you were making a move in *Words with Friends*?

Sure, sex is fun, but have you ever watched one thing on your phone while your wife watches a different thing on the TV?

Sure, sex is fun, but have you ever designed a new IKEA kitchen in your mind?

Sure, sex is fun, but have you ever texted your lady to bring you something upstairs when she was downstairs?

Sure, sex is fun, but have you ever refused to introduce yourself to the neighbors?

Sure, sex is fun, but have you ever declined an invitation to a baby shower?

Sure, sex is fun, but have you ever kept score of how much money you would be winning on *Jeopardy*?

Sure, sex is fun, but have you ever remembered to separate all the different types of recycling?

Sure, sex is fun, but have you ever tried to figure out what is happening with your 401(k)?

Sure, sex is fun, but have you ever deleted your voice mail without listening to any of it first?

Sure, sex is fun, but have you ever had your spouse cosign a loan?

Sure, sex is fun, but have you ever covertly fed the cat human food in an attempt to win complete allegiance?

Sure, sex is fun, but have you ever watched a young person try to figure out the twenty-five-year-old pop culture reference you just made?

Sure, sex is fun, but have you ever flirted with your friend's dad?

Sure, sex is fun, but have you ever licked a plate clean while no one else was watching?

Sure, sex is fun, but have you ever declined an invitation to a birthday party?

Sure, sex is fun, but have you ever tried a new anti-dandruff shampoo?

Sure, sex is fun, but have you ever . . . ?

Sure, sex is fun, but have you . . . ?

Sure, sex is fun.

Sure.

body negativity

I have been stuck with a smelly, actively decaying body that I never asked for and am constantly on the receiving end of confusing, overwhelming messages for how to properly care for and feed it. Healthy **hair** is lustrous and shiny. Those words I just used might mean the same thing. Healthy hair should also be strong, but, honestly, I don't ever worry about that because I shave my head, and it's not like I have to worry about it being strong enough to hold up a buoyant ponytail. I wish magazines and commercials talked more about scalps, because, wow, mine has been a horror show since the dawn of time and I am so very old and still find myself in public in a black shirt like, "Oh, please, excuse me for a minute, I appear to be molting from above the neck!" WHY WON'T CORPORATIONS TELL ME EXACTLY WHAT I SHOULD PUT ON MY HEAD? Okay, I can wash it every day, but I read websites and they tell you that's bad to do. But if I skip a day, I get itchy. If I skip two days, I start to develop dandruff in my eyebrows, which is thoroughly disgusting. I can oil my scalp, but it's already oily, which I've been told is also bad.

Then when my hair is washed and my scalp is glistening and flake-free for five minutes, which of the 132 bottles of styling products crammed underneath my sink is the nourishing, hydrating, frizz-controlling, root-covering, volumizing, texturizing, smoothing, sculpting, shine-enhancing, color-protecting, moisturizing finishing gel-spray mousse-foam that is going to get my shit looking together?

Let's talk about glowing **skin**. I don't drink water and my blood type is pizza, but my skin looks good from a distance, mostly because I put three different oils on it and occasionally rinse off my blush before bed. Your face skin needs to be smooth yet supple yet stretched like a fresh canvas, and you're supposed to pretend that you haven't thought about it since you were nineteen. You have to clean it, shave it (perimenopause gang, represent!), tone it, then use a treatment on it, then press a serum into it, then moisturize it, then screen it from the sun, and, bitch, are you kidding me, that is just the skin on your fucking *face*!!!!!

Eye care is weird, because you don't do anything proactive for your dumb eyes and, when there's a problem, you flip the fuck out and remember how delicate and sensitive they are and wonder why you never cared about them before you got some moldy mascara in there and made them pink. I have worn glasses since I was nine years old, so, by default, I have taken care of my eyes at least once every two years. I'm nearsighted with an astigmatism, so I go to an ophthalmologist and get that yellow light shined in my cornea and take that scary test where they blow bursts of cold air directly onto your eyeball while screaming at you not to flinch and ruin the test. I try to wear fashionable glasses and that shit is expensive? But worth it. Because of them, people will decide you are cool, before you open your mouth and shatter their illusion. Because I stare at a screen fifteen hours a day, I invested in UV-protection lenses, which serve as a constant reminder that I had to adjust something in my real life because of all the time I waste in my fake life. That's sad!

Your **eyelashes** should be long and fluttery, which can be achieved by painstakingly gluing faux mink ones on top of your own and jabbing yourself repeatedly in the eye with a brush coated in black wax, as you try to paint each individual lash with lengthening, volumizing, water-resistant color. Or you can fork over sixty dollars to a trained lash professional who will attach synthetic lash fibers onto your wimpy lashes with medical-grade adhesive. I have one tube of mascara that I bought from a vending machine in an airport when I was pretending I might be a different kind of person for the two days I was in Minnesota. I wasn't.

I have plucked, I have tweezed, I have shaved, I have waxed, I have threaded, I have microbladed, I have trimmed, I have tinted, I have filled in, I have styled, I have contoured, and I have microfeathered my stupid **eyebrows** and none of those things has ever had a discernible impact on my life. Now I do nothing, and it's fine!

I have my dad's **nose**. It has been covered in blackheads and tiny little, I don't know, blood marks ever since I can remember looking at it in a mirror. I know from years of training from the pages of *Glamour* that these blemishes are little spots of oil that come to the surface of your skin and oxidize, but after years of squeezing them privately at home and occasionally paying a licensed aesthetician to squeeze them out in public, I don't think I have ever seen a not-clogged nasal pore. You buy pore-shrinking cleanser when you're young and naive and believe that a six-dollar tube of over-the-counter face wash is capable of performing science on your face in your messy bathroom. After that, you graduate to the strips, which are extremely satisfying if you enjoy ripping shit and/or inspecting gooey things that come out of your body. As a devout Q-tip inspector, I understand the stomach-lurching appeal of looking at the little speckles of nose junk dotting a bright white pore strip. It helps to get the pores cleaned out, you see, because your nose is supposed to be smooth and matte, except at the tip, which should sparkle because that makes you look young.

Do you think about **ear** upkeep? I used to hang out with this dude who got the insides of his ears waxed, which was W I L D because we weren't even thirty at the time, and just imagine what his senior citizenry is going to look like! He was a fucking teen wolf with tufts sprouting from his ears, which I thought was kind of sexy, but it wasn't my body. Anyway, I produce a lot of earwax, and every time I go to my nurse practitioner, I ask him to look inside my ears. He does and says it's fine, even the times they feel pretty itchy and sticky. Honestly, something could have crawled in and died in there, but I never push the issue because (1) TRULY, what is more disgusting than talking to another person about your "excessive wax," but also (2) I feel like every medical professional I talk to is two degrees from saying "you're too fat" no matter what you've made an appointment for them to check. I don't know the correlation between gummy ears and weight, but if you give a doctor enough latitude, they will find one.

I do not have all my **teeth**. There is so much shit you have to do for your mouth alone that I refuse to believe anyone I've ever met is doing *all* of it. You're supposed to have: clean, straight teeth; healthy gums; a vibrant pink tongue; fresh breath. I have: zero things on that list. Teeth are impossible because you literally have to (1) have good genes or (2) BE RICH to have good ones, and even if you're blessed with both, it doesn't always work all the way out for you. I am the kind of person who deftly weaves *30 Rock* quotes into my everyday lexicon, and my favorite among them is when Liz says to Tracy, "How do you know I'm not rich?" and Tracy replies, matter-of-factly, "YOUR TEETH."

Whenever people accuse me of having money I am quick to point them to the damp, pulpy hole where the first premolar on my upper right jaw used to be or to my gappy front teeth and pronounced overbite. Baby, if I was rich, I would have all my rotted stump teeth cut from my skull and replaced with piano keys. I am *obsessed* with rich people who don't fix their crowded, overlapping teeth, because my teeth have always been a dead giveaway that I have nothing and came from even less. Just imagine the wealth and power you'd need to feel free enough to keep your brown teeth despite being able to afford an in-home orthodontist. It's staggering.

Who has time to take care of their teeth? I'm supposed to brush for two minutes, then floss, then rinse, then swish with Listerine for a full sixty seconds even though it makes my sinuses burn and my eyes water, and occasionally do a whitening strip? Come on. I'm not flossing because I will never floss, Listerine is painful, and two minutes is a very long time. I got this Aesop mouthwash that feels like it's doing something to my neglected, gingivitis-ravaged gum-line every time I swish it around, so that's something. That I can do.

At last count, I had no fewer than forty-two **lip** balms between my bedside table, tote bag, office, and car, and for what?

Uncreased, unlined **foreheads** and **cheeks** are a prerequisite for tricking people into believing you have a good life. But life is fucking stressful and too goddamn long, and I am afraid to get needles in my face, because I know me, and I know that the minute I make some drastic alteration to my face, my hands and neck and other dead-giveaway parts are going to shrivel up like a raisin and I'm going to be the only shiny, moon-faced bitch out here still looking old because the rest of her body immediately started running away from her doctored face.

Rarely do I feel myself channeling either of my old, country-ass parents, but one of the times I feel them the most is when faced with a tub the size of a Carmex container full of fancy wrinkle cream that costs upwards of five hundred dollars. I'm not cheap, and I love flushing money down the toilet, but nothing brings the "child, that's just overpriced Vaseline" out of me quicker than the skincare counter at Saks. I mean, there are multiple times during the day when I can actively feel my body dying (sitting on the side of the bed after I first wake up in the morning, checking my text messages at literally any point during the day, when I accidentally catch the evening news), and if there is a cream strong enough to counteract the existential dread woven through every cell in my body, I'd buy it. If it exists, I bet it's at NASA or some shit. They're using it to power rockets.

Your **neck** is supposed to be firm and long, but I thought that was only asked of penises. Why does my neck have to do anything other than hold up my head? I do not, and will never, use any specific treatments for my neck. I cannot be bothered to care about my neck. Of all the things I have to check off this endless list, "neck maintenance" is not going to be one of them. Between whatever slides down it when I'm scrubbing my face and hair and whatever is slathered across it when I'm trying to moisturize all the other parts I can reach before the bathroom gets cold, that is all I can fucking be bothered to do.

What's happening on your **back** right now? Do you even know? How much hair is on it? Is the skin soft? Has years of spending every day in a straitjacket-tight bra left weird marks on it? How are your moles doing? What's up with that weird scaly patch? Are you already so tired from all the other shit you have to keep track of that you can't be bothered to worry about the part of your body you can't even fucking see? I FEEL THAT.

I think the last time I actually thought to myself, "Hey, I wonder what's going on on my back?" was in 2002 when I was sleeping with this dude who lived in the apartment downstairs from mine. He would moan weird shit during sex like, "You are so warm inside," and "I love looking at your back" while *making love* to my rear end. I laughed the first time he said the warm thing because, I'm sorry, what? Have you been fucking corpses? Do I have undiagnosed measles?? Anyway, I'm not such an asshole that I wouldn't try to make my back nicer for someone who enjoyed looking at it, so I bought a back-scrubbing loofah stick and almost dislocated my fucking arm trying to scrape the dead layers of skin off my back with so much force that it bled. Then I would squirt lotion on the wand end after my shower and try to slather it on, because I hadn't anticipated how dry and raw the trickiest part of my body to reach was going to feel after having twenty years' worth of dead cells scrubbed off it. I ended up having to back up to the towel rack and gingerly rub myself up and down like a dog against a dry towel to try to get the lotion to absorb into my wounded skin. My freshly unearthed baby back ribs didn't feel right for weeks, but the next time homeboy tapped on my door inappropriately late at night bearing nothing but lidded eyes and a throbbing erection, he did stop accidentally slipping into my anus long enough to ask, "Ouch, babe, did you fall on your back? You want me to put some liquid bandage on this?" Good ol' thermometer dick reminding me that no good deed goes unpunished and you should never do anything nice, ever, for anyone.

Let's flip your bodies over and examine all the shit that you could do but won't, because who could possibly keep track of all this, to have a nice **chest**. I don't mean your boobs, because they should be addressed on their own. I'm talking about that piece of real estate between your neck and where your boobs *begin*. Here's how I take care of my chest: sometimes when I wash my face, but only after I've taken a shower, I'll accidentally squeeze out too much moisturizer or put too much oil/serum into the palm of my hand, and, as I'm frantically looking around the bathroom trying to find some way of disposing of it that doesn't include dribbling it all over the floor, it'll dawn on me through my morning fog that I could just rub it on my chest and have a weirdly shiny breastplate for the first few hours of the day. I know that back acne is a thing, but I'm pretty sure I also have chest acne? I don't know if that's what it is, but sometimes I get these little bumps, and what the fuck did I survive puberty for if thirty years later I'm going be squinting in the Clearasil aisle at the drugstore trying to figure out which of the options available works best on a saggy thorax?

Your **breasts** are supposed to sit right up under your chin from the moment they unexpectedly sprout on your chest until your ninety-ninth birthday, but you know what? I can't do it. I do not have perky tits, and that's okay. I think my "pinning my nipples to the nape of my neck" days are over, dude. One of the things that I keep telling myself, over and over again like a mantra, is "people already know what your body looks like, so you don't have to try anymore." MY BREASTS ARE SHAPED LIKE SUMMER SQUASH. Just as I am unwilling to fight with gravity as it ravages my face, these large bags of wet sand hanging below my clavicles are no longer going into daily battle against physics.

Are they even? Are they lifted? Are they separated? Does the band fit? Is the cup right? Does the underwire dig? Is the bra flat against your skin? Does it create weird lumps under your clingy sweaters? Is it lacy? Is it breathable? Is it scratchy? Does it wick moisture? (I heard that's a thing you're supposed to want.) Wait a minute, what were we talking about again?

Theoretically, everyone loves a strong, broad **shoulder**, but no one tells you how to get one. So, I guess you either have to be born with them or that's what those odd machines at the gym that make you look like a bird flapping its painfully heavy wings are for.

Michelle Obama is the gold standard for **arms**, and I'm sure there's a BuzzFeed interview with her trainer on how they got that way, but life is fucking short. Invest in some nice cardigans. Put Vaseline on your elbows. Wear sweat-shirts 365 days a year. Get arm definition lifting a coffee cup.

Armpit care and maintenance is a Whole Thing. You could, like I have, eschew all the possibilities and just let it go full lycan, occasionally spraying some herbal deodorant that doesn't work into your dark arm cave to keep wild dogs off you. Or you could wax or sugar or depilatory or shave or laser the hair off, dab it with something to prevent in-growns (?), powder it, and deodorize it. Every day? Every couple of days? Weekly? I guess that all depends on what kind of hair you have and whether or not you are taking beauty vitamins. I definitely am, by the way, because I love an easy fix even if it isn't real. The sheer number of available deodorants to choose from is staggering. I don't know how a person could be expected to make an informed decision without getting a bachelor's degree in chemistry first. It used to just be like, "Do you want to smell baby powder or cherry blossoms every time you raise your arm in class?" Now it's, "HEY, WOULD YOU RATHER BE SWEATY ONE HUNDRED PERCENT OF THE TIME OR DESTROY YOUR FUCKING BRAIN?"

My **hands** have been dry since 1987 no matter how much bag balm I rub on them, and for real, though, I don't even touch that many people, so whatever.

I got a manicure a few days ago, which is a thing I rarely do because—we're all friends here—I don't give a fuck. But I was going to a party that night and you know how parties are, just a bunch of people standing around in sequined clothes scouring the room to make sure one another's cuticles are pushed the fuck back. I walked into the shop midday on a Friday, and I had forgotten how bad it feels when you walk into a literal sweatshop of **nails**. I felt like I was actively participating in the oppression of another human being just glancing at the polish wall, and I'm not even a person who actually says shit like "oppression of another human being." Once you're in there, it's hard to turn around and walk out, mostly because some white lady's kid has wrapped his arms in a death grip around your legs while his mom dozes in the vibrating pedicure chair completely unaware, but also because they definitely need this twenty dollars in my wallet. I signed in and explained that there is not a universe in which I could actually maintain the shellac nails the manicurist was trying to upgrade me to then. I horrified him further by insisting he not snip my dry, ragged cuticles off because I didn't want to turn his workstation into a damn crime scene. I sat in silence, squirming in discomfort as I gazed down at the hair I should have shaved off my fingers, which is another thing you could do to try to have an acceptable body.

Your **belly** is going to be whatever it is, especially as you creep ever closer to the grave. For me, the most I can do is to maybe put lotion on mine. What else are you supposed to do, keep your belly button clean? I could lie, because no one is ever going to check, but that's not what this is about. I sometimes neglect my navel. One of these days, mushrooms are going to sprout in there.

Okay, no matter what you got, your **privates** have to be long or short, wet or dry, thick or sleek, and rough or smooth. I'm sure I could fill an entire book with all the ways you're supposed to keep your shit clean *alone*, without even getting into hair sculpture and removal and care. At this point in my life, I do nothing, which is apparently a theme. It's too much! How could I possibly keep up! I used to be young and optimistic and willing to shave hours off my sleep time and devote them to the preservation of my corporeal form, but now I enjoy "reading" and "lying very still not doing anything." I got a Brazilian exactly one time, in a cramped and overheated room in the back of an Ulta in Skokie, Illinois, and I involuntarily shit on the table when the woman yanked a giant strip of hot wax and cotton off my taint. What a fucking legend—she didn't even flinch, just wiped it up and handed me a giant wet nap, then went back to work while I chewed a handful of Advil, dry.

The man at whose behest I was re-creating *The 40-Year-Old Virgin* on my bush was fine, he was perfectly nice, but I was only going to all this trouble because he was flying in from out of town, and I wanted to do something nice because he was staying at my apartment, and I don't know shit about stocking a pantry. The most I've ever been asked to do before fucking a woman is shoo the cat off the bed beforehand, but I digress. Ugh, you have to mainline yogurt to kill off yeast, eat a whole cranberry bog to fend off UTIs, soak in a tub of vinegar to keep everything tight and balance your pH, drink a gallon of water a day, and after all this you're supposed to think about your eyebrows, too?!

> *My anaconda don't want none*
> *Unless you got **buns**, hon!*

I feel like smooth **thighs** are only possible for middle schoolers. Cellulite creams and washes and massagers seem like marginally fun wastes of money that you could otherwise spend on a jumbo buttered popcorn at the movies for all the good they're going to do for your cellulite. Do you wash your **legs**? Here is an act of radical transparency: sometimes when I'm running late, I just wash the parts of my body that stink, which means—now hold on to your butts—that I don't always wash my legs. I mean, they get wet, but I don't necessarily *scrub* them. Is that gross? I can use that extra minute to tap some pointless cream under my eyes with my ring finger (a thing you are apparently supposed to do) or stand next to the tub dry-brushing myself to help my circulation (yet another thing to add to the never-ending checklist). I start washing at the top, get real intense around the middle, then let the suds rinse off the rest. I know that is horrifying to you, I do, but have you ever considered this counterpoint? Your legs really aren't that dirty. I don't know that the skin on my calves has felt the rays of the sun upon it in the last five years, so how could it possibly be dirty? Sure, it could stand to be exfoliated every now and again, which I haven't even gotten to yet despite how often I'm told that my entire outer layer of my epidermis should be grated off like Parmesan once a week, but does it actually need to be cleansed every day? I hate even talking about this lest anyone confuse me for a hippie when what I actually am is EXHAUSTED, but this is a hill I'm willing to die on. With filthy legs.

Head, Shoulders, HOW MANY GLUCOSAMINE DO MY **KNEES** NEED TO STOP SOUNDING LIKE A SHATTERING WINDSHIELD EVERY TIME I STAND UP, and Toes.

Is there **ankle** care? I'm not sure what ankles are supposed to be other than "delicate," but, bitch, I have a heart problem, so my ankles bulge like hot water bottles at the end of the day. The most I can muster energy to do for them is buy the good kind of compression stockings.

I'm not sure how blocks of calloused skin housing blood and tiny little bones are supposed to also be supple and smooth and impeccably groomed at all times, especially when you just shove them into sweaty gym shoes all day and immediately put them in slipper socks at night, but here we are. My friend John runs a foot fetish porn site called Feetishes™, and when he told me about it, I wasn't grossed out or anything, because I would masturbate to two grandfathers fucking at a bus stop. I imagine how much intensive labor it would take to preserve perfectly fappable **feet**. Clipping and squaring up the toenails, filing down the heels, figuring out a way to seal that crevasse that always opens up on the ball of the foot, thoroughly moisturizing the webbing between each toe . . . And that's just what's expected of a normal person getting their barking dogs ready for flip-flop season! I can't even fathom what a nude foot model has to go through. Attaching tiny barbells to their phalanxes for daily strength training? Hanging upside down like bats while they sleep? I really just need these hooves to get me around from place to place every day and not hurt. I can't also make them beautiful. I mean, I can get a kick out of watching a woman wrap her impeccable soles around a slippery erection as much as the next guy, but what slobs among the rest of us has that kind of time?

I ordered vitamins, from Instagram, because that is the kind of thing I have the emotional bandwidth for. I don't take them every day (who do you think you're dealing with?), but I sometimes catch sight of the bottle on the kitchen counter and go, "Oh, yeah! A self-care thing I could easily do!" as I'm walking out the back door on a mission to Burger King. I've purchased many fancy water bottles while lying to myself that I would drink more water if the vessel it was served to me in cost eighty-seven dollars and Busy Philipps had the same kind. I'm trying out a new Vitamin C serum that's supposed to make my face light up like a fucking quasar because I heard the new trend is to be so distractingly shiny that no one can see all the things wrong with your hideous beast face. I tried to start using a facial roller, but using it was too embarrassing even when I did it at home by myself. I got some cream with acid in it from my sister-in-law who might have been trying to tell me something, but you rub it on your rough patches and it just dissolves the scales? Listen, I'm not a scientist, but my feet feel softer and look more pink, so I think it's working.

I got some bloodwork done and found out I'm deficient in Vitamin D, which I already knew because of ~extreme depression~ thank you so much. I don't even have time to get into all the shit you need to be doing for your dumb blood. And your organs, which you shouldn't even have to worry about since you can't see them. At least I might catch a glimpse of my back in a multi-mirrored room, but tell me, pretty please, when I might ever get a look at my pancreas? Folic acid! Potassium! Calcium! Turmeric! Zinc! B_{12}! Sodium! Magnesium! There are not enough hours in the day for all the motherfucking *beans* you need to be eating. The bananas, the kale, the eggs, the blueberries, the walnuts, the oats, the salmon, the broccoli, the oranges, the bell peppers, the plain yogurt, the cherries, the brussels sprouts, the flaxseeds, the celery sticks, the spinach, the tomatoes, the nineteen cups of unsweetened green tea. I need to know how to get some extra cow stomachs to hold all the shit that's going to keep me alive plus all the shit I actually want to eat.

Who are these people who somehow get the correct serving of carrots every day? Where do these positive bodies find time for all that sauerkraut and avocado? I know I have the same number of hours in my day as Beyoncé, but do I really have the same number as a person who manages to consume both a beneficial number of almonds and perform an adequate amount of cardiovascular exercise? I don't believe I do! All I could muster the energy for today was two sips of green juice (haha jk it was Diet Coke) and some accidental SPF.

Loving yourself is a full-time job with shitty benefits. I'm calling in sick.

country crock

Before we got married, I thought that my soon-to-be wife and I could pioneer a new type of marriage situation that some "relationship expert" would eventually dissect in *The New Yorker*, the kind of marriage in which she could continue to hang laundry on a line and churn her own butter in rural Michigan, while I spent the days counting down to my early death in a small, refrigerated apartment in Chicago. She could keep withering under the blazing sun while picking her own blueberries to make homemade jam and knitting socks to sell at the Christmas bazaar, while I ordered seventeen-dollar cocktails at swanky rooftop bars and waited four hours for a brunch table downtown. We'd meet up occasionally to talk about married shit (property taxes? which big-box retailer has the best deal on economy-size containers of powdered soup?!) and pretend we're still interested in having sex. Sounds like a dream, right? But, oh no, fam, apparently marriage involves a little thing called compromise, a concept I'd been previously unaware of while withering on the single-person vine. Compromise for my lady meant having to wake up next to a framed photo of Jheri curl–era Ice Cube on her bedroom wall, but for me meant GIVING UP EVERYTHING I EVER LOVED.

When I was thirty-seven years old, I packed a suitcase full of clothes that require dry cleaning and my unclean house-plants into a mid-size SUV with four-wheel drive, and drove through Indiana's industrial ghost towns to the sticky-sweet Southwest Michigan fruit belt, immediately regretting my decision to move to the town my girlfriend lived in as I drove past billboard after faded billboard advertising AM Christian radio stations and upcoming casino performances by smooth jazz has-beens. I grew up in a Very Liberal Suburb just north of a Politically Progressive City. My family did not have any money for frivolous things that might make childhood worth surviving (LOL, what is a lunchbox?) and qualified for every government assistance program in existence. My parents had the foresight to apply for section 8 housing in a Chicago-adjacent mid-size city where there were music classes and art classes available to me, and, sure, I might have gone to school wearing some classmate's dad's old work shirt because it had been in a donation bin at the Salvation Army, but at least when I started wearing all black and got really into Ani DiFranco junior year of high school, not a single one of my forward-thinking classmates was like: HA-HA, LESBIAN, GO KILL YOURSELF. I was lucky enough to grow up in a Super Nice Town, where it was okay if you dyed your hair purple and wrote mopey song lyrics on the white parts of your knockoff Chuck Taylors. It was a Cul-turally Accepting Haven where (Jewish or not) we learned about the Holocaust and got Rosh Hashanah and Yom Kip-pur off from school, a Promiscuity Province in which part of my sex education included the golf team's coach sternly watching my fingers as I carefully rolled a lubricated spermicidal condom down the rigid shaft of a lunchroom banana.

I can maybe give a rudimentary explanation of how evolution works (dinosaurs are birds!) and sing a nursery rhyme in Swahili if pressed, but I didn't learn any useful small-town shit while I was busy trying to look smart reading Vonnegut and pretending I was interested in skateboards. I didn't take home economics in high school. I took gender studies and shaved my head and started spelling *women* with a *y.* All these things are well and good for someone nestled safely between mid-rise buildings. But how are any of the limited number of skills I've acquired, like hailing cabs at midnight without falling into the street from too much tequila or having artisanal cupcakes delivered to my apartment before noon, going to translate in a place that has roving deer brazen enough to just walk up onto your porch and sort through your junk mail while waiting for you to toss the compost out. I get nervous being in places that are dark, without street lights, and where you can't get a pizza after 9 p.m. I do not possess the handiness to make myself useful around a toilet I'm responsible for fixing if it breaks. And okay, sure, pseudo-country life has its perks. Gas costs approximately thirty-seven cents a gallon. You can buy shoes at the grocery store. You're never going to stand shivering in your high heels outside in the cold trying to get in the club after midnight. The farmers' market is full of actual farmers instead of bearded hipsters in distressed flannel bloviating at you about peak asparagus season while criminally overcharging you for Pink Lady apples. These are all pros!

It sounds cute and all, but I am living in an actual nightmare. I hate nature! Birds are terrifying flying rats, and the sun will fry you and give you cancer, and large bodies of water are made up of mostly garbage and liquified human waste. I am a blue-state city slicker to my very core, content to ignore the outside world in favor of convenience apps and cable television. Everything here is dangerous and/or irritating: mosquitoes the size of a fist bite me through my practical long sleeves and leave itchy, egg-size welts in their wake; loud-ass frogs live in our backyard pond (why do we even have that?) and croak all goddamned night; bats hysterically flap their leathery wings while trapped in a woodstove; maniacal squirrels aloft in the branches over the deck hurl walnuts at our heads as we mind our human business grilling farm-stand corn for lunch. Sick raccoons fall out of our trees, fat groundhogs burst through the fence to eat the okra and tomatoes I refuse to help harvest from our garden but am pleased to know exist, and field mice scurry across the basement floor, sending chills up my spine with their scratchy-scratchy nails. This season on *Americana Horror Story*.

I have had very few encounters with the people who live in our surrounding towns since I moved, because I once drove past a house in which a person had literally built a makeshift wall in their yard made of Trump signs and I'm terrified the neighbors will sense the pro-choice vibes rising off me like steam and start inaccurately lecturing me about embryonic stem cells. One time, a man I'd never seen walked his golden retriever by our house as I was dragging the garbage can up the driveway from the curb, and he stopped and said, "You must be new here." How did he know I was new? Could he smell the lingering stench of unreliable public transportation on me? Could he see in my eyes that I couldn't really tell the difference between a cucumber and a zucchini without cutting it open? Did he register my smooth, uncalloused hands and instinctively know I had never driven a tractor?! What kind of sorcery is this? HOW DID THIS RETIRED MIDDLE SCHOOL PRINCIPAL KNOW MY SECRETS? Trying not to judge a Republican by his sensible dog-walking cardigan, I said, "I don't speak English!" And then I left the recycling bin in the street and slouched away before he could say "Benghazi." Although, in hindsight, I'm surprised there wasn't an ICE raid at our crib later that afternoon.

I have never really cared about voting. Until this year, I lived in a blue state and was always scheduled to work a twelve-hour shift on Tuesdays. Plus, I'm not really sure if this is real or not, but I don't want to be stuck for three days trying to think up ways to paint myself as an undesirable juror to overworked Cook County public defenders ever again, so I'd been like, "HARD PASS," when optimistic young people approach me on the street about registering to vote. I shouldn't admit this, but I am never going to read the qualifications of all the hopeful circuit court judges, and even if I did, how would I even know which one I should vote for? How does a statute work? What does adjudication mean? You're kidding yourself if you think a person who couldn't remember how the number of electors for each state is decided for the eighth-grade Constitution test is the same person who should be deciding who's the best candidate to interpret the law. Can you turn in a ballot if it's only one-third filled in? Seriously, does your vote actually count if you don't take the time to fill in every single school board bubble?! Since I had to move to a little blue dot in a big red state to participate in this cross-cultural marital experiment, when the post office asked if I'd like to register to vote as I filled out my change of address form, I sighed and said, "Girl, I guess."

I voted for Barack Obama one time, in 2008. Not that I wouldn't have voted for him again, but I didn't believe I could get my boss to buy the "new Black holiday" line two elections in a row. I had already gotten a pay raise out of him by citing reparations, but I am definitely not clever enough to pull off that kind of magic twice. I'll never forget all the winks and nods and knowing looks exchanged with every black and brown face in line as one by one, we cast our votes for our boy Barry, and I will also never forget walking what felt like 137 miles through downtown Chicago and Grant Park to watch the election results roll in with thousands of my new best friends, and, once Barack won and delivered that super-inspiring speech as African America's first president-elect, getting pushed and shoved and stampeded as I fought to get a spot on the northbound train after everyone realized it was two in the damn morning and we all had to be at work the next day.

The most exhilarating part of Obama's Post-Racial America for me was when salty white people taped Lipton tea bags to all the fedoras and straw hats gathering dust in their closets and started saying "nigger" with abandon in the middle of the grocery store. Remember when liberal whites tried to trick us into thinking racism was over, when every night their uncles were on the news, their DON'T TREAD ON ME and GO BACK TO KENYA signs on proud display? I was preoccupied sitting at home waiting for the mailman to deliver the reparations check Obama was surely going to sign himself and send out with priority shipping, but I heard that some of you idealists had your hearts broken when the secretly racist lady next door who called the police on your dreadlocked cousin that one time didn't start leaving her front door unlocked and inviting you over for a cold glass of milk and a warm slice of the American dream.

I can't reliably find West Virginia on a map, but I knew that eight years of the Socialist in Chief, or whatever people who watch Bill O'Reilly called him, was going to break bad as soon as America saw its opportunity. I thought for sure it was going to be Ted Cruz, but when Donald Trump won the nomination I was like, "Oh shit, these dudes ain't playing. And now I live near them."

My wife and I went out to eat the other night at the kind of place where you slop a pile of room-temperature food out of a chafing dish onto your plate while fogging up the sneeze guard keeping it safe. As I was raising an egg roll stuffed with pale mystery meat up to my mouth, in walked a group of rowdy dudes in unironic "Make America Great Again" apparel, ready to shovel ambiguously Chinese food you pay for by the pound into their freedom-loving mouths, and I braced myself for a conflict. I am a black lady with a white wife in a Red state, and I can't be sure that bro with the backward visor (LOL, WHY?) isn't about to start some shit with me just because I have the nerve to show my face in public.

This new political edgelord kind of bro is usually pretty easy to spot. He is wearing a North Face fleece and mirrored sunglasses made of neon-pink plastic, possibly multipocketed shorts, and definitely shower shoes. He's probably not saying any real English words, just grunting and whooping and huffing at varying volumes. He looks you right in the eye for an uncomfortably long time, and if you challenge him, he'll throw an unlandable punch in the direction of your face and grumble unintelligibly about your going back to Africa, a continent which you have never even visited. His friends are named Brody and Kevin and Kyle, and they punch one another a lot and call things they don't like "gay." These are dudes know what thirty-seven dollars' worth of Taco Bell tastes like, and nothing will get in the way of their path toward domination, not the opposition party media propagating their fake news, nor the shrill feminazis stepping on the white man's dick with their unsexy man-shoes. On a typical weekend, you'll find him kicking over Planned Parenthood barricades. Or he'll be shitting his cargo shorts in the back of an Uber on his way home from the college bar he's definitely too old to still party at. Or he's railing at anyone who will listen about the exorbitant taxes he has never actually paid. Or he's saying "state's rights" so you won't think he's actually racist. Or he's grabbing women by the pussy, and he will be back in the office denying you a lower rate on your mortgage bright and early on Monday.

I don't want to make it seem like I'm not well versed in unintentional racism, or latent racism, or hipster racism, or whatever you'd call "wow, I can't believe someone like you really read that new Ann Patchett novel" racism, but it's one thing when a lady in overpriced exercise clothes starts over-enunciating her order at the young immigrant man working at the coffee shop and quite another when a person dressed in the flag on any day other than the Fourth of July loudly reminds your queer ass that you currently reside in an open carry state. This, until recently, I thought was just a hilarious punchline to the joke of my new life. But a few months ago after I moved here, a guy with a salt-and-pepper '70s mustache casually wearing an inside vest with a laugh told me he might shoot me if I took my phone out to text in a movie theater from his assigned seat behind mine. And not that context matters (should I actually be shot for ruining a climactic scene in the live-action version of *Beauty and the Beast* with my tiny glowing rectangle of doom? well, probably?!) but it was half an hour before the movie even started. Like, the lights were fully illuminated and that *Entertainment Tonight* movie trivia that plays before the previews hadn't even started yet. My stomach fell out of my butt as I contemplated being murdered while Maria Menounos patiently waited for my answer to "What is the name of the kleptomaniac monkey in Disney's animated film *Aladdin*?"

You scoff at Miss Lululemon and her bone-dry latte, and roll your eyes behind her back as you mumble shit about "microaggressions" under your breath and hope that the Land Rover she left idling in the middle of the street has a ticket on it when she gets back. But I'm not yet ready for the kind of racism that screams: THE PERSON WEARING THIS RED HAT MIGHT HURT YOU. I don't have a plan ready if he spray paints a swastika on my car or loses his shit on the Mexican woman at the apple orchard while I'm paying the *real* price for a half-peck of freshly picked Honeycrisps. If a "fiscal conservative" asked me what my hair feels like in downtown Chicago, I could recite some Ta-Nehisi Coates or whatever to deescalate the situation, but what should I do if an American Worker Who Loves Winning decides to fuck with me out in the wilderness for fun?

I don't know—it's not even that rural here. And it's not

like I've never seen a tree before, but I've definitely never spent a lot of time around people who say the words "family values" in earnest. I drove up north once to spend a week writing in solitude in a cold, dark room (read: watch whatever movies were on Amazon Prime because the place I rented had a complicated TV system, so please be on the lookout for my new horror novel, *Help, This Airbnb Uses a PlayStation Instead of a Thing I Actually Know How to Fucking Use*, in stores this spring). In a tiny town, on the side of U.S. 131, I saw a billboard featuring a smiling Trump giving a thumbs-up with something like "We're so proud of our president!" emblazoned on it, and look, if you like borscht and economic depression, what do I care? Like who you want, do whatever the hell you want. But goddamn, that shit was chilling. I made a mental note not to stop there for gas.

Maybe I can just watch reality TV in the safety of my home and avoid eye contact with a newspaper for the next couple years. I mean, I talk a lot of shit and everything, but I'm a doughy creative, and I live with a lady who cans her own pickles and can't fight. I can't be out here defending the mainstream media against people wearing homemade "Lock Her Up" T-shirts. I mean, we just put a canoe rack on our Honda. I'm starting the paperwork to make our male cat an emotional support animal. There's no way we're getting out of a Freedom Headlock.

a guide to simple home repairs

what is that thing attached to the back of our house, a deck or a patio

what do gutters do

how do you clean a fucking screen

how many smoke detectors do you have to have? Like, is it a law or is it just up to your discretion

can I just try to step around the squeaky stair when I'm coming down, or is that the kind of thing that eventually needs to get looked at

what do you mean "store the hose"

sheesh, do I have to become a goddamn electrician to put this stupid Home Depot ceiling fan up

the dishwasher stinks—is that a real problem

what is that damp-looking shit on the ceiling

weatherstripping???

at what point can I just throw up my hands and concede this shredded chair to the cats

are houses supposed to be washed on the outside?

Over the last couple years I have had to learn to live in a house, and that is one of the hardest and most boring things I've ever had to do. There's a lot of basic shit I absolutely DO NOT KNOW as I uncomfortably masquerade through life in the body of a human adult and the brain of one of the aliens from *Earth Girls Are Easy*. I'm not going to remind you yet again that I grew up in a trash-filled possum nest with intermittent basic cable, but in case you're unfamiliar with the plight of my youth, let's just say that the first time I had to work my own thermostat, I was thirty-five years old.

The house my eight-pound infant self was brought home to was a two-story, six-bedroom, two-and-a-half-bathroom single family home whose current value is listed at $723,988 on Redfin, which is $359,000 more than it was worth twenty years ago, which is probably *even more* than it was worth when my dad bought it in the late '70s with help from a VA loan that he earned cooking beans and shirking any actual responsibility for his fellow troops during the Korean War. I will never actually know how Samuel Irby came to own the big, beautiful house down the street from Mason Park, but if I had a time machine and the stipulation on my using it was that I could only go back to one specific point in history, I would 100 percent choose to go to the bank office the minute before my dad and his tidy little Afro strutted through the doors to buy that fucking house. How did he get it? What earnings potential did he show them? Why was there no background check? Did he know the loan guy? Were they just giving suburban houses away in 1978? Did my dad pull out a shotgun in the middle of the bank?!

I have very specific memories of that house, where I lived until my parents divorced in 1984:

- the record player with every Barbra Streisand LP lined up in the cabinet it sat on top of (to this day I can sing *Color Me Barbra* from start to finish, and, trust me, that's my best party trick)
- I had a little television set in my room that I used exclusively to watch *Soul Train* and the *Lou Rawls Parade of Stars* telethons
- we had many pets, the grossest of which was an Alaskan malamute my dad loved that lived in the garage and once killed another dog while I was playing in the yard next to it
- a giant Chevy Caprice gleaming in the driveway
- the many, many bottles of 1980s-style 50-percent alcohol NyQuil from when my dad got big into AA and pretended he was going to stop drinking but basically just mainlined cough syrup instead
- my oldest sister had a bedroom in the back of the house a bit removed from the rest of us, and that felt very glamorous to me, because I had zero idea what she did in there

When I sweep away the mental cobwebs hanging over that time in my life, I can't find a single memory of either of my parents hammering anything or using a tape measure. There was never a table saw set up in the driveway on which my dad handcrafted a replacement cabinet door. My mom never stood in the paint aisle at True Value, clutching swatches of the various shades of marigold she was considering for the kitchen. Once, I locked myself in the downstairs bathroom and was too scared and clumsy to get it unlocked, and my dad told me to crouch in the bathtub so I wouldn't get knocked unconscious by the falling door as he kicked it off the fucking hinges. For the rest of the time we lived there, that bathroom just *didn't have a fucking door.* And now you expect *me,* a feral dog with PTSD who had to maneuver a heavy door haphazardly against a splintered frame to poop in relative privacy, to know my grout from my caulk?!

Shortly after I was born, my dad, (a terrifying, unstable person and hypothetical entrepreneur) got it into his head to convert the basement of his starter home into a rooming house for his wino friends. This is the ideal living circumstance for a helpless baby! He constructed makeshift walls out of plywood to make "rooms" and stuck twin beds between them. I wish I could say he was on some benevolent hippie community-living type of shit, but this was about getting drunk and loan sharking and playing dice, and more than one person died under suspicious circumstances in that basement. I'm not being dramatic. I don't mean *murder* or whatever— I mean something like "drowned due to a malfunctioning water heater" or something like that. Bad but not, say, investigation bad. All his tenants were men who weren't allowed in the rest of the house, and I'm honestly surprised that this isn't a story about how I was kidnapped and trafficked by a man missing his front teeth and doused in Cutty Sark.

do I have a septic tank

whose responsibility is the sidewalk

if we never attach the water hose to the icemaker, is that bad

is there a way the mailbox is supposed to, you know, *be*

I thought hard water was just a made-up thing to get me to buy shower spray

the washing machine stinks—is that a real problem

why does the lawn have to be mowed so often, and how do you oil the mower or put gas in it, and if so, do you pay a guy to do that

how many types of batteries do I really need to keep on hand at all times

"vacuum the freezer coils"?

try to replace this interior door ourselves or just move into a hotel for the winter

when was I ever supposed to learn how to measure blinds

how often do I really have to go in the garage

is defrosting the refrigerator still a thing

When my parents divorced, my mom and I moved from that house to this two-flat on the other side of town, across the street from both the church and the middle school I would eventually attend. My mean grandma owned and occupied the first floor of the building. Other than a man who occasionally came by to mow the lawn, no actual care-taking of the house took place. At least not in an explicit way that I can remember, and certainly not in a way that translated to me. There was a shed at the back of the house that my grandma made me keep my bike in. Remember, this was firmly in the Jason Voorhees/Freddy Krueger era, so I was 100-percent prepared to get murdered when having to retrieve my sky-blue Schwinn Stingray from that crumbling outhouse because she didn't want me tracking in any "out-side dirt."

There was a crawl space under that frightening-ass house, too. A perfect forever home for your local killer clown! I had to go to church all the time because we literally lived across the street from it, and one Halloween, instead of let-ting us take to the streets to partake in the devil's holiday, the church threw an "autumn party" at which we sat very chastely, dressed up as good boys and girls, listening to the Christian version of "Monster Mash" and eating sugar-free candy. Someone had snuck in a VHS tape of *Silent Night, Deadly Night*, and when the septuagenarian chaperone fell asleep, we crowded around the TV and I got to see my very first soft-core boobs. Then I watched in horror as they were impaled by a murderous Santa Claus. (What kind of psycho would do that to boobs?!) I walked home later that night with my heart hammering in my prepubescent chest toward the darkened shed no one really knew what to do with and the crawl space no normal person would have a real use for, then went upstairs and slept fully clothed with all the lights on, breaking at least two of the Top Five Black Mom Rules.

I remember being a teenager in the summers, and absolutely roasting in the third-floor walk-up Section 8 apartment we moved to when my gram decided to buy a condo because not taking care of that scary old house had grown too expensive. I filled old Snapple bottles halfway with tap water and crammed them into the freezer, pulling them out a couple hours later to drip melting ice on my forehead and tongue, trying to convince myself I felt less hot even as my flesh bubbled away from my bones like pieces of fried bologna in a hot pan. I had no idea what a window-unit air conditioner even was, let alone that there was an alternate universe in which I could not spend every July morning afraid to eat breakfast on the cracked vinyl of our kitchen chairs for fear of ripping the heat-fused tender skin off the backs of my thighs when I got up. I would watch Cubs games on WGN and suck on Fla-Vor-Ice popsicles that I was too impatient to let get fully cold, counting the days until I could go back to my school lunch and air-conditioned classroom.

does the air conditioner have to be cleaned, and if so, who does that

do people clean their roofs or does the rain just take care of it is a storm window just the regular window or is it some special kind of extra window

what is that steam coming out of the side of the house that smells like laundry detergent

do you actually have to clean out cupboards or is that just a thing that happens in magazines

who washes walls

how organized is the deck supposed to be

is it better to flush, or just toss that runny leftover pasta from three nights ago

am I supposed to do something with the heat thing (??) when it's not winter

no really what is a crawl space for and do I have to go in it

is one fire extinguisher enough for a whole house or is there like a square-footage requirement

what is a grounded outlet

must I really learn things about grass

I lived in a high-rise dormitory for one year after I got out of high school, and maybe that experience was useful for learning about how to deal with unrepentantly loud neigh-bors you're not in charge of, which seems to be a running theme of adulthood. The geeky senior in the double room next door to ours was basically a hall monitor in pajama pants, and not an actual authority figure to whom we paid even a scrap of respect, so I learned nothing about running a grown-up home, especially since there were no courses offered titled Intro to Property Taxes or Wait, How Do I Fix This Mailbox? in Northern Illinois University's catalog.

After I expelled myself from college, I was homeless for a hot minute and lived out of my car, which meant that the only home maintenance I needed to stay on top of was remembering that if the gas needle dropped to half a tank, that meant that at any moment my car would grind to a halt in the middle of the street and I'd be forced to lug a red plastic jug to the nearest Citgo. I eventually moved into my friend Jon's childhood bedroom in his stepdad Mel's house while Jon was away at college, like a good kid, and it was the first and only time I have ever lived in a rich person's Really Nice House. In rich people's houses, you know that things will absolutely be taken care of. Work has been and will be done. But it's done by a contractor who doesn't really talk to you and seemingly shows up whenever he feels like it. At the end of it all—voilà!—there's a second bedroom and the banisters and chandeliers have all been replaced!

Jon had his own wing that I was allowed to take over, a bedroom suite with a full bathroom (and a kitchen!!) above the garage, connected to the building that housed Mel's graphic design and photography studio. This meant that I spent a lot of my time there listening to Jon's old A Tribe

Called Quest mixtapes and imagining how different my life would have been if I'd grown up with my own bathroom. I don't think it occurred to me in high school, when I was smoking bowls and playing Aphex Twin in that very room, what a coup it was that this kid had his own separate outside entrance. In high school! Seriously, what is a curfew when you have a key to your own door? I am still the exact same person I was in 1995, so I'm sure I was mystified by how close his bed was to the ice cream in his very own personal kitchen. But wow. What a fucking flex. Anyway, I got to live in one room of a multimillion-dollar house with Italian marble bathroom floors I was afraid to breathe on, a stainless steel Viking hood and range I knew I was too broke to even glance at, and bottles of expensive sparkling water in the refrigerator at all times because these fancy motherfuckers couldn't even *hydrate* regular.

if I want a new banister, do I just google "new banister person"

why does the dishwasher sound like that

which neighbor is responsible for the fence neither side asked to be installed

I would love to install a dimmer switch but I also love not being electrocuted

what is a property tax

a lawnmower costs HOW MUCH

how did the neighbor decide exactly on which invisible line between our homes his snow blower was going to stop? Like, would it kill him to help me out with a few inches of clear sidewalk

the faucet can just drip forever, right

wait, what is this sticky . . . ? Never mind

should I set traps for these mice or just burn the fucking house down

I have lived with exactly ONE handy person. And I don't mean handy by trade. I mean my old roommate, a regular woman with a job at a bank who knew how to use a stud finder and also how to put up shelves. It's pretty amazing to be around the kind of person who envisions a thing they want, and then goes to Menards and figures out how to make it real. I'm the type of person who thinks, "Wow, that table would be gorgeous in a deep teal," and then walks past it every single day for the rest of my life without once considering going to the hardware store and getting sandpaper and a drop cloth. I would love to replace my kitchen cabinets, but how am I supposed to get the old ones down? And, even if I developed some herculean old-man strength and ripped them clean off the wall, what am I supposed to do with them? How do you throw cabinets away? Who do you get to put up the new ones?!

My roommate taught me things I still might not know about if she hadn't been there to drag me kicking and screaming into rote domesticity:

- what air plants are
- that teriyaki chicken wings at the hot bar in Whole Foods are incredible
- that it's good to leave boxes of Kleenex out
- that switching out the knobs on an IKEA dresser from the bumped-and-bruised section for prettier ones is a real thing
- that you can place a rectangular piece of finished wood on top of your radiator to make it a shelf
- that vacuum cleaners have bags that you have to throw away
- that I needed to learn to use a goddamn hex key
- that you should occasionally run some white vinegar through a hot cycle in a top-loading washing machine
- that it's legal to put up a new toilet paper holder in a rented apartment

In my twenties I would dog-sit a lot, because living with roommates is emotionally exhausting when you're the kind of person who never stops worrying that someone might be mad at you for a thing you hadn't even realized you'd done. Plus my job at the animal hospital meant I had unfettered access to the kind of people who lived in mansions and didn't even blink at paying seventy-five dollars a night for me to eat their cheese and introduce their dogs to *Law & Order* reruns, especially because those people believed that my proximity to veterinarians made me some kind of pet expert. At the very least, they could sleep tight in Tuscany knowing that I wasn't going to spoon-feed onions and raisins to their borzois. The best part of that job, other than knowing that finally no one was around to judge my consumption of peanut butter straight from the jar, was getting to live in the kind of house I'd otherwise never have access to.

I had never had an alarm system (I accidentally set off several, and definitely almost got arrested when more than one dog was like, "Bitch, I don't know her," when the cops arrived to shut it off. Gee, thanks a lot, Lucy.) or taken a bath in a jacuzzi tub or seen recessed lighting in someone's home. I thought dimmer switches were the height of elegance! I used to sit for this family that had speakers built into the ceiling of every room. There was a central command system with all these knobs and buttons and lights, and if you knew what you were doing, you could set it up so that whatever CD you put on would be playing in every room of the house. And when I tell you that my mind was *b l o w n*, I'm telling you that I ran from room to room up and down the stairs, mouth agape, as Dave Matthews warbled "Warehouse" in the bathroom and the den and the library. AT THE SAME TIME. I never wanted to own a place like that of my own, because, holy shit, it just seemed like so much *work*. How much money were they spending on light bulbs? When your house has seven faucets, how do you make sure that none of them is leaky? How many hours must you set aside specifically for dusting? How do you keep everything in order? The sheer enormity of keeping a house the size of my grammar school heated and clean would make bile creep up the back of my throat. I am not cut out for that life. Imagine me with an alcove.

I lived in my last apartment in Chicago for six years or something like that, not long enough to become a legend ("don't go near apartment 309, that weird cat lady who gets all those quarts of soup delivered will cast a spell on you!"), but definitely long enough that every other apartment got rehabbed as people cycled through over the years, and I had no idea that mine was the only one left with crumbling asbestos windows and a neon-pink bathtub.

The seal at the base of the toilet wore out, and occasionally when I flushed, dingy water seeped out the bottom, just slowly enough that I wouldn't notice until the next time I went in there and nearly broke my teeth on the sink from slipping around in my own waste. The ceiling in that place fell in, twice, because homeboy upstairs was growing hydroponic weed and his hoses got backed up or some nonsense (what am I, a farmer?), and the leaky water built up and came crashing down on all my fucking books and electrocuted my television. The utensil drawer stopped sliding all the way out. The overhead light wouldn't work unless the ceiling fan was also on, but in the winter that's annoying, especially in the daytime before the orchestra inside the radiator banged and clanged to life. My door would bang and whistle if whoever last smoked a cigarette out the hallway window forgot to shut it after they'd finished. The freezer just up and quit, on a regular-ass Tuesday. All these problems were solved with e-mails to a faceless gentleman named Joe whom I never met, a man who started his day after I left for work and would always have the problem "solved" before I got back. I would leave my crib at 7 a.m., e-mail Joe from the train, and by the time I got home twelve hours later, there would be a new fridge installed. Or the toilet seat would be replaced. The ceiling would be back in one piece. The utensil drawer would move like greased lightning. I never had to pretend to have an opinion about fixtures or discern the infinitesimal difference between two shades of blue paint. I would go do my job, and Joe would make sure that the walls matched whatever shade of industrial eggshell was in everyone else's tiny, sad apartment by the time I got back. This is how life is supposed to be lived.

do postal workers just want money at Christmas or do they need a gift from the heart

what happens if I never ever *ever* launder this rug

am I too old to tape posters on the wall

that cherry tomato that rolled under the unreachable corner cabinet: what's gonna happen to it

where is the circuit breaker and why didn't I think to look for it before plugging in the window unit and a hair dryer in the same outlet

how old do I have to be before I get to literally yell "get off my lawn" at the children trampling my goddamned grass

can "drafty" be an aesthetic

is the UPS man judging me

LMAO, I'm not ~pruning a tree~

why is so much furniture made solely for decoration

do I have to wash this mop, and if so, where

how long before someone calls the police on me thinking I'm breaking into my own damn house

I got my lady a biweekly cleaning service last Christmas (in
case you don't feel like googling "how can I be romantic").
I can feel your judgment, like, "OH, OKAY, MONEY-
BAGS," but even if I had to go clean someone else's house to
pay someone else to come clean my own, I would do that,
because is there anything more horrifying than having to
confront your own dirt or acknowledge the things you've
resigned to remain in a state of "kind of dirty"? Like, how
clean can that tight spot behind the toilet actually get? Can
I really be expected to regularly dust the top edge of every
picture frame? I'm afraid if I inch the refrigerator to the right
just enough to force a mop between it and the cabinet it's
stuck to, a creature is going to jump out and bite me. Am I
the one who should be trusted to get the grates clean, and
more important, does it matter if they aren't? Even if I bleach
that plastic mat we leave the winter boots on, some moron is
going to sneeze some deadly strain of influenza directly into
my mouth the next time I go outside, so what difference
does it actually make?

Have you ever purchased blinds before? I mean, have

you ever sat in the place where you live while a person with a Trapper Keeper full of *faux bois* blind samples comes to your home and presents the options for you as if you have any idea at all what the fuck he is talking about? It's magical! Yesterday, a gentleman named Jeff came into this house, whose gutter debris I am actively ignoring, in a truck with his phone number printed on it, and slowly and methodically hung blinds that he'd cut specifically for windows he'd precisely measured. If I could bottle and sell the feeling I had watching him complete this task I knew I wasn't cut out to perform no matter how many times incredulous home improvement experts had scoffed in my face while shouting, "Just go to Lowe's," I would have Bezos money.

is it ever worth it to try to fix something in my home myself like what is really going to happen I should just hire a guy right

who the fuck do these squirrels think they are?

if this table is not real wood, do I actually have to polish it

I thought HVAC was a slang term for a badass, like HBIC

take the shower head off? With what?!

is a linen closet supposed to be organized in some other fashion than "rifled through"

at what point do you just throw away the stove

what's really going to happen to that bacon grease I poured down the drain

what is "insulation"—or wait, is it called "installation"

Listen, I don't know how to live in this house I live in with my lady and her kids now, and I know that. I mean, I knew when I arrived with a car packed full of books I'm never going to read and placed open bags of cat litter spilling all over it in the driveway—whose cracks I wasn't aware until two weeks ago that I am now expected to monitor and fill and pave over—that I wasn't cut out for living in more than four hundred and fifty square feet of space. I'm reminded of it every time I go visit a friend who's, oh, you know, just doing a DIY remodel of the guest bathroom. LOL, WHAT. How did you learn to make a wall? We learned colors and shapes at the same time in elementary school! When between Elmer's Glue and yesterday did you figure out how to do a baseboard? (I'm still over here hoping beyond hope that no one will notice that I don't actually wash those.) Life was so much simpler when I could look at all my possessions at the same time from my bed, when my kitchen touched both my bedroom and the closet, and I didn't have to worry about a beeping noise coming from the basement after I'd already climbed all the way to the top of the second-floor staircase to go to bed. I like it when the wiring is someone else's problem, when I can submit a maintenance request through the management company's website and come home at the end of the workday to a faucet that doesn't drip anymore. I don't have "Turn the Broom Closet into a Home Office in Seven Easy Steps" money just lying around! And even if I did, who is going to tell me which pliers to get? When am I going to have time to learn how to use a level or pour my own concrete? Girl, I am not Bob Vila. I don't know shit about crown molding. And I'm not building a temperature-controlled cellar for this cheap-ass Costco wine.

we almost got a fucking dog

Helen died and immediately began haunting me from cat hell.

So I don't know what I actually believe about ghosts. Basically, I believe in them when it works in my favor, and the thought of them doesn't make me feel uncomfortable. For example, if I feel an odd breeze in a windowless place and can't immediately locate a silent fan or heating vent, I am willing to believe that maybe a ghost is blowing on me. If I'm home alone and feel a little prickle on my scalp and can determine that there aren't any bugs crawling on me . . . Okay, sure! Maybe there is a benevolent spirit floating around reading that *Atlantic* article I'm pretending to understand over my shoulder! But if you were to suggest that my dead mother might be looming, invisible, overhead, disgustedly judging what I eat and choose to masturbate to, then I would confidently inform you that *Ghost Dad* isn't a real movie and that most of the clips with "mature" tags on Pornhub that I have bookmarked on my phone are very tastefully shot.

The morning after my cat Helen was euthanized, I was in the kitchen performing some well-deserved self-care by making myself a delicious and nourishing meal (microwaving something from the Hot Pockets family of products) while drinking a diet water and minding my own fucking business, when I felt the air around my swollen ankles grow cold. I looked around, shuddering as I waited for the thing that had obviously come to kill me to show its evil face. Sunlight poured through the window over the sink, heat radiated from the hot oven, Peabo Bryson warbled warmly from the countertop speaker that doesn't really work: all in all, I was in a downright pastoral setting, straight out of a '50s-era sitcom, and definitely not in the kind of place you'd expect some rotten, rapidly decomposing corpse to come shambling into. I mean, do ghosts even like Crystal Light?

For weeks after that, I'd walk into a room and see a clinically obese gray shadow lurking ominously in a corner near the floor, or catch a whiff of off-brand tuna in the air where I'd least expect it. Could a pair of my moldy underpants that had accidentally fallen behind the hamper and been lodged there for days be the cause of the fish-market smell wafting from my bedroom? Of course! But is it also completely plausible that it might be the stench left behind by a rancid cat ghost? Absolutely.

An aside:

Years ago, right after I moved into my last apartment in Chicago, the one I expected to die alone in to the soundtrack of an *NCIS* marathon, I thought I had a ghost. Several nights a week, I would be awakened from a dead sleep by this—I don't know how to describe it without sounding like a fuck-ing moron, but I'll try—vibrational energy? I'd be knocked out atop a pile of pizza boxes and magazines, then be jolted fully awake by a humming and swaying feeling in the air.

I am a dumb person who doesn't understand building structure or architecture, but it didn't seem like the kind of thing a fucking mid-rise apartment building should be doing. It was like my room was droning at me. Every morn-ing while getting ready for work in those days, I would listen to this ridiculous show on Kiss FM hosted by a dude I'm pretty sure called himself Drex. You know what makes me wistful for a happier, simpler time? Thinking about when I could actually crack a fucking smile at prank mother-in-law calls on drive-time radio shows before living turned to hell and I had to be mad about everything all the goddamned time. You know what I listen to now? *Pod Save America*, on a phone I come perilously close to dropping in a toi-let full of feces every single morning. Because we live in a fiery hellscape, and I don't know what the three branches of government do exactly, so I need three IPA bros to explain our crumbling democracy to me between ads for sheets and Bluetooth speakers while I wonder which of the six wash-cloths scattered around the shower is mine.

So early one morning Drex on Kiss FM tells this riveting story to the other hosts (you know how those shows are: pop hits interspersed with prank calls and ticket giveaways, and they feature a woman of color who is funnier than the host is, but who is forced to play sidekick, and featuring "my old pal Clown Car with the traffic and weather on the twos!") about how he had a ghost in his place. And he knew it was a ghost because he'd come home after work and cabinets would be hanging open and shit would be rearranged, and no one else had a key to his apartment. I immediately glanced around my clothing-strewn apartment and wondered, *"Was that novelty Taco Bell bag filled with Corn Chex cereal on my nightstand when I left yesterday?"* Drex had consulted with a paranormal expert who told him that the best way to deal with a ghost is to firmly yet politely demand that they leave, because apparently ghosts have some strict moral code that they are required to adhere to. And so, the day before, when he'd gotten home from work to find yet another rearranging of his belongings, he yelled at the ghost to leave him alone, and lo and behold, IT DID. I was gobsmacked.

I was brought up in church, but taken there by people who smoked and drank and had multiple children out of wedlock. Whatever lingering side effects I have from my many years of being expected to recite the Apostles' Creed from memory by a woman who was probably high with a cigarette in her mouth, manifest themselves in this way: I'm not really religious and I am ambivalent about church except for the music, of which I have many secret playlists that I listen to on the regular, but I also don't like to mess with "the devil." I mean, he's definitely not real, but just in case? I'm not fucking with a Ouija board or pretending to cast spells I don't actually understand. I *do* believe ghosts can be real, especially because I have very little tolerance for "science" and like to leave inexplicable things unexplained. Life is just sexier and more mysterious when the flickering lights could be a poltergeist rather than a fluctuation in voltage or a loose cord.

Okay, so, in the wee hours of every morning, I would be jostled awake by this low-pitched hum, literally feeling my bed swaying beneath me like Rose clinging to that *Titanic* door. My brain, molded by years of grainy exorcism videos on *20/20*, immediately leapt to the conclusion that my apartment was haunted by a pissed-off demon. This was pre-cats, before I full became a spinster witch, so it wasn't like I had a creature around who could tip me off. By the third or fourth night of this, I was sufficiently spooked, trolling Craigslist for mediums on my lunch breaks and googling "can you legally break a lease due to supernatural inhabitants." Then I remembered Drex. And his advice to, you know, politely ask a ghost to leave. Sure, I could've looked up banishing spells or bought some potions from the occult store, but this is where I remind you that the lingering effects of Many Years of Bible School kept me from dabbling in any Satanry. Or perceived Satanry.

That night, I performed my usual evening routine: dinner for one consumed zombie-style over the sink; many episodes of reality television devoured with rapt attention, my face pressed against the television; falling asleep fully clothed, with my phone in my hand. And there it was again, at two or three in the morning, a loud humming slash vibrating that made my bed quiver so hard I bolted upright the minute it started. I lay there massaging the sleep out of my weary eyes and suddenly remembered what Drex had said to do: acknowledge the ghost's presence, then politely demand that he leave. Easy, right? Please pack your things and get the fuck out, sir, I have to be at work in four hours! I sat up and looked around to see if I could make out any floating Big Gulps or candy wrappers in the dim light provided by the streetlamps in the alley my apartment overlooked. There were no tipped-over bottles or clouds of ecto-mist swirling near the baseboards, nothing other than that weird, ominous moaning and the rattling of the walls that accompanied it. I cleared my throat and in my most authoritative third-grade teacher voice said, "Okay, I hear you. I'm tired of this. Please leave me alone."

The wailing continued. Louder, I declared: "I pay six hundred and ninety dollars to live in this asbestos closet and I don't need a roommate. You have to leave!" The droning paused, and for a millisecond I felt like a capable person who could solve her own problems; then it came roaring back even more intensely. I am not so attached to living that I would willingly survive a supernatural terror that would torment me for the rest of my days, so I started feeling around in the sheets for a stray sock to asphyxiate myself with in case some monster with dripping fangs rounded the corner ready to eat me. Bitch, I can't fight! When the zombies come or the aliens land or whatever dystopian shit that is bound to happen in our lifetime happens, I'm not stockpiling buckets of slop and batteries or any of that doomsday shit. I will be in the fetal position somewhere waiting for them to lobotomize me. I gave it one last try, plugging my ears with my fingers and shouting, "SHUT THE FUCK UP!" at the top of my lungs. The noise stopped immediately. I couldn't even believe it! First, I couldn't believe that I had anything in my useless collection of trash and novelty gifts that would be of any interest to someone who had actually been to *hell*, but more important than that, it seemed unfathomable to me that I could then convince that someone to leave my apartment! I am a horrible negotiator! I pulled the blanket over my head and slept the sleep of the saved and thankful.

The ghost appeared to be gone for good; make me an

honorary fucking Ghostbuster! A week later I was down-stairs in the lobby deciding whether or not to take someone else's *Cosmopolitan* magazine upstairs when this good-looking young dude in a cardigan smiled and said hi to me. He flipped his locks over his shoulder and noted my open mailbox door, then asked if I lived in 309. I don't trust the motives of attractive people, so I just stared at him with my mouth open, hoping he would walk away and forget that he caught me reading someone else's steamy sex tips. "I'm in 409," he said, unprompted. "Right on top of you." Hot men know what the fuck they're doing when they say shit like this, with their perfect teeth shimmering through their perfectly groomed beards. I was supposed to think about him grind-ing on top of me, WHICH I IMMEDIATELY DID. "Any-way," he continued, "I heard you yelling the other night. Sorry about that. I didn't know you could hear the reverb from my bass amp so much. I had a friend come soundproof my place. Has it been less noticeable?" And this is why I stopped taking my ass to church. Would a loving God actu-ally humiliate me like this??

Obviously, I am an expert on ghosts. And Helen was *clearly* still hovering in the drafty corners of the house, clucking softly to herself about my disappointing choices and willing the other cats to do her bidding. Speaking of Bootie and Coco, and their staunch resistance to my soppy desperation, they are my lady's cats. I live with them, I tag along when they have to go to the vet, I brush them off the counter-tops when they're trying to get at whatever waterlogged food is rotting in the sink, but they are not *my* cats. I didn't pick them. I didn't lock eyes with them through the bars of a shelter cage and feel that little furry paw wrap around my heartstring and gently tug at it. They were already living here when I arrived from Chicago. They had their own nooks and crannies and hideaways, their own schedules and patterns and antipathy toward another human taking up the space they'd already designated as their own. So after Helen died, I needed to get a new Helen.

But what if I replaced her with a dumb, happy dog? What must it be like to come home to an animal who is overjoyed upon your return, who is grateful for you and the wonderfully cozy and sheltered life you have provided for them? Imagine coming home at the end of the day to the aggressively wagging tail of a creature who spent the entirety of their waking hours dreaming of your tires crunching over the leaves in the driveway! What a dream to have a companion who not only worships the very ground I walk on, but also would rescue me from a well if I happened to slip and fall down one!

As I have mentioned too many times, I worked in an animal hospital for fourteen years, which means I know everything there is to know about pet ownership. I wish I was exaggerating. In a job where every day presented a new and confounding horror, one of the things that continued to surprise me was how often people would pick up the phone and actually risk embarrassing themselves in front of another person to ask basic pet care information they could just google to figure out without having to suffer through a painful human interaction. Because countless people decided to waste their anytime minutes calling in to ask me whether plastic food bowls would be harmful to their beloved dachshund, or if prong collars are safe, or what prophylactic flea and tick topical treatments work best, I am full of useless trivia about the most basic shit a child could probably tell you about dogs.

"Tell me all the things I need to have a dog!" was a common request, especially from people who shouldn't own one. The answer generally boils down to these things:

- a crate large enough for the dog to comfortably stand and turn around in
- a soft, adjustable collar that fits snugly, but that you can get two fingers under
- several leads, but not a retractable one, especially if you're going to text or do some other distracted shit while walking your dog
- bedding
- puppy pads, because that dog is definitely going to shit all over your house
- large water and food bowls
- food and treats, which, wow oh wow, the fucking rabbit hole you could go down. You can kill yourself researching the best organic, grain-free kibble or buy logs of raw food for upward of a hundred dollars a month, and no matter what you choose, there will still be some asshole on the Internet trying to convince you you're doing it wrong
- a ton of chew toys
- medicine! Your dog will need all kinds of medicines! It will not be cheap!
- baby-proofed kitchen cabinets
- a better hiding place for your delicious rat poison

- plastic baby gates to keep the dog from ruining all your shit
- while you're doing that, put a fence around your house!
- a good groomer, because have you ever tried to wash a goddamn dog?
- a trainer and/or classes
- day care! Dog walkers! Boarding facilities!
- a city license, if you're a little Goody Two-shoes
- a washer and dryer
- a commitment to picking up anything you don't want destroyed by slimy dog teeth every single minute that creature is loose in your home
- the firm discipline to put all your food and drugs away the minute you are finished using them
- an unlimited credit card
- no discernible social life
- stamina to walk several miles a day, in the rain and snow and cold
- the patience of a saint

Sure, you don't have to have or do all those things to be a dog owner. Crust punks on the street in Seattle have dogs! But to be a good dog owner who isn't annoyed all the time, you have to do/have/be at least most of them.

I remember one snowy day I was driving to work, and I used to live on top of the fucking lake, because in Chicago it was possible to get an apartment on the beach for cheap if you really lowered your expectations for what the words "beachside living" can mean, and this person (midwestern winters render everyone genderless; in the month of January, we are just amorphous shapeshifting piles of down filling and wool) was waiting for their dog to poop in horizontally blowing ice spittle while struggling to remain upright against the biting wind as icy waves crashed onto the frozen sand behind them, the tattered end of the blue newspaper wrapper clutched in their mitten barely visible through the storm. I sat at the stoplight where Sheridan Road curves and turns into Evanston, fingertips pressed to the heat vent from which a whisper of anemic warm air trickled out, and chuckled softly to myself. "Man, *fuck* dogs."

But I've never had a cat that let me put clothes on it. Or performed any cool tricks. Or came running when I called. Or accompanied me on a long, peaceful walk at dusk. (I'm never actually doing that, but I would like to have the option.) I've done all this exhausting work for the animal hospital, and been in this field for my entire adult life, and I innately understand what a bad idea it is to commit to an animal if you have any intention at all of living a normal, carefree life. And yet I was waking up thinking: "Wouldn't it be cute if there was a little doggie snoring on my pillow right now?" Then I'd get up to go to the bathroom and survey the home that is a dangerous canine death trap littered with poisonous, flammable choking hazards and mentally stitch together all the outstanding accounts receivable it would take from my new life as a "freelance writer" to pay for a visit to Animal 911 in the wee hours of the morning, and I'd laugh myself almost to death.

How many times have I dropped half a Vicodin on the floor and then spent twenty minutes blindly stumbling around in search of my glasses before locating them and spending another half hour looking for a tiny yellow stump of a pill? If a dog lived here, he'd find it and wolf it down before I'd even have a chance to realize it had slipped from my gnarled grasp. My days of carelessly leaving loaves of raisin bread on the dining room table would be over! Can I live in a world where the peanut butter has to be put away while I'm thinking about whether or not I want to make another sandwich? Am I cut out for the kind of life led by a person who doesn't forget there's an irresistible pack of Trident in the bottom of a tote bag tossed in a heap next to the back door? I don't think I am! I know that cat people get a bad rap, but do I really have it in me to become a dog person?

We went to the SPCA on one snowy February morning, a couple weeks before my birthday. I talked my lady into looking at a dog, with no pressure to bring one home, unless I saw one that I fell in love with and couldn't live without. I'd gotten myself worked up in the weeks before, scrolling through dogs on Petfinder, fantasizing about little dogs I could dress up in teenie-weenie jackets and train to be mean to everyone but me. I even went so far as to e-mail the foster parent of a fat gray-haired Chihuahua mix named Coraline who was a million years old and had cancerous mammary tumors that needed to be removed and who was so stumpy and cute that I almost cried while reading her bio. I was so smitten, I considered letting a dog interview me for the opportunity to destroy my furniture and checkbook!! But she got adopted (are there other completely naive and irrational people in this town?) before I could put on my best suit and tie to go to whatever meth lab she was staying in to see if they'd consider letting me pay two hundred dollars to take her to my house.

That's really how we ended up at the shelter, because I

had been rejected by a dog who couldn't read the love letter I'd tapped out on my cracked phone screen to win her over. As Lois at the front desk led us to the kennel, I felt my heart clench. I was powerless against the slobbery little beards and juicy sad eyes of the whimpering dogs. As we walked in, some kind of giant ridgeback mix launched himself at the cage door, gnashing his teeth and barking, up on his hind legs. "Not him!" Kirsten squeaked, hopping away from the spittle flying out of his cage. We walked by bored bulldogs and hyperactive hounds until finally we reached a heartbreakingly adorable cattle dog mix who had, judging by the size of her swollen nipples, definitely given birth in the recent past. She had some country-ass name, Backhoe or Wheelbarrow or some other farm shit, and I wanted her desperately. She looked at me like I was made out of sausage. I signaled to Lois that we wanted to take her to one of the soundproof *SVU* interview rooms, where I assumed she'd grill me on my whereabouts before slamming my head into a table and offering me a Styrofoam cup of coffee from which her partner would later extract my DNA to use in court to convict me of a crime they framed me for.

I watched the dog trot shyly down the hallway as I imagined her scampering through our sun-dappled house with the Sunday paper in her teeth. The three of us were left alone while Lois went to locate her history and vet records for a little background. I sat in one corner with a bag of treats and held them lovingly toward her. Kirsten sat in another corner with a different type of treat, shaking the bag gently in her direction. Tractor looked from one of us to the other, then back again, and did nothing. I scooted closer from my corner, Kirsten scooted closer from her corner, and ol' Hog Oiler retreated farther into her corner.

"If I wanted to be rejected, I would just get another evil cat," I said, and pouted.

We sat there for what felt like ages, cooing and singing and trying to coax Pitchfork out of her shell. Kirsten rewrote her thesis while I did the last four years of my taxes, and still . . . nada. Lois eased the door open and slid through a crack so the dog couldn't take off running. Why she was concerned about an animal that had basically wallpapered herself to the farthest wall making a mad dash toward the exit was beyond me, but I guess you can never be too careful. Lil' Wheat Chaff had come from dubious origins, and no one was quite sure of her age or how many babies she'd had or whether or not she liked jazz. The one thing they did know was that she "doesn't really warm up to people and has noise sensitivity."

"Aw, shit," I grumbled, packing up the copy of *The Iliad* I had read in its entirety while we were trapped in the padded dog room. "They should've told us that from the jump. No thanks, Corn Stalk!" Kirsten shushed me and motioned for me to take my coat back off. "What does that mean exactly?" she asked.

Lois explained to us that dogs like Cotton Gin would be best served in a house where people make little to no noise, and didn't try to engage with her too much at first. But, seriously, no noise. Like, no loud music and no shouting and no turning the television up because your ears are bad and no accidentally dropping anything on the floor. Girl, what? We have a drum set in our basement! "Goodness, I used to have a dog just like that," Lois sighed, scanning her paper.

"I couldn't even put dishes in the sink without him flipping out!" Kirsten looked at me in disbelief and I smugly put my jacket back on like, BITCH, I TOLD YA. At this point, the dog gathered up her hobo bindle and headed back to the sanctity of her cage. Satisfied with having at least tried, and heaving an internal sigh of relief at having dodged a bullet, I decided to make a big donation that could maybe cover a pair of noise-canceling headphones for my would-be dog daughter. But wait a second, hadn't we walked by a cat room?

I felt a cloud of cold air envelop me as Lois led us into the darkened kitty sanctuary. I could hear Helen's deadly groan of disapproval in my ear, and I knew immediately that I was making the right decision. Am I really going to schedule my entire life around the scatological needs of a creature who will chew through all my fancy toys? Will I really have to pretend to care about notes the dog walker leaves, or worse, will I really have to spend my red wine and magazine money on a dog walker?! What if the back of my CR-V was filled with dirty Chuckits and chewed-up Nerf toys and filthy rubber balls? Picture me flinging a frisbee into a lukewarm lake full of dead fish, then actually standing there while waiting for a sandy, muddy dog to bring it back to me! That cat room smelled like my future, like damp pine litter and tuna casserole and the moldy inside of an L.L.Bean moccasin, and I walked directly to a large cage housing a tiny tortoiseshell kitten who was scaling the bars with her razor-sharp claws, face pressed hard against them as she strained to grab for my finger. "If you take me home, I will end you," she whispered, as a bright spot of blood appeared on my fingertip. "Lois, I've found my soul mate. Ring her up!"

Jackie Brown came home and immediately claimed a dark corner in an upstairs closet as her own. She is not nice. She is not sweet. She hates my fucking guts. She is full of kinetic energy and skitters across the slippery floors, crashing into shit because she can't pump her little brakes in time to stop. She prefers to sleep in a vent in the basement and emerges several times a day sleep-drunk with giant dust bunnies hanging from her whiskers. We've had her almost a year, and she hasn't gained an ounce, weighing in at a mighty five pounds at her last checkup, which the doctor said is fine. I believe it to be further evidence that she is demonic and doesn't require food to live. She sits at the window in the sunroom all day chattering the avian equivalent of Parseltongue to the birds. She stares without blinking for minutes at a time. She refuses to be in any room I'm in. She only purrs when she's knocking something fragile off a high shelf. She sleeps during the afternoon, then gets up after dinner and spends all night breaking things. She's a menace and a scourge and she is going to spend the next ten years minimum ruining my life. But that's fine, because at least she's not a fucking dog.

detachment parenting

I jump away from children the way most people jump back from a hot stove. I don't dislike them. As a matter of fact, a lot of them are funny and smart and tuned in to all the cultural shit I don't know, and are usually more than willing to very slowly explain things to me as I nod and take notes. I didn't know what a TikTok was until a ten-year-old explained it to me, and I'm guessing that shit is already obsolete, which is why I didn't even bother embarrassing myself by downloading it. The power that young people have is amazing, because neither I nor ANYONE I HAVE EVER MET has reached that mythical age at which you "stop caring about things." Here's a tip: it does not exist! Most of us are barely concealing our desperation to understand exactly what the fuck these young people are talking about. Not because I want to participate, but just in case there's some sort of entrance exam for cool olds.

I'm forty now, and the hilarious thing about being forty is this: I don't know anything. Before you try to convince me otherwise or try to make me feel better, you should know that I know that *you're* forty and trying to reassure yourself that *you* know something. You don't! Here's a word problem one of my lady's kids brought home the other night:

The ratio of two numbers is 5 to 1. The sum is 18. What are the two numbers?

I'm sorry, what? First of all, am I dumb? Don't answer that. Did I ever, at any point in my miserable existence, learn how to solve this problem? The kid, a girl, didn't even ask me to help; I just happened to glance down over her shoulder as I was walking by huffing a marker and making paper airplanes out of all my letters from the IRS, then walked right into the wall because I was so confounded by her homework. Is she a fucking wizard? My lady's other kid, a boy, had to write a paper on an ancient Chinese dynasty! Excuse me?? He was sitting at the dining room table casually shuffling through pages of meticulous research, and, okay, was I actually in some kind of remedial program or are these kids straight up SAVANTS?

I'm terrified to be at home alone with these children. I have a lot of basic knowledge and have committed thousands of random facts to memory: Did you know that an individual blood cell takes about sixty seconds to make a complete circuit of the body? Maybe if a fire started in the kitchen, and I made it to the fire extinguisher before the flames had a chance to set my cheap, flammable clothing ablaze, I might be able to put it out, but I don't know a lot of useful child information. I was home a few weeks ago during the day when they had friends over (remind me to rent an apartment) and the neighbor's kid looked up from his homework and asked me if I knew who the thirty-third president was. I thought we were playing that game where someone knows the answer to the question they're asking because it's right there in the book they just happen to be reading, so like a dummy I said, "No! Who?!" as if I knew and was just playing along. And then we just sat there blinking at each other like idiots until I realized he was waiting for me to come up with the answer and help him pass the fucking GRE. Dude, why are you asking me that shit? Wouldn't you rather learn which household cleaners you aren't supposed to mix with bleach? Please ask me something about a television show!!!!!!!!

Here are some things I could teach a kid:

- *maybe* thirty-eight states on a blank US map
- how to mute mean tweets
- not to mix wine and Norco
- how to file a tax extension
- who's who on *Game of Thrones* (sort of)
- the best hangover remedy (Drink more. JK! Drink a Coke and walk around the block.)
- Forest Whitaker's filmography
- how many forks each person needs on the table
- which cat litter to buy (Feline Pine)
- the best Instagram accounts to follow
- how loud to scream if the cat catches a bird and tries to bring it inside.
- which candle scents are good, for ~ambiance~
- the benefits of an Epsom salt foot soak
- how to turn your laptop, iPad, and television into a picture-in-picture-in-picture situation
- how to play spades

- how to avoid making an unwise tattoo decision (just make it, who cares!)
- where to eat in Chicago (Maude's!)
- fantasy football draft mistakes
- how to make a frittata
- health-food-store snack hacks
- codeswitching
- where to find the best compression socks on sale
- how to make fake phone calls to get out of public interactions
- not to stick a fork in the sink disposal
- clean your air-conditioner filter
- how to google a meme
- that if you just make a new e-mail, you can get multiple discount codes when shopping online
- that beets are gross
- how to avoid people you hate
- that making toast in a frying pan is the only acceptable way to make toast
- how to write a personal check
- the lost art of ironing

Is that enough? Don't you also need—I don't know—a strong character and moral center in order to guide a child through life? These two children in my house are not my children, so I'm off the hook I guess, but y'all know my luck is bad. One day, they are inevitably going to ask me what they should study in college, or who not to invite to the slumber party, or when to open a Roth IRA, and then: WHAT AM I GOING TO DO? I have not lived the kind of life worth emulating! I didn't have the kind of childhood I can look back on and draw wisdom from. I had bad parents! Sometimes my lady and I will be sitting side by side in bed in our matching Vermont Country Store nightgowns like we're in a sitcom. She's rubbing lotion onto her hands (every woman who ever goes to bed on television is always thoroughly lotioning—what the fuck?) while I peer over my reading glasses and frown at the newspaper (again, TV executives, who reads the fucking paper at night?), and she'll set her alarm and casually ask, "Hey, what would you do if [insert totally normal naughty child behavior that a black child with a black mom would never get away with]?" Now, most times in situations like these, I would just fake my own death and pretend to rise like Lazarus the next morning, but sometimes I'll set the old *USA Today* aside and say, "Have you ever thought about digging your long, red press-on nails into the tender fat on the back of their upper arm while threatening their life under your breath?"

See? *That* is how I was raised! Once I threw a fit in the Barbie aisle at Toys"R"Us because I wanted a new doll and my mom said no. I howled and screamed and rolled on the floor, drawing a bunch of unwanted attention to us like I'd seen some other kid doing in the past. My mother calmly picked me up from the floor, patiently led me by the hand outside, then RAN ME OVER WITH HER FUCKING CAR. A tantrum? In this economy??? My mom and dad didn't know shit, and I turned out fine (just kidding, there are still vegetables I haven't heard of!), and I'm okay to sit quietly in the corner playing Fruit Ninja or buying these kids nuggets at the drive-thru for the duration of their teen years, but even *that* is setting a terrible example.

. . .

I'm a good cook, but the thing about cooking meals for children is that sometimes sophisticated ingredients and techniques are wasted on them, and as a person who expects an entire parade after taking the time to BRAISE! A! MEAT!, I knew I was going to have to adjust my expectations and practices. Listen, it's not like I would otherwise be making consommé every night, but I have been known to attempt my own pad thai, and those are not hours that should be spent on a second grader. Maybe, if I was a chef. But I write a blog. It's not even a fucking food blog. I write about sadness! So I decided to arm myself with a bunch of kid-friendly meals so that I might convince my lady's children to like me, or at least convince them to tolerate me enough not to delete my saved shows from the DVR. I grew up poor, so I know all about those meals where your daily servings of grain, protein, and vegetables are all mixed together in the same murky chicken water. On that note, here is my recipe for a wholesome Midwestern casserole called "Cheeseburger Macaroni."

CHEESEBURGER MACARONI

Step one: I'm going to let you know that, to start, a lot of these ingredients should already be in your cabinets. Did you know that children eat all the time? My memory of eating as a kid is that, sure, it was constant, but it was also secretive, shame-filled, and carbohydrate-based. My lady is not a "box of Little Debbie Oatmeal Crème Pies from the dollar store in your pajama drawer" kind of mom, which means that every available surface in our tiny kitchen is piled with food, but it's also the kind of food that I never want to eat. It's all shit that has to be prepared. Even the snacks! Even if you were trying to have a *healthy* snack! Even if you wanted to come home and fill your belly with nutritious carrots and a legume spread of some kind, first you'd have to find the organic reusable produce bag with the purple carrots from the co-op, and wash them with the fruit wash before trimming the tops off. Then you'd have to root around in the tool drawer for a peeler—she frowns upon those delicious pre-peeled baby carrot nubs—and then go take off your shoes and lie down, because all you wanted was something to stress-eat over the garbage, and now it's a goddamn production. Sometimes I think to myself, "What do I miss about my old life?" And you know what? It's not hot dates or anonymous doggy-style sex. It's *refined carbohydrates.* It's *mouth sex* with *a cookie I didn't have to bake.*

Gather these items:

½ stick unsalted butter

2 red bell peppers, diced

1 yellow onion, diced

2 tablespoons of minced garlic FROM A JAR
    (why torture yourself?)

1 tablespoon kosher salt, plus more to taste

1 teaspoon dried oregano

1 teaspoon paprika

¾ teaspoon freshly ground black pepper, plus more to taste
    (okay, listen, never measure this)

2 tablespoons tomato paste from a tube

1 pound lean ground beef (or turkey? textured
   vegetable product?)
1 pound elbow macaroni
¼ cup all-purpose flour
2 cups whole milk (kids go through so much
   milk and it is truly revolting!)
1 15-ounce can crushed tomatoes (with the juice)
1 cup chicken broth (or veggie, if that's your thing)
3 cups (about 8 ounces) shredded sharp cheddar cheese
   (from a bag—are you kidding?)

Step two: I like to watch old episodes of *Top Chef* while I chop vegetables because—now, hear me out here—it takes the pressure off and lowers my expectations. There's no way for me to watch master technicians balancing microgreens on a spoon with tweezers and also worry that my tater-tot hot dish is somehow not going to turn out right. Oh, I'm sorry, did I not tourné this zucchini you spit all over the floor? Should I have prepared a chiffonade to go atop your Annie's mac and cheese? Do you need a coulis for your Go-Gurt?! Man, fuck that. You're gonna get these jagged chunks of slightly undercooked potato and this ice-encrusted frozen corn, and maybe you'll hate it, but you're also only going to eat three mouse bites, so I'm not stressed. You don't like my chickpea patties? Fine! I've seen you eat a popsicle with bugs on it! Who cares?!

Salt a pot of water and bring to a boil over high heat. Heat the oven to 400°F. While that's working, melt the butter over medium heat in a Dutch oven, then add the peppers, onion, garlic, some salt, oregano, paprika, and a few grinds of pepper, and cook, stirring occasionally, for seven to ten minutes. Add the tomato paste, stir to combine, and cook for one minute. Add the meat, season with salt and pepper, and cook for about five minutes. Break up the meat while it cooks. Cook your pasta in the pot of boiling salted water until it's still chewy and underdone, usually a few minutes less than the package directions suggest. Drain the pasta and rinse with cold water. This sounds like a lot of work, but I promise you can do all this at the same time. If I can, you can. I mean, I have to take two Aleve before I stand in the kitchen for even ten minutes, but this I can suffer through.

Step three: Okay, so, when I was growing up, if my mom ever went to this much trouble (she usually did not), then there definitely wasn't going to be an extra THING on the table. She wasn't going to snap a bunch of green beans or roast a squash to serve with it; this shit has all the food groups in one bowl and that's what you get or you can go to bed. Well, I don't live in that kind of house now. I live in a "we ordered a pizza but I also made a fresh herb salad and roasted some brussels sprouts and shallots to go with it, and since I had a little extra time, I also made a loaf of bread and whipped up a fruit tart including homemade pastry cream" house. That ain't me. I like to leave the car running outside Chipotle, not prepare supplemental foods to accompany carryout! "What kind of shit is this?" I asked the first time a leafy watercress home salad was gently placed next to my Popeyes Spicy Chicken Sandwich.

My lady handed me a bottle of home dressing, which, for the uninitiated, is something people who grow up in loving families that put limits on the TV make. "It's cute you think I'm going to eat this unsalted vinegar spray on this bowl of damp lawn clippings you're trying to serve me but, no, ma'am, I will not."

Add flour to the Dutch oven and cook, stirring occasionally, for two minutes. Add the milk, the canned tomatoes and juice, and the broth, then bring to a simmer. Add the cooked pasta and 1½ cups of the cheese and stir to combine. Season it to your liking. Sprinkle with what's left of the cheese, then bake in the oven until it's bubbly and browned on top, twenty-five to thirty minutes. Remove from the oven and let it cool for five minutes before you serve it so you don't burn your goddamn taste buds off.

Then you eat it, preferably out of a plastic shatterproof bowl. I'm not an expert, but kids love this shit. It's just fancy Hamburger Helper! It's not even good for you; it just seems like an upgrade because you had to cut up some vegetables to make it. And children love it! I once made it for a post-soccer "can all my friends come over?" kind of party, which was very scary, because there were now an exponential number of tiny brains floating around waiting to soak up all the colorful combinations of swear words pouring out of my mouth as I get steam burns and accidentally cut my hands. Also, what if they had decided to band together and rise up and overtake me? A gussied-up meat-and-cheese soup was not going to save me! How would I bat ten pairs of cleated feet away from my precious face? It didn't matter, because they happily gobbled it up. Kid tested, evil stepmother approved.

I bought a car, because you have to have a car in the Midwest. Only, when you live with children, you don't need a car as much as you need to have a ROLLING VEHICLE FILLED WITH MISCELLANEOUS SHIT FOR THEM TO SPILL FOOD IN. The last car I owned ten-plus years ago was almost as old as I was. It had a tape deck and no heat or air-conditioning, and its most impressive feature was ~very fancy~ automatic seatbelts that could decapitate you if you weren't paying attention when you got in the seat and shut the door. If I came to pick you up, there was no working horn to honk. I'd have to double park in the middle of the street, because there is never a spot anywhere you need one, and ring your buzzer until you yelled into the intercom that you were coming down, while a line of furious drivers spewing creative strings of curse words formed behind my car on your one-way street (FUCKING CHICAGO). Then, after I'd circled your block a few times or put my hazards on in a nearby alley, you'd come down and have to climb over gooey bowls of half-eaten cereal, an extra pair of shoes for the club, and a self-defense crowbar just to get in. Then I'd drive us to dinner bumping Smokey Robinson on V103 with the windows partially down no matter the season, because they did not roll all the way up. I'd self-park in a sketchy lot two blocks away from our destination because I was too embarrassed (and also poor!) to explain the literal wreck I was driving to the valet while paying him in dimes: "You have to pump the gas six times, then you really gotta lean on the ignition when you try to start it, then immediately put it in neutral for at least six minutes."

That was back in the good old days, before time ravaged my body and spirit. I swore that if I ever got another car, especially one that hadn't come off the lot of a combination car dealer/burrito stand, I would keep it pristine and full of both oil and coolant. No more changing my own windshield wipers in the parking lot of an AutoZone, no more buying bald tires from dudes who just happened to have one lying around the garage, no more climbing in my own trunk with a Dustbuster I'd "borrowed" from work. I was going to take care of this new car better than I had anything else I'd ever owned, including my body and pets. When my old car died in the middle of Lunt Avenue on a Sunday morning because it needed a new alternator (a what, now?), I walked away from car ownership and spent years riding late-ass buses and overcrowded, sweaty trains, grocery shopping with a camping backpack so I could lug my food home on foot, and negotiating with cab drivers outside the Target in Uptown about whether or not they could fit an entire dining set into the back of a Crown Vic. And that's fine, you do what the fuck you have to do, but that's the baggage I dragged into the car dealership with me one day after moving to Kalamazoo, the baggage that dissolved under the watchful eye of Eric the Used Honda Salesman, in the armpit sweat that soaked my T-shirt during the test drive he forced me to go on. I would've bought the car without his demonstrating the moon roof on a busy fucking highway, but I digress.

I put a down payment on this car, a used Honda CR-V, which is the single most expensive purchase I have made in my life other than the many uninsured medical procedures I have paid for out of pocket. I'm excited and also scared. I drive it home in awe of all the knobs and buttons that aren't already smeared with another human being's sebum. There are no salt-crusted mittens jammed next to the seat-belt or warm bottles of Diet Coke rolling under the driver's seat. My car is empty and clean, and I make a silent promise that I will always keep it that way no matter what. I am going to buy weatherproof floor mats and go to the car wash every week and do responsible shit like "winterize" it, even though I don't really know what that means. Eric sees me off with a wave, proud dad style, and I try not to back into any of the newer, nicer cars in the lot, because it's stressful when somebody is watching you drive.

It's a beautiful day and I connect my phone to the Blue-tooth, which wasn't even an available technology the last time my name was on a car title, and then I pull into the driveway feeling like a real adult, my nostrils filled with that glorious new car smell, the triumph of my personal check having been accepted at the dealership rolling off me in waves, and immediately my lady flings open the gunmetal metallic (their words, not mine) doors and just starts filling the car with . . . MOM SHIT.

I got out and stood there horrified as she expertly, in seconds, stashed mason jars filled to their brims with bulk nuts and sugar-free trail mix in every hidden cup holder and secret cubby hole; bundles of reusable grocery bags, some with actual farmers' market dirt littering their bottoms; pic-nic blankets and bungee cords and bike pumps and maps; a first-aid kit and jumper cables; a fanny pack–looking thing that clips to the visor filled with "important papers." I sank to the ground in the yard, helpless, watching in slack-jawed horror as my New Clean Thing was defiled by grimy soccer cleats and a skateboard. Bitch, I don't ride a fucking skateboard! Why are you putting one in my fucking car?! She smiled with all her teeth as she cheerfully stuffed both seat-back pockets with granola bars, and not the good Quaker kind with candy and shit, but the nasty health kind that taste like dog biscuits. "What are you doing to my car?!" I yelped. I could make out a trail of oats and chia seeds or whatever the fuck this bitch eats dotting the passenger seat of my rapidly devaluing New-ish Clean-ish Car, and my throat constricted. She paused in the middle of trying to shove a Costco-size package of tissues into the center console and smiled at me even harder. "What do you mean, babe? This is a family car!!"

I don't tell these kids a whole lot about myself, because, listen, I'm not sure what is and isn't good for them to know about a greasy old dirtbag who spent ten years writing about her pussyhole on the Internet. When you know you are eventually going to have or raise a kid, you have years to start getting your shit together, i.e., burying your real self under a bunch of arbitrary rules and a fictional explanation of your past. You don't have to tell them about that time you choked on your own beer vomit in high school; you can just say, "Don't drink." Okay, wait, there are laws that prohibit underage drinking. How about this better example: your kids don't have to know that your room was so disgusting that mushrooms grew in your closet sophomore year; you can just say, "CLEAN YOUR ROOM," and look like a good, caring parent without ever divulging your past. And your kids just trust you, you know, because you're their mom.

Every book and movie and country song about step-parents is fucking TERRIBLE. No one is ever like, "Wow, this new bitch fucking my dad is so nice. I love her so much. I would never even *think* about murdering her." It's always: "Damn, the dude from *Nip/Tuck* moved in with Richard Kimble's dead wife and now they are fighting each other with knives!!" These fictional stepmoms sweep in, seduce the defenseless widowers with their lies and charm, then lock the children in a tower and make them sew clothes with talking rats for eternity. There is literally no* depiction of stepmothers that doesn't make us seem like bloodthirsty monsters, and while that description is the embodiment of everything my heart strives to be, in reality I understand that once I inevitably have a stroke,† these kids might be the ones in charge of whatever home my body is deposited in, so it would serve me to be nice.

It took me a long time to even decide to get married because just setting up a life with another consenting adult is a harrowing enough decision. (We still don't share a bank account, because, look, I have plenty of shame by my damn self and I don't need somebody seeing how much I actually spend on magazines; plus, there's all the other shit you have to consider before taking the eternal plunge, like, "Do we

---

* I am not doing research, but I'm reasonably sure this is accurate.

† I'm taking atenolol, but, come on, can you really trust science?

agree on essential condiments?") Then you factor the kids into it, and that adds an even trickier set of questions. At least for me. Because I'm not a parent, I had no desire to ever be a parent, and up until now I never thought I would have little eyes watching everything I do, which is mostly nothing. I am self-conscious, and I hate for anyone to be watching me, and kids notice every-fucking-thing. I don't need these young, impressionable people out in the world quoting Mike Epps's stand-up and saying "bitch" all the time, which are two things I very much enjoy doing, especially while talking on the phone to all my old bitches back home. I am 100 percent not concerned with helping the children chart a course through life. They have white parents who understand interest rates for that! But I do think a lot about how many times they might have overheard me watching *The Hateful Eight* at top volume on the big TV in the back room and shudder.

I'm not a monster. I know how to keep my shit in check when in front of a son-of-a-bitching *child*, okay? I just don't want to accidentally teach one how to ignore a parking ticket or that you can actually survive on jalapeño Doritos and smoothies for days at a time. What kind of role model am I if I literally show them how you can watch TV all day and still occasionally make money and contribute to society? Or that it really doesn't matter if you eat dessert before dinner? I'm nice to the animals and I have a lot of fun gadgets, but I listen to the classic rock station in the car instead of NPR. Am I a bad influence? I have a lot of plastic soap bottles in the shower, and I don't always remember to compost my banana peels and eggs. Will this negatively affect the futures of two youths who don't even know my middle name?

They are not allowed to read my books. I refuse to expose them to my scumbag friends, and if they had to name three facts about me, I have no idea what they'd say other than "she likes mango vitaminwater," which they only know about because they know they aren't allowed to drink mine. Is that bad? My sister sent us an Easter card last month, and they were like: "SAM HAS A SISTER?" (Sam, in fact, has *three* sisters. Oops.) On the one hand, this is great because the fewer of my family members they can pick out of a lineup, the better, but on the other hand it makes me think: Am I *too* private? Is this nuts? Am I so worried about having a negative impact on them that I won't end up having an impact at all?

God, I don't know, you know what? For now, I think it's fine. I don't want anyone to ever get the upper hand on me, even if it's a miniature one that hasn't yet touched a steering wheel or a beer. I'm not going to give them my Netflix password, but I also won't give these dudes any poisoned apples. We'll see how my detachment parenting style works out for everybody. Maybe we'll never know, or maybe they'll take a page from my book and write about how I sold their voices to a sea witch or made their beloved spotted dogs into a coat.

After my first book, *Meaty*, came out, I got an e-mail from a Very Famous Person. I was sitting in the breakroom at my animal hospital job slurping down old soup (probably) while my coworker Lori and I placed bets on which *Maury* contestants were indeed the fathers of the children they were loudly refusing to claim. I checked my e-mail and there was one that read (this isn't exact, because it was a long fucking time ago and periodically I just clear out all my e-mails in the hopes that doing so will make my problems immediately disappear):

> *Hi, my name is Abbi and, dude, I loved your book! If you're ever in New York, I would love to meet up for coffee and talk about some ideas. Best, Abbi Jacobson*

I thanked Abbi in my mind and forgot about it for approximately eight months.

. . .

In my defense:

1. She did not say: HI, I AM A VERY FAMOUS PERSON WITH A TELEVISION SHOW at any point.
2. I had seen maybe three episodes of *Broad City* because I couldn't pay for cable, so her name did not immediately ring a bell for me, and I am not in the habit of googling people, because that's intrusive.
3. Not to be a dick about it, but I get very vague fan mail all the time and I always feel weird about whether or not people actually want me to write them back. Sometimes I will send an e-mail back thanking them for reading my stuff and then I will end up in a months-long thank-you loop that can only be broken if one of us dies, but then other times I will write a brief yet passionate response and hear nothing, then I find myself checking back like, "why didn't she respond, did I say something offensive?" when really it's just that that person has normal boundaries.
4. She specifically used the words "if you're ever in New York," and I rarely happened to just *be* there. It's cute that you like my book, sister, but I'm not getting on a plane. Listen, I don't mind telling you how to get in touch with my agent or anything else I can do to help, but I'm not going to fly to you, you have to be fucking kidding me

So eight months later: I'm responding to a bunch of e-mails and hers is in the queue and I write back some form of my standard response when I'm not sure what a person really wants from me. I proved that I read her e-mail, was grateful that she enjoyed my book, and imparted that I really would drink a kale smoothie with her if we're ever in NYC at the same time.

She responded almost immediately. And this is not exactly verbatim because I have very little memory retention, but it's pretty fucking close:

> *HEY, STUPID, my name is ABBI JACOBSON and I star in A TELEVISION SHOW that is beloved by MILLIONS OF PEOPLE who would probably burst into tears upon receiving an e-mail FROM AN EXTREMELY FAMOUS PERSON who wants to talk to their POOR, REGULAR ASS. Like I said, I have some ideas I would like TO TALK ABOUT WITH YOU. Why don't you go WATCH MY VERY POPULAR SHOW and maybe READ SOME GODDAMN ARTICLES ABOUT ME and then maybe you'll understand THE MAGNI-TUDE OF THIS CONNECTION I AM TRYING TO MAKE. And then, next time you're in New York, LET'S GET THAT JUICE.*

I sat there slack-jawed, blinking at my computer screen. I was like, "yes, wow, very cool way to be a moron, Sam." And I downloaded some *Broad City* episodes from iTunes and then spent the next weeks feeling too anxious to write her back.

A redirect, your honor:

Okay, sure, I'm an asshole, but she kept stipulating that we had to meet in New York and my life at the time was: wake up, eleven-plus hours of cat dilemmas and dog vomit, go home and watch old episodes of *Grey's Anatomy* while eating a burrito, bed. Hell, that's basically my life *now*. Lather, rinse, repeat. I didn't have any reason to go to New York. Also, I don't know if you can just, like, suggest a phone call or Skype to a bitch with a security detail, so I just decided to put it off until I came up with a realistic reason to go there, or she forgot about the whole thing altogether and I wouldn't have to spend a week agonizing over what to wear to meet her. I watched every available episode of her show and felt very special and overwhelmed (and also kind of terrified of Ilana?), but I still was too anxious to respond. Then, six months later, I wrote back *again* saying what a pleasant surprise it was to hear from her and I would for sure reach out the next time I went to New York, which would probably be never.

Her e-mail response was like lightning: *I'M COMING TO CHICAGO.*

The hardest I've ever pursued anyone romantically was probably this ruggedly handsome dude named Roy, a dude who first approached me on the dance floor at this Latin restaurant in the West Loop that served exorbitantly priced tapas and also turned into a full-fledged disco after 11 p.m., which is weird to me because I don't like to watch people dancing while I am eating or running the risk of knocking over someone's skirt steak with my vain attempts at salsa. Anyway, this dude came up to me and introduced himself, then clocked my drink and went to get me a fresh one, which is a very seductive thing to do for a poor person. The entire time

I was standing there waiting for him to return I was thinking, "this must be a trick," because I was the least coordinated person on the dance floor plus I kept pausing every couple of minutes to run over to my table to eat bacon-wrapped dates. What was he even interested in? He came back and leaned in to give me a fake compliment, and I could clearly see under the flash of the intermittent strobe light that he was at least ninety-two years old. But he was funny and wore shiny church loafers, so I was fine with getting murdered by him when it eventually came to that. He gave me his number at the end of the night even though I know from all the magazines that I was supposed to give him mine, and I called him as soon as I woke up the next afternoon because, bitch, I'm thirsty!!!

Roy answered on the Bluetooth in the car, which is truly Big Dick Energy of the highest magnitude, and we had a good, funny conversation while he glided through the streets of Chicago on his way to his many important senior errands. He had a son my age and a daughter my mom's age (maybe his daughter *was* my mom!), and I could hear him listening to the Chi-Lites in the background. Yet I remained undeterred, because I was in an emotional place where I believed validation from an older man would fractionally improve my self-worth. That was also a point in my life when I thought I liked sex, when what I *really* like is contracting all my muscles so they remain perfectly taut and not squashing all nineteen of my chins flat against my neck while someone who doesn't care what music I like grinds around on top of me for ten minutes.

This dude was obviously cool—I mean, he owned at least one suit jacket that he was confident enough to wear to the club. He didn't flinch even once at my evening-wear Birkenstocks. I thought this would be an impressive notch in my bedpost. Which really means a notch in his, because at the time, I was sleeping on a mattress that had come rolled up in a cardboard box that I caught my neighbor trying to steal off the UPS truck.

We gradually increased the frequency of our phone calls until we were talking to each other every other day, which was a milestone in my life that I have yet to achieve again, even though I now have an actual wife. But he wasn't asking me to go out. He told me how he watched the moon landing in real time and where he was the day man discovered fire, but never once did he try to get me to swing by the retirement village for sex. Instead of employing the "he's just not that into you" wisdom instilled into me by one Miranda Hobbs, I started doing dumb shit like calling him from other people's numbers (what) and dragging my friends to the club week after week, looking as sexy as possible (sure), trying to accidentally run into him. I want to remind you that this was a visceral-fat-compressing-bike-short-under-a-dress time in fashion history, so "getting dressed up" meant "binding my ribs to my spleen," and that is way too much effort to ever put into anyone, especially someone who clearly had a wife at home or happened to be in witness protection. The silver lining is that I eventually developed a decent bachata from all those Latin nights at the club; the storm cloud being that I did all that work moisturizing my calluses and shaving my finger hairs for a gentleman I talked to for weeks but never saw in person again.

. . .

Looking back on that experience now, I really do just shake my head and think about how lucky I am that someone like Abbi saw something in me and my diarrhea book worth exploring, because I am the Roy in this scenario, and, seriously, WHO HAS TIME FOR MY SHIT? I made Abbi chase me for months, and I'm not entirely sure it was worth her effort.

But she caught me like a slimy, garbage-filled, oily-whiskered catfish on a hook! She got on a plane and came to Chicago, and I rifled through all the horrible clothing in my closet to find something remotely appropriate for brunch with a TV star. We made plans to meet at this restaurant called Little Goat that I like because it's owned by Stephanie who won *Top Chef*, and I will do literally anything anywhere that has a TV tie-in. I was surprised by how normal Abbi looked, and I processed everything I wanted to say at least three times in my head before I allowed it to come out of my mouth. We got a booth in the back, and I noticed waitstaff noticing us, which is a thing I've grown used to after having known her. It hadn't even occurred to me that people would actually be trying to take my photo while I was with her. By "take my photo" I mean, "catch me unawares with my mouth open and my shoulders hunched and my neck looking like a pack of hotdogs in the blurry background of their pictures of an actual famous person."

I did this show in Chicago called *The Paper Machete* a couple weeks after *Meaty* was first released in the fall of 2013. It's a weekly live lit show that takes place at the Green Mill cocktail lounge in Uptown, and it's kind of hard to describe, but I'll try: it's a modern take on an old-fashioned salon; writers and comedians and poets and actors write essays on the news of the week, and sometimes there are sketches because fuck you if you want to see a live show in Chicago that an improv troupe hasn't weaseled their way into, and there's usually one or two live musical acts, plus a talking bird puppet who is very good at reporting the latest science stories in the news. It's hosted by Christopher Piatt, a tall and hilarious alien who used to be the theater critic for *Time Out Chicago*. And it's one of the most popular theater-adjacent attractions in the city. If you're ever in town, you should fucking go. The *Machete* is a reliable place to get to work on the kind of material I don't usually write (topical, newsworthy shit that requires at least a skimming of CNN dot com), in front of a giant, tipsy crowd. I did the show consistently enough and performed well enough to work my way up to staff writer, which just meant that if people dropped out at the last minute, Piatt could send me a desperate text begging me to come up with a tight five about Bill Cosby going to prison or about how the Cubs finally winning the series turned the North Side of the city into a human garbage disposal.

The best thing about the show, other than my scorching hot takes on local politics I don't understand, is that Piatt somehow can always convince Very Famous People Who Happen to Be in Town for Something Else to swing by the Mill at 3 p.m. on a Saturday to do the show. The week my first book was published, I was slated to read a piece I'd written about the forthcoming *Fifty Shades of Grey* movie and just how much I would die for Charlie Hunnam to step on my neck. When I got to the bar after racing around through pouring rain and on unreliable public transportation, Piatt told me that the day's very special guest was none other than Janeane Garofalo.

I don't need to tell you how much Janeane Garofalo's body of work means to me. You could probably flip through my old DVD collection and answer that question for yourself, which is to say that I own at least TWO original copies of *The Truth About Cats & Dogs*. I spotted her by the bar, this pocket-size person (every famous person is approximately four feet, two inches) in a puffy winter coat, and my intestines liquefied, and I had to steel myself to keep from crying. I just love her that much. Before the show started, the stage manager told me that I would be reading right before Janeane went on. No pressure, of course. I cashed in my drink tickets and hoped that a couple drinks would settle me down. I read my ridiculous, disgusting essay and people laughed and I could make out Janeane chuckling appreciatively in the shadows next to the bar and my heart skipped about a dozen beats. After she did her set (do real comedians still call it a set?), shuffling through her notes while apologizing incessantly, the show ended, and she was immediately swarmed by people thrusting old VHS copies of *Reality Bites* in her face for her to sign. Which, in hindsight, was a brilliant idea, and I'm mad I didn't do the same. I waited my turn at the end of a line that inched forward so slowly that it honestly felt like I was moving backward, and when I got to her I vomited a bunch of words that sounded something like, "You are a goddess, I love you. Is there anyone you need me to murder?" and she was very gracious and told me my thing was funny, and then I said, "Hey, can I give you a copy of my book?"

I had two copies of *Meaty* in my bag because when you put out a book with a tiny independent press, one thing you have to do is constantly carry copies of that book on your person while alienating everyone you meet as you beg them to please buy one, and she very graciously accepted them and thanked me by saying, "I don't use social media or e-mail, so I have no way to tell you if I like your book," which is hilarious because feedback isn't even a thing I had considered. Also hearing what people think about your book is excruciating. I was just super stoked to be able to put them in her hands and watch her walk away with them. She could have thrown them in the garbage right after for all I'd know, but that wouldn't matter because Vickie Miner had a copy of my dumbass book in her purse and I could die happy, whether she tweeted at me about it or not. I walked next door to have my usual post-*Machete* dinner of Three Chili Chicken and Dan Dan noodles at Lao Sze Chuan and then went on living the rest of my boring life.

At breakfast the day I met Abbi, in the back booth at Little Goat where I ordered the Fat Elvis waffles and Abbi had the spiced apple pancakes, she told me that she had been gifted my book by Janeane. Excuse me? I'm sorry, what did you just say? I knew she had guest starred on the show because I had watched a bunch of episodes to prepare for our meal, just in case famous people do shit like quiz you on obscure trivia from all their projects. What if you met Tom Cruise (GOD WILLING) and he was like, "Before we get down to business, I need you to tell me the name of my character in *Collateral*." I would drop dead. And pass the test. (It was Vincent.) Anyway, Janeane did the show, and to thank them for the pleasure of having her, she gave both Abbi and Ilana copies of my nightmare book about *puking and dead moms*, then Abbi read it and loved it and tracked down my e-mail and sent me a message that took me eight months to respond to.

The idea she wanted to pitch me was this: Have you ever thought about turning your book into a television show? And, reader, I had absolutely fucking not. I had definitely thought about making a show about an imaginary person who could be on-screen all the things I am not in real life, but the idea of that person being the actual me had never crossed my goddamn mind. I am neither beautiful nor smart. My most impressive skill is being able to quietly shit in unexpected places. And the closest I'd been to Hollywood at that point was going to several tapings of *Judge Mathis* during his first couple years on the air. I immediately started doing the one thing I'm best at: making a mental list of all the reasons a thing that has just been suggested to me absolutely will not work.

I didn't want to piss off an actual celebrity, but I also was never going to quit my job or go on a diet or get fillers injected into my lips or do any of the things I imagined were keys to Hollywood entry. I seriously thought, "Would it be possible to have a show on television and also still go to work every day? I need this fucking prescription coverage." It's not cool to act like you're not excited about a big opportunity but, come on, dude, I don't have the kind of life that has been conducive to ~dreaming big~ or whatever. I wasn't in a place physically or financially to throw caution to the wind and risk it all for the chance to maybe possibly have a TV show four years from now. Because that's what "developing a show" actually means, that a network gives you a little piece of money to guarantee that for a year or two they are the only ones that have the right to refuse to produce whatever the thing is that you spent months of your life fine-tuning to their specific tastes. I didn't even know that then, at Little Goat, vainly trying to think of a nice way to say, "Thank you for getting on a plane, but can I just pay for your pancakes and we'll call it even?"

But what if I spent the rest of my life going to parties and telling the same old story of how I met the girl from *Broad City* one time and never capitalized on that experience? What would my friends think if I told them I had turned down an opportunity without even trying it first? Honestly, I have the kind of friends who would be like, "Who cares? Do what you want," which is why they are my friends, but I'm sure I could find *someone* in my circle who would turn up their nose at my letting a possible half-hour comedy series slip through my fingers. So I did what I always do, which is to say "YEAH, SURE" and then hope that later on, if it sucks, an escape hatch will open up for me and I can get out of it.

I e-mailed my Hollywood agent (a man I had never met whom I thought I would never have a reason to really know) to inform him that I might finally be needing his services, and he wrote back, "Wait, I'm sorry, who???" and then I melted into the earth, and that is the end of this story.

Just kidding, kind of. He e-mailed something positive because he is relentlessly optimistic, which is a feature of this industry that can be very confusing to a normal, realistic person who does not mind the truth. I have grown used to being ruthlessly edited and have zero ego when it comes to having my work corrected. My calls about my writing from NYC are always like, "Hey, dummy, this thing you wrote is a turd. Wow, do you need new medicine? We refuse to pay you for this ridiculous trash. Rewrite the whole fucking thing by tomorrow or we'll see you in court." And my calls from LA are like, "Hi, sweetie, great meeting feedback! They really vibed with you and totally want to have your babies! It's just that they're pivoting to hardcore computer-animated docufiction, so your project isn't a fit right now, but the good news is they think you're hilarious and would love to circle back if you ever come up with another idea in the future. P.S. The entire network is now following you on Instagram!!" COME ON, WHAT. Just tell me to fuck off!

The first thing Abbi decided to do when we started to organize everything was to find someone who could also write the pilot with me, because I had never written a script before. I had never seriously written dialogue before. I'm not even sure that with most of my TV diet being made up of shows like *RHONY* and MTV's *The Challenge* that I'd even heard enough scripted dialogue to be able to properly *mimic* it. I also didn't know what an act break was or what the words "cold open" meant when put together like that.

Next, we had to put the story together. Which basically means that we had to look at the broader stories and themes in my book (. . . my life??) and extract one main one that we would use as the basis for the pilot and essentially a thesis statement for the whole show. That's a wild-ass undertaking, because how the fuck do you decide what part of your life is the most interesting for an audience of people who have never heard of your messy ass before? I tried to pull way back from this thing I'd lived and written, and to disconnect emotionally from it as much as I could when it was about my painful breakups and my dead mom, and tried to figure out how to package it into something I could convince strangers to pay Comcast for.

SEASON 2, EPISODE 3

So what were the themes in this book that we were trying to make into a show? What would the book look like when translated to TV? If I wasn't me, and I had thirty seconds in an elevator to convince a network president to give me millions of Viacom's dollars to play make-believe, I would say: **Meaty** **is about a morose orphan too old to elicit sympathy for her parentless-ness who drops out of college to grieve said dead parents while scamming as many meals/free places to crash as she can, trying to scratch together a living by working odd jobs, poorly managing a very confusing autoimmune disease, and also getting broken up with all the time while constantly trying to stay soft and open in the pursuit of romance.**

Right? Kind of? Something like that! Here's the basic pitch bible I wrote and memorized and recited in a very chill and casual way for a show loosely based around my butthole and my worst exes.

inflammatory bowel disease
I don't treat my Crohn's like it's an albatross around my neck, like I'm laboring under the weight of this oppressive disease.

I'm just having diarrhea in airports and sometimes taking Medrol to settle my inflamed large intestine. I'm not going to google what percentage of the population has an IBD, but I'm sure the number is significant, at least according to the number of people who come to my readings bearing gifts of quality toilet paper. If I'm going on a date that might be a sex date, then I know I have to eat saltines and bananas all day and stay away from coffee. But that doesn't really matter because I still get bloated and gassy and have to shove a wad of toilet paper in my butt to mask my farts while this person I really want to fall in love with me has the movie paused in the other room and the apartment is eerily quiet and they think I'm just peeing. It's a serious topic that can be dealt with in a really funny way while also repping for the chronically ill and constantly medicated, like me.

a kind of careless bisexuality

I have never been the kind of person who felt in control of her dating life, but I also didn't slip and fall into any amazing relationships, either. Throughout my twenties, I basically dated anyone who asked me out and let them dictate the terms. Not having parents meant I never had any pressure to date with intention, and I never had to worry about the gender or personality or life goals of anyone I was sleeping with because it wasn't like I was going to bring anyone home to meet the people in charge of my trust. Lesbian relationships are often treated with such treacly tenderness and no thank you to that. It's not all hand-holding and heartfelt conversations. I've had a number of relationships with women that were defined by casual "hey u up?" texts that resulted in sex and ended with my foraging through her old takeout containers in the morning, then wearing the exact same clothes to work that I'd been wearing the day before. Why don't we see relationships with women and nonbinary people treated without the preciousness? Like, yes, it's possible for non-men to ghost on you!! No one is a monolith!

fat people doing fat shit without crying big fat tears about it
I can't watch *This Is Us* because even though the brothers are hot and the dad is a smoke show, in the first couple episodes the fat girl doesn't get to be much more than "fat," and wow, no thank you! Maybe there are fat people sitting around silently weeping about being fat every minute of every day, but that is a redemptive arc thin people like to see on television, and it's just not the fucking truth. And I like physical comedy as much as the next guy, but it's also super gross to watch a fat bitch just *bounce off shit* all the time? I don't know, dude, sometimes the chair with fixed arms isn't going to work for me, but it's not like every time I sit in a desk, I get up and take the whole thing with me, or I'm sighing wistfully as everyone else at brunch joyfully eats their quiche while I pick at a piece of boiled lettuce. The shit is called *Meaty*, and sometimes I hate my body not because it's fat, but mostly because I never wake up in the morning to discover it has transformed into a wolf or a shark overnight. When is the last time you watched a show with a fat woman who didn't at some point reference a new diet or some ill-fitting old jeans? Also this idea that fat people only get pity sex from recent parolees or whatever is bullshit; I've never fucked a repulsive loser ever in my life. JUST THE HANDSOME KINDS OF LOSERS.

intergenerational friendships! but not the gross kind!
mentorships? fake adoptive dads!

I am still friends with a shitload of my friends' parents. They've shown up at my readings looking hilariously awkward and beaming with pride and I love that. And there's definitely an element of them having guided a kind of rudderless person navigating a tricky early life? But, also, I went on vacations with them, hung out with them watching TV, cruised for dates, all that shit. One of the most fascinating things about my life to other people seems to be the many years I lived with and worked for Mel, my not-dad who found me toiling away in a job that was just barely keeping me afloat and brought me into his home to give me a second adolescence, even though I was almost out of my teens. I don't want to get all *Diff'rent Strokes* reboot about it, but: Mel and I have a father-daughter witty repartee kind of thing. I'm black and he's Jewish. I have chubby cheeks and he has a long, winding staircase. The whole thing just naturally lends itself to a half-hour situation comedy!

the fronts we put up

I'm bored by cool, icy girls who are effortlessly hip; quirky, adorable girls who are effortlessly hip; and brassy, sexy girls who are effortlessly hip. Why don't we get to watch an awkward mess pretend that she makes her own osso buco bone broth to impress the self-described "foodie" who messaged her on Tinder even though he wore a fedora in his profile picture. I spent a lot of my twenties trying on new personalities, especially when convincing people to either be my friend or to have sex with me. Nothing drastic, just shit like going to experimental music shows or being really good about regular eyebrow maintenance.

TV Sam lives in a shithole (so did the real one) and eats meals on the bus (ugh, I did this, too), but definitely has an Instagram corner in her tiny apartment. I feel like this is who I *still* am, posting soft-focus pictures of the clean and organized corner of my desk when just out of frame there's a book and paper avalanche threatening to overwhelm me. We get a lot of messy girls on TV, but let's add more. Someone who is buying a candle at Barneys downtown then is facing that shit LABEL OUT in the bathroom so when you go in there to fix your face and carefully look through her prescription bottles (wow, so does oregano oil really work? Does Zoloft???), you will know that you are in the lavatory of a classy bitch. Yes, she just split an oat milk latte between three different credit cards, but have you tried the Clé de Peau face cream she just casually left sitting on the table by the couch, next to some first edition Toni Morrison books arranged *just so* against that vintage-style milk bottle vase filled with fresh tulips? Has she had her teeth cleaned in the last seven years? Fuck no! But have you tried one of the vitamins she purchased at the suggestion of a targeted Facebook ad and has never taken but has beautifully displayed on the kitchen counter? Why, you simply must!

depression/anxiety

I am a high-functioning depressed and anxious person. I know it can manifest in myriad ways, but mine are these: (1) extreme inertia, but never at the expense of my employment, so mostly bailing on friends who want to hang out and feeling extremely apathetic toward doing "fun" things that aren't lying very still; (2) self-soothing with food, though never in shocking amounts, mostly just staring into the void while eating ice cream over the sink, then realizing, "oops, the pint is finished"; (3) fear of trying new things or venturing out of a comfort zone, clinging to childhood demons as a means of never actually having to move forward; (4) blistering resentment for the outwardly happy and seemingly well-adjusted.

I have a running inner monologue recounting every horrible thing I've said or done since I can remember first publicly humiliating myself, and the voice never shuts the fuck up or goes away even for a minute. Even my dreams are anxious. Last night I had a dream that I was walking around with a baby, a white one who was old enough to walk, and we were trying to catch a bus. Not a regular bus, but a Greyhound to who the fuck knows where. And in the dream, my heart is in my throat because I'm desperately trying to run-walk while holding hands with this stumbling baby and not miss the bus, but also I don't want to set anybody off because I am yanking a blonde child through the streets and I've never tried but I assume if you get caught kidnapping a white kid they send you to Gilead for that shit. So, we finally catch up with the bus, and I toss the kid on, and I'm searching for a bus ticket in my giant bag and freaking out because everyone is watching me, and then this woman in a fancy daytime outfit pushes past me and sneers, "I don't need this, I'm going to get on a Delta plane!" and then I woke up in a panic.

My brain outlines every possible disaster that could befall me at any given moment: "Don't cross against the light. If a car comes around the corner you'll never move fast enough to beat it. Okay, fine, you made it across, but then you tripped on the curb. Did anyone see you trip on the curb? Yes, that guy in the blue shirt pretending not to have seen you trip on the curb definitely just saw you trip on the curb and was mortified that he might have had to help you up . . ." and on and on ad infinitum. Not that I need to make another *Herman's Head* with all this, but have you ever watched *Herman's Head* because that show was fucking funny.

self-sabotage/eating trash/not taking meds

"Food is a temporary solution, but to a person with Crohn's, it can be a dangerous one." Doesn't that sound like the first line of a future documentary I'm making about the time I almost fatally overdosed on garlic bread? Anyway, the initial Crohn's diagnosis takes a battery of tests over the course of several months, and even then, once you're diagnosed, it can take literal years to figure out the right combination of medications to take while also using the process of elimination to discover what foods trigger you. It's different for every person, and while an anti-inflammatory diet can be beneficial, that shit is super hard and expensive to maintain. Not everyone can afford to eat an organic wild-caught salmon every single meal. And, it also isn't a matter of just eating healthy. If I eat brown rice, I will be prostrate atop a river of undigested grains within hours. The basic beginner plan is to avoid milk and cheese and fibrous vegetables and take it easy while figuring out your trigger foods. Which, for a person who eats to feel better emotionally, is murder because what if popcorn ends up putting you in the hospital? The medications to treat IBD are outrageously expensive, and even when you are taking the best care of yourself, if you don't have one hundred and eighty dollars for a month's worth of Pentasa, you're fucked. So sometimes model patients end up sick in the ER because they can't get their meds. It's a struggle.

How does this fit into a comedy, you ask? Honestly, I'm not 100 percent sure. I've managed to make a career out of LOL, I SHIT MY PANTS, and so I don't think it's that hard to translate to another medium. More important than that, even if it's not knee-slapping funny, it would mean a lot to me to put chronic illness in people's faces, especially the silent kind that you might not even know a person is struggling through. I bet if you met me on the street, you wouldn't automatically think "sick," but if you looked at my last CT scans you would, and I want to represent for all my people taking twelve pills a day with bald joints and intestines lined with scar tissue.

being okay with just being okay

When rocking the boat and taking a leap of faith seem like the most terrifying things you could ever do, why try them? Isn't everything just fine as it is? I think we all buy into the lofty ideals set by our teachers and parents, but there are actually people who are just fine punching a clock every day and then coming home to stare at their phones until their bodies are completely overtaken by sleep. I have never related to someone whose main goal wasn't just getting a table at a good restaurant and being able to pay for it. All I wanted for myself at twenty-seven was to go to clubs and drink Coronas and watch people awkwardly flirting with each other while hoping that someone would flirt with me. That's it. That was all I required of my life. Not everyone has the secret desire to be a pop star or climb their way up the company ranks, and wouldn't it just be D O P E see black girls on TV not doing shit?

SEASON 3, SERIES FINALE

The first time I flew to LA to sell this dumb show to executives, I was armed only with a backpack and a laptop and some Klonopin in case the West Coast's chill vibe was no match for my stomach-churning Midwestern anxiety. Abbi, Jessi (who helped develop the show and was going to cowrite the script), and I had spent months and months building a skeleton of this idea and scrambling to get meat on its proverbial bones, while living and working in three different regions of the country. There are characters to invent, and those characters need backstories, and they need families, and they need to have places to live, and they need to look like something, and they need to have clothes, and they need to like bands, and they need to have allergies, and they need to have a signature cocktail, and they need to get laid and THIS is all the minutiae you have to devote energy to when you are populating a new world that has before never existed and have fifteen minutes to convince a Hollywood Person to buy it from you. Which, on the one hand, is thrilling. But, on the other, how do you confidently decide that this dude who doesn't exist outside of the old edition of Final Draft I'm writing him in is the kind of dude who wears cardigans and has intentional facial hair. Am I allowed to write a fictional Latina character or is that appropriation? What does it mean to be the god of a make-believe universe?

To this day, I do not own any impressive show-pitching clothing, and a thing about me that I am slowly learning is that no matter how much I attempt to go against my own grain, I will go right back to the thing I am most comfortable with no matter what. Which means that when I was faced with packing to go sit in a bunch of intimidating boardrooms, my closet yielded very few options that read as "professional" or "a solid investment for your streaming service." So I just packed my regular pajama-adjacent cozy clothes, the shit normal people put on when they get home from a long day working outdoors in the rain: loose, comfortable exercise pants that you just sit in; a thin, worn T-shirt that might have some faded words on it; a soft cardigan. If anyone questioned my attire, I could pull a "there's too much good stuff in my brain to also think about clothes," and see if they'd buy it. Worst-case scenario: I could summon a few tears and sob, "I'm sorry, Mr.Showtime, I lost my luggage!"

Pitching is weird because it feels like being a used-car salesman, except instead of cars you're trying to sell a niche program that you definitely can't prove anyone will ever want to watch. I can't even guarantee that my nine friends will watch it. Do you know how many people who have been in my home have never purchased one of my books?! Several!!!! Our first pitch meeting was at Netflix and I tried to pretend I was relaxed and cool, which was surprisingly easy because I didn't have to tone down my nerves as much as I had to dial back my dread. I am not a person who automatically thinks, "This is gonna be great! I'm totally gonna kill it!" It's always like, "I hope the bottom of my chair doesn't collapse," or "Are any of these women tigers? Is it possible they can smell my fear?"

In the waiting room, three young guys with identical haircuts wearing matching blue-checked button-down shirts and pleated pants were earnestly rehearsing their spiel, and I looked down at the Old Navy sweatshirt I was wearing to meet these Vice Presidents in Charge of Development and wondered if I had maybe played it too cool. I had washed, yes, but I had bought my shirt for three dollars using Super Cash and my toes were exposed: Was it too late to change my idea to a surefire hit like a reboot of some '80s show like *Empty Nest* or *Amen*? "Oh, I'm sorry, I didn't mean 'a fat show about diarrhea.' I meant, 'What if we made a black *ALF*?'"

It works pretty much the same way at all the networks you go to:

1. You walk into the lobby slash holding pen slash upscale waiting room, then you either show or give your ID to a security person in a suit behind a desk who has some sort of appointment book or computer situation with all of the day's hopefuls listed on it. They locate your name and determine who you're meeting, then you either get your identification back or they remove a pointless organ (a gallbladder, perhaps . . . ?) to deter you from stealing any *Game of Thrones* plot points that might be just lying around on a designer coffee table and hang on to your ID for you to collect after you've finished crying over your silly dreams in front of strangers.
2. Someone takes you to the room where you're going to meet the decision-makers, which is always

uncomfortably quiet and has too many chairs. Or maybe we just showed up with not enough people? I'm not sure. When we were at Amazon, there were literally 126 seats crowded around the conference room table, so we had to play musical chairs to figure out where we should be nonchalantly seated by the time everyone else came in. Do we face the door? Should we crowd around one end? At each stop on our first tour of Santa Monica conference rooms, I would just loom awkwardly in the corner, too nervous to take the incorrect seat, and then start willing my armpits dry and wondering when someone was going to bust in on us with bottles of water.

3. Maybe it's the person who deposited you in the room, but sometimes a different person will enter with water and ask if you want something else to drink. I never drink the water because one meeting might be in Beverly Hills while the next one is in Santa Monica, and having to pee while mentally rehearsing a sales script during a long car ride is a nightmare. The drink person leaves, and then you get many minutes to sit and wait for people who know a lot about you and who you've never met before to come in and wait expectantly for you to make a good impression on them. I am afraid to talk during the waiting minutes, because I assume every place I go is bugged, so I just nervously look at all the posters and mourn all the shows I could be watching if I never went to sleep or wrote books. This is also a good time to try to adjust yourself in

the chair, which nine out of ten times has fixed arms that painfully stab your hips.

4. The show purchasers come in! These people are always very nice. The nicest people you have ever met. Sometimes they hug you, which is a very LA thing that I immensely enjoy. I love a hug! I'm very soft and easy to snuggle up against in a non-sexual way. They are always dressed casually, but in a way that lets you know their clothes are still expensive. (I make a mental note to try and find upscale sweat-shirts for next time). Anyway, the meetings start informally. They ask you what your dog's name is and if you've had dinner at _____ yet, real friendly and low stakes. So there's some easing in, which is good; I like to give the sweat glands a good five minutes to simmer down before I have to launch into selling. At TBS, we talked about astrology (they brought it up, I swear!) and I instantly regretted not getting my chart read so I could sound ethereal and informed, but since I hadn't, I just said, "I'm an Aquarius!" and poured a bucket of water out on the table.

5. Before you get the meeting, your agent sends in all the stuff you've put together about the show you want to sell which, honestly, I never fucking saw? We might have to fully break the flaws in my oper-ating system down another time, but I am not a control freak in even the most liberal sense of the phrase. I pay zero attention to detail and have very few accounting mechanisms, so if you say you're going to take care of it and send a thing, then I'm just going to believe you did that and watch this

cat video for the hundredth time. Pretty sure my
agent's assistant sent PDF copies of my book, or
some chapters, or possibly a couple paragraphs? I
never asked. But also, how much can you reasonably expect a person with access to unlimited *Search
Party* reruns to read about your failed relationships
and diarrhea before you meet them? Abbi, Jessi, and
I had written a pitch document (read: a typed-out
version of all the stuff we were planning to say about
our show, the fine points of which we would probably mess up without notes). I paid very little attention to the staggering amount of miniscule details
involved in this process, because the more things I
could anxiously obsess over, the more "sell a major
television network a show about my fictional life"
felt like a thing I shouldn't be attempting. The execs
have a general idea of what you're selling, so after
the chitchat you just seamlessly transition into the
sales pitch, which is so awkward it caused me physical pain. I am an awful salesperson. I would very
much like to sell a show that is not about my life,
because nothing sounds dumber than telling people
who have to be polite to you why you are interesting. Also, I have to sit there in my regular-fat body
(as opposed to television-fat, which is less fat than
me but more fat than a GAP model) wondering
if I need to reassure someone across these various
tables that I had no plans whatsoever to star in this
imaginary show. At FX, we were sitting in these
low-slung chairs that were very fucking cool just
shooting the breeze and at one point I realized I was

in full shit-squat and had this sickening thought: "What if I can't get up from this chair?" followed by an even worse one: "Does anyone in this room who is eyeball measuring my thigh circumference at this hideous angle think I *actually* want to be in this?"

6. After you say your thing, do your little dog and pony show, they ask you a lot of very smart and thoughtful questions that often feel like a trap. This part is the most interesting to me, because you're getting insight into both what they're considering when it comes to their programming and also testing the weak spots in your ideas. I had never done this before, so I had no point of reference and stammered through every answer like it was my first day saying words. They use a lot of superlatives when they speak, which makes you feel like they're tapping you with a magical TV wand that all but guarantees your massive commercial success. Either way, I don't care, it's fine. Even if no one wants to see Fake Sam sweating on an emergency room toilet, I got to fly first class to LA, get cupcakes out of a vending machine, pretend to drink many fancy bottles of water fetched by people from Kansas with Big Dreams, try not to bleed on the pristine couch at Apple, look at lots of Emmys in glass cases, take pictures of *Sons of Anarchy* posters while stopping myself from asking if I could have one, make the joke "we could just call it *Fat Insecure*," which nobody at HBO laughed at, walk through a movie set on the Fox lot, poop *twice* at Amazon, and maybe at the end of two days of flop sweating in various conference rooms,

someone would take a chance on a true moron and offer to buy our zygote of a show.

After it's all over you don't have to hand out business cards or leave behind any brochures for their perusal. You do your choreographed dance number, everyone shakes hands and/or hugs (they love hugging!), you stop by the front desk to get your liver back, then you find your way down to the parking garage and you get in your rental car and sit in traffic for an hour and a half trying to get back to the east side of the city where everybody cool lives. Pitch meetings are always mostly good and positive-feeling, at least the ones I've been in, which makes it really hard to know what the two to six smiling people on the other side of the table *actually* thought. I call my Hollywood-specific agent at the end of each meeting to give him the same rundown every time: "Yes, I was very charming. No, no one visibly reacted to my psoriasis. They seemed to really like the voiceover idea. I'm pretty sure I left some condensation on that leather chair. Yep, okay, follow up with them. If they don't want it, please just murder me in my sleep." This whole process is so strange and disconcerting; it's not like a job interview where you follow up or sit by the phone, and no one tells you whether or not you've actually done a good job. You just go right back to your regular life. I have gone two rounds through this ringer, and both times my return was met with the people covering my duties at work shrugging while saying, "So what?" No one in the hospital breakroom gave two shits that I drank a coffee across from a dude who worked with Triumph the Insult Comic Dog.

Our final pitch meeting ended late on a Friday afternoon,

and my friends and I drank cans of rosé like good Californians and ate meatloaf like good Midwesterners to celebrate, and then we went to a fancy boutique patisserie with an overwhelming number of ice cream choices that was packed full of wailing children who were frustrated with how long I was taking to decide on my expensive, well-deserved treat. Which I get, but come on, man. I've never seen cornflake ice cream before, I need a minute to fucking think about it! Two hours before I had been in a glass-walled suite making a case for queer POC representation on primetime television, and now a child named Salinger was fully standing on my feet to get a better look at cone varieties in a stark white acrylic box crammed with toddlers and cooled roughly to the temperature of the arctic circle. Life is so fucking weird. I'm glad I wore my sweatshirt.

hollywood summer

"Do you want to come to California for a couple months to work on the television show of your dreams?" is honestly the most exciting non-food-related thing any other person has said to me. When Lindy West sold the adaptation of her book *Shrill* to Hulu and it immediately got picked up to series—which is a dumb Hollywood term that basically means "we will give you money to make several episodes of a show, sight unseen, that we don't know if anyone will actually watch"—she called me on the phone (a crime), and we unintelligibly screamed high-pitched nonsense words at each other for a full minute and a half.

At that point, I had been circling the drain of my own rapidly disintegrating development project (another showbiz glossary term that essentially means "maybe we'll let you make a show for our network but probably not. Please enjoy existential uncertainty and a years-long low-grade panic attack as we reject every single one of your slightly different drafts") for 730-plus anxious, emotionally draining days. I'd sat in many hip conference rooms with sockless guys in boat shoes trying to convince them that my Fat Diarrhea Show would make compelling television, and I'd received almost an equal ratio of meetings/calls from my therapist/agent during which he tried to let me down easy in his gentlest voice by explaining that "[redacted streaming service and/or basic cable network] just really isn't in a *comedy* space right now."

Anyway, wow. Lindy had her very own television show! And it wasn't on a website or, and I'm just being hypothetical here, acted out by the discarded dolls growing moldy in the playroom in my basement! I was fucking jealous (duh) and wondered, "Maybe my thing really is just too stupid for TV," but I made myself feel better by remembering RACISM, oh and also by thinking about how I wouldn't have to worry if someone from E! News would scrutinize my chin hairs on any red carpet premieres. I'm not shaving, I'm tired!

Lindy told me that she was allowed to pick one of several people who would join the *Shrill* writers' room that summer in Los Angeles, and she wanted that person to be me. I had zero experience in a writers' room and zero experience working on a television show other than the soap opera running a continuous loop in my head, starring myself. The only screenwriting experience I had was the pilot I had cowritten for my own optioned book, which ended up being flushed down a FOX toilet with a runaway alien from *The X-Files* and several unaired episodes of *24*, so I was incredibly flattered and 100 percent positive that I was grossly unqualified for this job that I was absolutely going to accept. I'm not going to let a little thing like having absolutely no fucking idea what the fuck I'm doing get in the way of possibly getting a coffee enema at the same spa a Real Beverly Hills

Housewife goes to; my threadbare yoga pants and I were getting on that plane no matter what. BUT:

- where was I going to live?
- how do situationally impoverished go to Hollywood?
- does Hulu have a dorm? You know, like a lil' writer farm? I cannot afford to even think about California real estate!
- how do Midwestern people like me get around? Should I just get one of them star maps?
- do people still take the bus there or do I need to make friends with someone who owns a plane or what?
- can I somehow negotiate a Lyft stipend?
- should I just rent a car?
- wait, yes, I *should* rent a car. But will they give me one for two months or do I have to go renew it every week? Jesus what a hassle.
- how do I decide which is my new grocery store?
- a follow-up: Do the stores there actually sell food with cholesterol in it?
- can I make short-term friends as an adult or should I just subscribe to every single channel available on Earth?
- people there only drink oat milk, right?
- seriously where the fuck was I going to live???

I hadn't even gotten the job officially and already I was worried about whether or not I was going to find a bed to watch shows in (because meeting people is daunting), whether I would have a tall-enough toilet with many-plied quilted toilet paper, and if California supermarkets carry gluten-based snacks. These are the kinds of things that matter to me, not learning things or being prepared. What was I supposed to do in the week between finding out about the gig and dragging my battered Samsonite full of sweatshirts and pajama pants to the airport: Take an Aaron Sorkin masterclass on the fucking Internet? Join my local improv troupe? Fuck that. I skimmed Lindy's book again and memorized some surfing words and left the rest up to Satan.

I fucking love LA (dog birthday parties! spiritual healers on every corner! unironic oxygen bars!). You might not think so because I'm a misanthropic depressed person with menopause acne whose hips are too wide for every single restaurant chair in Silverlake, but you would be wrong. I'm a Fat Bitch from the Middle West and I love accidentally running into minor celebrities with my cart in the wheatgrass aisle at the Rock 'N Roll Ralph's on Sunset. I love being in the neighborhood where *Vanderpump Rules* is shot but never getting out of the car and just cruising around hoping to see Kristen popping into the spray tan shop because when you are on reality television, that is a part of your job. I love walking through the Americana with sweat pooling under my arms as I imagine how great my life would be if I could live in a shopping mall in a place where it never snows. I love witch doctors and blond topknots and designer sunglasses and how everyone is friendly until they figure out that you can't put them in a movie. I love being served a twenty-one-dollar fresh-squeezed juice with zero irony. I love wearing my gross, real-person clothes to a breakfast meeting at the Four Seasons because that is not humiliating at all! True story: there was a for-real Bentley with a driver sleeping behind the wheel parked in the circular drive out front when my Uber driver's rusty Toyota Celica dropped me off and I was like, "Wait, am I actually Pretty Woman?" and then the hostess gave me directions to a soup kitchen while beating me about the head with a broom.

I love horrifying all of the miniskirted assistants at my TV agent's office by eating carbohydrates in public. I love going to a ritzy spa and suffering first-degree burns on my labia while getting my yoni steamed, a procedure I didn't need that provided no benefits. I love when someone recommends their shaman to me, a mean asshole who won't even put that astrology app on her phone, in earnest. I love that no one ever talks about how LA is the actual desert, and there's just lizards and shit skittering around everywhere and everything is actively burning to death in front of you. I love how many adorable ice cream shops and bakeries there are all over a town where nobody eats ice cream or baked goods. I love how, while sitting at a restaurant gazing out at the ocean and casually mentioning that your back has been bugging you, people will offer a little NBD nibble of shrooms the way someone in, say, Milwaukee would go fishing through their bag for a dusty Advil.

Here's a list of things I did that summer in my Fancy Hollywood Office after I took the job:

- sat in my chair
- turned on the massive computer, got scared when a pop-up window announced "OFFICIAL PROPERTY OF WARNER BROS," and then turned off the computer

- wondered if anyone needed me or if I was missing a meeting or something and they'd forgotten I was supposed to be there
- whispered into the receiver when my friend Fernando called me (During my "job"? A hate crime!) because I didn't want anyone to hear me being all loud on the phone
- spun around in my chair
- put a plant on my desk that I forgot to consistently water and couldn't bring back to Michigan anyway so who even knows what happened to that little guy
- ordered too many things I didn't need to make up for not having any friends
- watched the valet guys moving around the cars in the lot in an intricate pattern I could never figure out
- did my writing assignments while wondering, "Am I doing this right?"
- scooted in my chair
- diligently wrote while wondering, "Are they going to make fun of me?" every ten goddamn minutes

The first day of my new job as Lowly Staff Writer on an American Comedy Web Television Series, I got to the office and couldn't figure out how to get into the building until a woman who worked at the reception desk—she must have smelled my bad taste through the walls—came to rescue me and pointed out the unlocked door, which was literally five feet from the locked one I was yanking fruitlessly on while hyperventilating. I was several minutes late and covered with a thin sheen of musky flop sweat at ten in the morning, my palpable impostor syndrome causing my stomach to lurch acid up the back of my throat. That is the perfect way to show up for your first day at a new job! "Nice to meet you, fellow comedy kids! Would you like to shake my damp and clammy hand? My body smells like a dog's teeth!"

Our office was in a squat, nondescript building in the actual neighborhood of Hollywood, which sounds fancy but is mostly just dusty and hot and unexciting. I can't decide if you'd want me to go into detail about how it was all set up, or if that's the dumbest idea I've ever had. Okay, here's an abridged version:

I approach most endeavors with zero expectations, which is a skill I have honed after forty years of fairly regular disappointment. I learned early on that if you just expect things to be bad, not even bad but the worst thing that could ever happen to anyone, then, unless someone gets murdered in front of you, whatever it is usually turns out to be fine. Bearable, at worst. It's a good skill to have, and it makes new things, for the most part, pleasantly exciting? I had no idea what was in store for me, so I packed a sack lunch and brought a refillable water bottle just in case, because I assumed there wouldn't be food or maybe at best we'd have access to a vending machine that you had to walk up four flights of stairs to get to, and, honestly, I was fully prepared to fill my water bottle up in the bathroom and eat my room-temperature string cheeses while confidently saying dumb shit like, "I'm just pitching here, but what if we sent that character to the moon?"

Everyone else seemed bored and unimpressed so I tried to imitate their nonchalance as we were shown to our INDIVIDUAL OFFICES. A real office! With a desk and some chairs and a couple windows plus a computer and a file cabinet! I farted a giggle out of my mouth, then immediately shut it down because no one else seemed fazed. Oh, sure, of course. They were bona fide showbiz professionals (*jazz hands*) who'd probably had dozens of offices throughout their careers. Meanwhile, I wrote my last book in the handicapped bathroom at my old job during my lunch breaks. "BE COOL," I warned my inner tuna casserole. Nothing is more embarrassing than unbridled enthusiasm. I was shown to a designated office, I shrugged like I didn't give a fuck, and then I walked in and set down my JanSport backpack filled with shrink-wrapped portable snack cheese. "This'll work, I guess," I said coolly, pretending to inspect this room that was bigger than my last apartment. I snuck a picture, my hands literally vibrating with glee, when I thought no one was looking and sent it to my friends in the heartland, who are all potatoes.

We were led on a tour. From the name tags on the various doors, it looked like there was another show being written on our floor, which didn't mean anything to me other than that there would be more people to avoid shitting in front of in the communal bathroom. There was an open-plan kitchen with a large conference room off it, and as we approached I saw that it contained a nice-size fridge, a wide sink, a coffee maker, some cabinets, and a tall island surrounded by stools with a bowl of fresh fruit in the center of it. "Whose perfect bananas are these?" I wondered. "Who gets to eat these shiny, unblemished apples?!" my brain screamed. Then Lindy reached out and nonchalantly plucked an orange from the arrangement and began to peel it. I would never do that, because I am self-conscious to the point of paralysis, but I bubbled inside with excitement. Holy shit, Mister Hulu himself buys us produce!!!!!

Coffee, too. And lunch. So much lunch!! Listen, I know you want me to tell you that my coworkers were glib Hollywood assholes and that we spent every day committing microaggressions against one another while daring someone to call HR, but I *can't* because maybe one murdered somebody and maybe another burned the building down with us inside and maybe yet another took us hostage and maybe Kate stabbed someone in the stomach, but I never saw it because I was too busy weeping over the menus that would magically appear in the middle of the conference room table at ten thirty every morning.

Do you know that there is not a single Thai restaurant where I live? Okay, no need to cry for me, it's not like larb is a basic human right, I'm just trying to illustrate why the fact that we could just, you know, have dishes from Night + Market Song delivered to us in the middle of the day was cause for celebration. I'm a rube, okay? I'm used to living that "packet of expired Swiss Miss cocoa in the break room if you can find it" kind of life. I've never had a shared assistant before! And, frankly, an assistant is a lot of pressure, and I would never want to have access to one again. Every time someone young and eager (whose job it was to remember how much Stevia people like in their tea in the hopes that one day that would translate to a writing job) offered to get me a drink, I would be like, "Wait, can I get *you* a drink? What kind of kombucha do you like?" and then I'd melt into a thick goo of inadequacy. I have never not had a job where I wasn't the one whose job it was to fetch the ____ or clean up ____ with a mop. I love a cold drink and I hate walking, so what dream to not have to do that, but it felt weird not to give the person who committed to memory that I like that one weird soda a tip or the keys to my rental car. You know, to make it feel even. I honestly cannot tell you shit about how to make a television program, but I *can* tell you that we got to make a shopping list every week of things to have on hand in the kitchen. This is an unbelievably amazing gift that immediately devolves into the most stressful decision you've ever had to make in your life!

Someone would slide the notepad with GROCERIES scrawled at the top over to me and I'd have a complete internal breakdown.

You know, this office would be great with gummy bears. Should I write gummy bears? Is everyone going to know that I'm the one who requested a child's candy? Is Lorne Michaels going to see this list? Did Craig write "chia crackers"? I am so impressed. That is a person who actually cares about his life, even in the face of complimentary snack foods. What if I put down "yogurt," and they get the unsweetened health kind? Is it more depressing or less depressing if I write down the specific brand and flavor that I want? Why do I always want the shit called low-fat chocolate cherry cupcake yogurt?

When you buy it yourself, you can just scan your own shit at checkout and nobody knows other than you and your debit card. When you're adding it to a shared list, beads of sweat pop up on your upper lip when the assistant calls on speakerphone to regretfully inform the room that whoever ordered the "Yoplait Whips! Vanilla Crème Mousse" is shit outta luck. You'll be embarrassed, but you'll also be a little sad that they don't have your fucking yogurt.

Wow, this is an inordinate amount of pressure and I am taking too long and looking incredibly weird! I have to hurry up with this. Ha-ha, how mad would everybody be if I just wrote "a single onion." How do I decide on something that I definitely want to eat, but nobody else will so I won't have to pee on it so they know it's mine? How do these people know their snack needs so well? Who the fuck wrote "turmeric tea"? I thought we were here to party. Okay, fine, pretzels and Diet Coke.

Writing a television show is like hanging out with your friends in the same room every day, arguing about what should happen on a show you haven't watched yet. After the first week, I waited for someone to show up and tell me, "Okay, hoe, it's cute that you thought we were just gonna let you sit in a chair and get paid to think about imaginary people. Here's your scrub brush, you remember where the toilets are, right?" And . . . I would do it. I would scrub those toilets. When I worked at a bakery, I had to mop the floor every night and scrub down pastry cases, and I once burned an entire layer of skin off my arm on a trayful of fresh millet bread. For that I was paid $7.25 an hour, and I gladly cashed those checks. I'm no stranger to thankless grunt work. I almost prefer it. There is nothing to prepare a person who once accepted twenty bucks cash and a gift certificate to the on-campus coffee shop to make three hours of grueling telemarketing calls for the idea that someone with a palm tree outside their office would pay you ninety-two dollars an hour for snarky joke ideas from your tiny, incompetent brain. Every day I drove to the *Shrill* room in my Toyota

Camry—turns out you can rent one for a month at a time in Los Angeles for approximately the cost of an entire car in Iowa—and wondered if that would be the day someone saw through my ruse and ordered me to go pick up lunch or ask me if they could use my back as a table.

I used to pick up dog shit for a living; I had no reason to believe I would ever sit in a room with people who make decisions about what other people get to watch and be taken seriously when I suggested, "WHAT IF WE THREW A FAT BABE POOL PARTY THAT WILL COST A MILLION DOLLARS."

I wrote my episode, season one episode four, in its entirety in an ice-cold room at the Standard Hotel in West Hollywood the night before my script was due. And I know that *sounds* glamorous. I know it conjures the sexy image of a sleep-deprived chanteuse with a hint of deep, exhausted purple shadowing each eye, a mountain of wadded up sheets of yellow legal paper on the floor beside the antique desk on which sits a well-worn typewriter and a juice glass with a dried-up circle of wine staining its bottom, and me slumped over the fancy desk chewing pensively on the arm of my glasses.

What really happened was the power had gone out in our rented summerhouse because Los Angeles is a flaming hellscape and it was 105 degrees for many days in a row, and the power grid just could not compete with all those cranked-up air conditioners. GOTTA KEEP ALL THE INJECTABLES FRESH.

Lindy and I were living in Martha Plimpton's ranch house (bitch, I know!!) at the top of this inconvenient mountain in the Hollywood Hills at the end of a hazardous two-way winding road that was 100 percent blind corners, closer to the sun than I have ever been or will ever be again. The afternoon before my big important television script was due, just before I was about to sit at my borrowed desk and really get to work I swear, the lights blinked off and all the whirring and buzzing and clicking, the house's steady heartbeat, ground to a halt. I knew immediately that it was my punishment for always leaving shit until the last fucking minute. Give me a week to work on something, I'm doing it the night before it's due. Give me a month to work on something? I'm doing it the night before it's due! Give me a day to work on something, I'm starting it at 2 a.m.

I wish I had a more exciting and glamorous answer for the question of how I came to write the pool party episode of *Shrill*, but it's pretty simple: I wrote it because someone told me to write it. In the beginning, when we were coming up with the arc of the season, we all pitched ideas to build the narrative for the main character, Annie ("Really, though, *should* she go to outer space???").

The basic premise of the series is this: Annie is a fat, single woman in a situationship with a loser, and she's also unfulfilled at her job, where she is underappreciated. Our goal was to figure out a way, in only a handful of episodes, to evolve her from a whiny doormat (sorry!) to a bitch who owns her shit. Or a bitch who is maybe on the path to owning her shit? Anyway, while talking about a tangible way to shift Annie's perspective from the beginning of the season (unhappily eating special weight-loss foods and putting up with shit from a shitty man) to where we wanted her to be at the end of it (fat and fine with it, or at the very least on the way to being fine with it, and dumping said piece of shit), all of the writers were throwing out ideas (we didn't want to resort to a cheesy makeover montage or hit her over the head with an exercise bike), and I said maybe she could go to a fat girl party, and maybe that party could be at a pool, and maybe seeing half-naked fat people enjoying themselves could be the catalyst for this change in her attitude toward her body and herself. In Chicago I would go to these dance parties and clothing swaps and exercise classes that were made specifically for fat women, and I thought it would be cool to see Annie seeing all different types of bodies unabashedly enjoying decadent party snacks while wearing crop tops and bikinis poolside.

Before naked Tumblr models were pervasive in the culture, hanging out with size 28–plus girls at the club dressed in miniskirts with their upper arm fat exposed was my gateway to being like, "Oh, okay, I don't have to hide or hate myself, got it!" because the Internet wasn't invented yet when I was a child (probably) and had to seek out my own flesh-and-blood affirming spaces. I was a kid in the '80s, so Nell Carter and Shirley Hemphill are the two fat women who come immediately to mind when I think about who looked like me on television growing up, and Nell wore billowy caftans (fuck me up, sis) while Shirley preferred bell-bottom jeans and tight T-shirts (absolutely my shit), which was cool, but it wasn't like I was seeing a whole lot of loud, joyful embracing of their "curves."

Then along came the Internet, and I'm no longer stuck in 1992 with fashion magazines that would lead you to believe that no bodies above a size 6 even *exist*. There was suddenly this wide world of fat girls in stylish clothes living their lives and being free and I just *galaxy brain* started to feel like the tide was turning for people with bodies like mine. Just because I had suffered through my tens and twenties in long-line girdles and Spanx that came up to my chin didn't mean the next generation had to.

I showed up for fifth-grade picture day in a business suit from JCPenney because there was nothing that fit me in the juniors section, I went to one middle school dance in a "blouse." I did it, I crawled in oversize acid-washed denim jumpers with pastel mock turtlenecks underneath so that these girls in their neon mesh crop tops could run, and nothing makes me happier. As I pull my high-waisted jeans up to my ribcage and resign to throw out every bra with an underwire I've ever purchased, it's seriously fucking thrilling to have fat girls in bra tops strut past the bus stop bench on which I have paused to rest because, listen, I'm ninety-four in elder gay years.

I don't want to LOSE MY FUCKING MIND ABOUT THIS, but do you know how revolutionary it is for a person who once upon a time ate those Olestra chips that made my insides ooze involuntarily to my outside no matter how tightly I clenched my sphincter to stem the tide to click on the Universal Standard website and see a woman modeling size 40 jeans? You hear people talking about the importance of seeing "someone who looks like me" And it's like "okay, sure, who cares, shut up." It has always been obvious in regards to race, but with size I guess I'd never really thought about it that much because, well, that's just the way things have always been. Sometimes, it isn't always clear what you don't have until Lane Bryant puts on a lingerie fashion show and throws a billboard up in Times Square, and Tess Holli-day is on the cover of a widely distributed magazine with her back fat out and then it's like, HELL YES, BITCH. SHE HAS THIGHS LIKE ME, OPEN UP MY LARGEST VEIN AND INJECT THESE IMAGES DIRECTLY INTO IT.

I wanted to write a moment like that for the show. Frankly, America needs more moments like that. More fat people, yes, doing normal stuff that isn't "dieting" or "being sad." But also, more young fat women deserve to look at a mirror image of themselves on a television screen (I know, I know, the youths watch TV on their computers) without the attached self-loathing and parroting of diet culture that we're used to.

I think everyone involved came to *Shrill* wanting to tell this story but with a nagging voice in the back of all our heads shouting, "BUT NOT LIKE THAT." As a consumer of popular culture you can't help but be exposed to all the typical fat girl stereotypes and tropes: She cries on the scale! She's a great friend to skinny protagonists! She has a closet full of adorable cherry-printed skirts! But for me, *Shrill* was an opportunity to put a bitch fat lady who can't sing on TV, and it made people so fucking mad, and I love that.

We wrote the show in LA over the course of two months. I ate more delicious free lunches then I could count; I went to many, many shows and left early; I saw Jeff Goldblum on the freeway and almost drove my stupid fucking overpriced car into oncoming traffic. I also:

- spent a not-insignificant amount of time at chain restaurants in Sherman Oaks
- went to a psychic in Santa Monica who got some things so right that it scared me

- micro-dosed psilocybin mushrooms every day
- got recreational IV treatments
- left a restaurant for being both too small and offering no parking, which made me feel like the fucking mayor of the Midwest
- saw the dude who played Ryan on *The Office* at a fried chicken spot
- hung out at Skylight and Book Soup too much and had to ship books home
- introduced Lindy to *Catfish: The TV Show* and created another lifelong fan of Craig from the Craig and Zoe episode
- went to Sephora in Pasadena and let the handsome salesperson with very smooth skin shame me into purchasing six million dollars' worth of tiny bottles of oil
- slammed my hand in the door of the rental car and pissed my pants from the blinding pain
- stocked up on powerful crystals
- tried fruitlessly to find a quality bagel
- sat in the car listening to "In My Feelings" on repeat in a parking lot in Long Beach while watching other people frolic in the water
- ordered tacos a thousand times
- pretended I was starring in *La La Land* and made unironic jazz hands in public
- went to several vegan restaurants, on purpose

After all of us writers turned our individual scripts in, we spent a week or so punching up one another's jokes. I learned so many things on the job, meaning I faked like I knew what the fuck people were talking about then looked it up on my phone when they turned their attention elsewhere, that I am retrospectively quite proud of myself for never obviously shitting the bed during this whole process. I got off the plane in LAX, not knowing what it meant to offer up a "quick pitch" in a meeting, and now I would never fucking say it without fear of looking like a total impostor, but I know what it means if *you* say it. I didn't know how to write "this scene happens in the house at breakfast" in a script a year ago but now I know it's "INT. HOUSE—MORNING." "Punching up" basically means that other writers go through your script and try to come up with lines that are funnier than yours, and you get to do the same thing to theirs; then everyone submits them anonymously and the producers who get final script approval pick the ones that they like best and they're probably not yours but whatever, bitch!

When the scripts were all punched up and edited, it was time to leave. We worked June and July, and shooting started in August, and the cast and producers had to dip off to Portland for pre-production and location scouting, and look at me pretending I know all the technical shit they had to do! There was a table read (the actors, some of whom you will recognize from fucking *Home Alone* and try not to humiliate yourself in front of, read through the scripts while sitting around a big table while other people who aren't actors watch them and try not to breathe distractingly loud while laughing too hard at the jokes) at Warner Bros., during which I sat thunderstruck by Julia Sweeney as she sat two feet from where I was trying to prop a complimentary breakfast sandwich on my lap while juggling scripts. I mostly spent my last week watching *Sharp Objects* in the air-conditioning at

Martha's house and avoiding all the Gila monsters prowling around outside. Then I went home, where I no longer had to talk about weed or pretend to understand fashion.

My life snapped right back to whatever it was before I left. I ran my usual errands, picked themed snacks for our monthly book club, and let my muscle memory lead me right to the gastrointestinal distress aisle at my beloved local pharmacy. I didn't have to learn the layout of a new store anymore!

I don't ever want to be the kind of person who is not fully blown away by the magnitude of getting to make a big, dumb, shiny thing that doesn't cure disease or whatever but brought people some joy! I got many positive tweets! I never want to take for granted that a person in a big corporate office pulled out a giant cardboard check for millions of dollars to buy mini hot dogs and fake margaritas, just because I typed it up on my old, junky laptop. It still feels like a fucking coup, like "Do they *actually know* that they let a person who regularly falls for fake news stories write an entire episode of their television show?!" I'll never be too cool for all those coffees a kid with a master's degree had to spend his summer running to get for me. I am a garbage person who has taken a shit in the street before! Do you think that, when I was spreading my frozen ass cheeks open to force hot diarrhea through my trembling haunches as a blizzard raged around me, I could have ever imagined, twenty years later, I'd be wearing those flat headphones you only see around the necks of directors in behind-the-scenes DVD extras of your favorite movies, watching actors read words that I wrote from a monitor? I DID NOT. I thought I would be living in a windowless apartment above a Jamaican restaurant, married to a small hairless dog. I may still end up there, fixing Mr. Little Jeans his dinner as reggae pulses through our floor from the restaurant below, but as long as you keep letting me use your log-in, I will always have my Hollywood Summer.

⚡⚡⚡

Our mailman, Erik, is a very sweet young man. He always appears to be happy while delivering stacks of Amazon boxes and slippery piles of magazines to us and the other people on our street, despite the fact that we live on a hill with an incline so steep that cars just slide down to the bottom of it during icy weather. He does yoga and is friendly and smiles at me even though I get dozens of books in the mail and, like I said, we live on a treacherous ski slope at least three months out of the year. He's a straight-up delight! We had a horrible winter storm; school was canceled, roads were blocked off, the movie theater app on my phone messaged me to tell me that the matinee I'd planned to see was a no-go since the theater was closing for three days due to snow and subzero wind chills. There was a knock on the front door that I assumed was going to be the Abominable Snowman dropping by on his way home from the indoor farmers' market to warm himself by the woodstove until the roads cleared up, but alas, it was dear Erik, who'd apparently climbed a glacier forming downhill to deliver a certified collection letter to me from the goddamned IRS.

The first thing I did when I got a paycheck for writing a book, which still feels like a joke sentence the eight-year-old inside of me wrote, was to recklessly spent the entire thing in a week and a half. Maybe. Probably. At least that's what it felt like. I first did some responsible things: I looked up my credit report and paid off all the old balances for goods and services I didn't even remember having received, which is particularly painful for me because I do not delight in participating in responsible things. I bought a travel sleep machine, which, while it offends me very deeply to make decisions that are good for my well-being, has come in very handy while trying to live through the night in LA guestrooms and New York City hotels, but was shockingly expensive and also decidedly NOT FUN. I paid for a new hot water heater and a guy to install it, and sure you could cook pasta in my shower, but that's not exactly my idea of a great time. And who knows what I spent the rest on, normal life stuff, I guess: Amtrak tickets and synthetic oil changes and a Hulu subscription and shirts.

These days people are always like, "Aren't you rich now? You pick up the check!" And, first of all, no! My books cost, I don't know, ten dollars (?), and I know from Instagram that you borrowed yours from the library because you tagged me in the photo. And that's fine, who cares, I support my local library, but we're gonna have to go half on this pizza. Another thing: I don't actually have a job! Plus the government gets the lion's share of everything I make?? My lady is a social worker! Listen, you don't have to cry for me, but I'm not rich enough to buy you a trip or a nice bag.

I recently met this asshole who wanted to bond with me over our shared impoverished childhoods and while, ordinarily, screaming "GIRL, WE USED TO GET THE BAGGED ALDI CEREALS, TOO!" in a new friend's face is one of my favorite pastimes, the minute she slipped and admitted that her mom tucked name-brand Jell-O pudding cups into her trademarked Heathcliff lunchbox, I held up a disgusted finger to silence her. "What are you, a Rockefeller?" I cried in disbelief. If you don't understand what the words "shelf stable Snack Pack" mean, you have to, excuse me, get the fuck out of my face. On the rare occasion I wasn't forced to settle for the free hot lunch, my mom would take a piece of rinsed-off previously used tinfoil, flatten it out, lay all the components of whatever she was cobbling together for a barely edible meal next to each other on the foil, fold the sides envelope style, then hand me that lumpy rectangular blob to shove into my Inspacktor Gorgett (that's clearance rack Woolworth-speak for "Inspector Gadget") backpack where the congealing food blob (canned tuna mixed with boiled macaroni *actually touching* a slice of stale 7UP cake!! The horror!) would immediately begin to leak all over my homework. I was always turning in worksheets stained with Salisbury steak runoff. Then she'd pull up to the playground outside school gunning the engine on her Chevy Celebrity with an unlit Kool clenched between her teeth, shouting, "Don't forget to bring my foil home!" as I shuffled, hot and flushed pink, toward the swings.

Anyway, just in case you mistakenly think for even a second that I'm stuck-up and making so much money that I don't remember using five-dollar calling cards well into adulthood, please enjoy this guided tour of some of the stupidest and most desperate money moments of my life before I get dragged to prison for not understanding how to pay the taxes on a royalty check I used to buy a fucking lawnmower.

My first-ever roommate, who was otherwise a very kind and thoughtful stoner, got me (and herself) evicted for selling shitty weed out of our apartment but not actually using any of that money to pay her half of the rent. It was a surprisingly nice place: hardwood floors, gigantic windows overlooking a courtyard, a kitchen big enough to put a table in (which I do not even have now, as a seemingly successful adult). I'm not even sure how we got approved for it because I was definitely nineteen and had nothing to my name other than a very nice iron. But we moved in and got the electricity turned on and then a house phone we agreed to split equally until the first bill came, and it was three hundred dollars, because homegirl had a best friend who lived in California. Neither of us had three hundred dollars, or one hundred and fifty dollars each, if we're keeping it all the way real, so we did what broke people do and made nighttime plans on the phone before we left work and hoped no one changed the location while we were at home in the shower getting ready. At that time, I worked in a bakery and had no one to come home and call anyway, so who cares? But can we please just stop for a minute and think about the stone ages when a person you met three months ago could just, like, fuck up your life in this way? I'm sure that my biggest dilemma in 1999 was worrying that I wouldn't be able to call JB's and get a pizza. Looking back on it now (mystified that somehow we survived), I'm like, "WHAT IF I HAD NEEDED A FUCKING AMBULANCE, SHARON."

We didn't get *evicted* evicted; we got a notice taped to our door that we were so far behind on our rent that authorities were about to get involved, which was a surprise to me because I had been sending floral-embossed checks from my first-ever bank account faithfully every month. My roommate had not. We self-evicted to avoid the embarrassment of the sheriff setting our meager belongings (I had three different dustpans and a futon with a Beatles cover on it) out on the curb. That was when I started to live out of my car, driving around in a bedroom on wheels (there was a broken coffee maker and my iron and some lamps under a blanket in the back seat) and sleeping and bathing in hourly motels.

This is the kind of thing that seems cool in a movie. In real life, I made friends with the greasy creeps who worked the front desks of hourly motels, and they'd sometimes charge me for five hours if I'd actually been there for seven, but that is not a sustainable way to live. I didn't have an address, but, as I said before, I eventually started living with slash working for my homeboy's stepdad at his graphic design studio, and he let me use his address since I was opening all his mail anyway. One day, while I was working, there was a knock at the door and I answered it. This nervous-looking dude is trembling on the steps, and he's like, "Is Samantha Irby here?" And of course, because I'm an idiot, I'm mentally running through all of the possibilities of who this could be: Have I fucked this person? Do I owe this guy money? Is he my dad??!?!! I nod at him, and then he shoves an envelope into my hands and yells, "You've been served!" before literally jumping off the porch and sprinting away. All I could do was laugh because, what the fuck is this, *L.A. Law*? I never went to court (I do not advise this legal strategy), so I got a judgment entered against me, and instead of calling a lawyer (again: don't live like this!), I saved up the money to pay it and mailed a greeting card with a check made out to my old landlord with "this wasn't even my fault" scribbled on the memo line.

Not long after that, I had another roommate situation fall through, as they inevitably do. You know what's always seemed fucked up to me? People who move through the world as if shit doesn't keep them up at night. I wish I could feel the freedom, even for a minute, of someone who bails on shared bills and fucks another person out of a place to live. The other night, I was lying in bed wide awake at two in the morning with an anxious knot in my stomach thinking about this group project I had been assigned my senior year of high school in a goddamned *elective* economics class (I MEAN, WHAT?), and we were supposed to do a presentation in front of the entire class about what NAFTA was and its economic impact on the United States, and are you asleep yet? This was 1997, okay? If it was now, I could just say the word NAFTA three times in the vicinity of my phone, and the ghost of Steve Jobs would have an A+ PowerPoint loaded onto my computer in a matter of seconds, and all my Instagram ads would be for Canadian plastics and Mexican corn. Back then, we would've had to go to the *library* and pore over *encyclopedias* and then type everything up in the *computer lab*, and maybe you've never met a high school senior, but none of us were doing any of that. The day of the presentation, standing in front of the board looking at our shoes while the teacher (a stone-cold fucking FOX, my god) shook his head sadly as we carried on nonsensically about "North America . . ." I felt like a dumb bitch!

Twenty years later and I'm still thinking about making the one kid who actually tried get a D on a group project that didn't matter, so, yes, it is wild to me that more than one person has caused me to do the "pack whatever you can carry because we are leaving *tonight*" shuffle. Am I a bad judge of character? Probably! But is it naive to assume that this friend of a friend who seems nice and has a job wants to have a safe place to sleep and keep her shirts? It can't be. BANANAS ASSUMPTION: This stranger I barely know won't mind if I get two pet snakes and take all the doors off the hinges and play the piano at three in the morning. REASONABLE ASSUMPTION: This stranger I barely know who works at the same job I do will pay her half of the bills so neither of us has to sleep on the street. Who knew this was a risk?

So that's when I moved in with Mel, the graphic designer I worked for and my friend Jon's stepdad, because my parents were dead and I had dropped out of college and I was making $7.25 an hour working at a bakery and it was going to, umm, take me a minute to come up with first and last for a new apartment. I had nothing, less than nothing, a backpack full of a few worthless things plus a bunch of CDs and my mom's old couch crammed into the smallest/cheapest storage unit I could afford. I can't cite credible sources and exhaustive studies to prove that growing up poor is basically a financial death sentence no matter how well you do later in life because I'm not a sociologist writing a textbook but . . . if I had access to generational wealth I probably could be a sociologist writing a textbook!

I remember going to see the late showing of *The Sixth Sense* one Saturday night and tiptoeing in the back door like I wasn't a whole-ass adult, wondering why my parents had chosen to fail me. Abortion was legal in 1980! Spare me the humiliation of trying not to make noise on my friend's mom's stairs!! I was working for Mel part-time when I wasn't cosplaying as a rebellious teenager, so I'd go sell opera tortes at the bakery on some days and walk downstairs in my pajamas to organize Mel's accounts payable and get paid to stumble through Whole Foods doing the grocery shopping on others. It was a pretty good gig, and I learned more about being a person and trying to create a nice life in the years I lived with and worked for that family than I had from birth to when I first realized that rich people actually take their shoes to a fucking cobbler.

Mel had a bunch of store cards to places like Shell and Barnes & Noble. One Christmas, I gave everyone I knew those giant discounted art books that no one buys and classical music CDs, because he never checked the balance on those cards and could write off all the purchases anyway (another concept I could not and did not understand until very recently when my accountant friend told me that if I eat lunch with someone who mentions a book to me, I can declare that meal as "work"), and I lived on gas station beef jerky while pretending to be Lelaina in *Reality Bites*, because he never checked those receipts, either. He had a house account at several small shops and boutiques in town that just tally everything up at the end of the month and send a bill. Did you know rich people can just *do* that? So I started taking all of my shitty jeans and T-shirts to his dry cleaner, who was visibly repulsed by having to launder gigantic bootcut late-'90s jeans, to save money, i.e., cost my fake dad money. I'd order gourmet sandwiches at this super fancy grocery store called Foodstuffs and charge them to his account, because I was not raised on twelve-dollar tuna sandwiches and once I had one I couldn't imagine going back. On the one hand, this feels fabulous, but on the other I was scamming sandwiches.

In a fit of impoverished desperation, after I moved out of Mel's house (the first time) and rented this ugly, carpeted (gross) apartment in a shitty neighborhood that had a bus stop directly below my window and an el station a few blocks away, I sold my first useless car ('88 Ford Escort, hatchback, manual transmission) to a junk dude for like eighty-seven dollars after finding his ad in an actual phone book I found buried in a closet at the bakery. Here's the thing, though: I didn't know I wasn't going to get two thousand dollars for that car. Because I don't know anything!! I once went to pawn a relatively new, super clean microwave whose sole purpose had been heating up sad, low-calorie frozen meals, and, because my cursory knowledge of pawn shops had come from television and not actual lived experience, I was straight-up insulted at the owner's meager offer—less than twenty American dollars. I had the box it came in and everything, and I remember clear as day needing one hundred dollars and thinking, "I know how I can get it! I can pawn this microwave!" before carefully cleaning and boxing up this literal piece of trash and hauling it down to my car (in the olden days, commercial microwave ovens weighed no fewer than sixty pounds and had to be installed by a licensed electrician), then driving to this pawn shop nestled between a Popeyes chicken and a twenty-five-and-over bar that required three forms of ID for entry (what), stumbling through the door with the unwieldy box, and setting it on the counter in front of your bored uncle, then standing there hopefully as he barely glanced up from his newspaper to assess it and declared, "Twenty bucks." I felt like a deflating balloon—the cheap gross rubber kind and not a beautiful shiny mylar one—as my heart sank from "ooh, maybe I can pay the light bill and go see a movie!" to "would this even buy me popcorn?" But that's how you learn lessons in life, right? Having outsize expectations based on courtroom dramas, and then having reality smack you in the face.

Still, I wasn't prepared to be handed the junkman's vending machine money in exchange for an actual car that had newish tires and a recently replaced clutch. I just stood on the gravel in the junkyard, shocked and embarrassed, surrounded by warm refrigerators with the doors hanging off like loose teeth and pickup trucks without hoods, clutching this pittance I needed too badly to refuse. I thanked him and shoved the cassette tapes I'd forgotten in the glove compartment (Wu-Tang, De La Soul, Violent Femmes) into my bag. But I hadn't considered how, exactly, I was going to get home from this remote land of rusted dishwashers and broken lawnmowers. I figured I'd catch the bus, but after doing that hopeful combination of waiting and walking, none came. I ended up at a pay phone by a Home Depot and called a cab. It cost almost forty dollars to get back to civilization. I am a moron.

Between periods of functional homelessness and living in places too depressing to go home to at the end of the day, I used to house-sit for obscenely wealthy people with purebred dogs that cost more than a semester of college. Most of the things I learned about fancy living came from generously helping myself to the luxurious face creams and aged liquors of people who could afford to both go away for weeks at a time *and* pay someone to live their life for them while they were doing so. I would pack four pieces of clothing in a bag (they always had easily accessible washing machines and dryers), my cell phone, and a pair of beat-up gray New Balances (to blend in seamlessly with my surroundings), then go to their houses after work and pretend to be Eloise at the Plaza. I would walk a mile picking up shit behind a Portuguese Water Dog, then spend the rest of the evening in a jacuzzi tub with Fiona Apple moaning out of Bang & Olufsen speakers. It felt like the greatest grift of all time! I never threw parties while house-sitting because I don't give a fuck about parties, and also because none of my friends were going to dodge cops all the way up to Kenilworth to eat pizza rolls cooked in a restaurant-quality wood-burning oven. So, by default, I looked like an incredibly responsible person. Maybe it seems unremarkable to you that I got to stay in a house with dimmer switches and MTV, and all I had to do in return was walk a nice dog around a pretty neighborhood and drag the recycling out to the curb once a week?! Honestly, I'd do that shit now.

Speaking of falling asleep in front of a massive flat-screen TV with cable I didn't have to pay for while a helpless creature with limited language skills banged its food dish around inside a playpen, I babysat way past the acceptable age for that to be a regular income stream for an adult person, and had several regular gigs during which I would not only cram as much HBO into my eyeballs as I could but also go shopping in the parents' Costco-size pantries. These were, like, rich people with a fleet of nannies and housekeepers who drove around their armies of Jeep Grand Cherokees just buying shit all day long. No normal person could keep track of that without a meticulous inventory list. I, too, am wasteful and terrible and have no idea where all my stuff is, but I'm talking about that lip balm I bought on a whim at the pharmacy and various frayed and knotted phone chargers. Not whole laptops and shit! I would roll up in my busted Ford Taurus on a Saturday evening, put the kid(s) to bed at seven, then spend half an hour smelling the eighteen types of cheese in the massive brushed-steel refrigerators in the remodeled kitchens of people who were cool just, you know, not knowing who has the Lexus right now.

Not a single one of them ever noticed the missing packages of frozen tortellini or boxes of granola bars, because the moms didn't eat and what the fuck did the dads care about dinosaur-shaped nuggets? (I care, very much, about dino nuggets, and if someone takes so much as a Coke from the garage without my permission, I notice. I mean, I don't freak out or anything, but I definitely know that there are four Feisty Cherry Diet Cokes on the bottom shelf of my fridge right now, and if there were three I wouldn't rest until I figured out who drank the one that's missing and make them vomit it into my upturned palms.) There's definitely no shame in this but at one point I was thirty years old, getting paid in fresh ATM twenties by people who were basically my same fucking age, who'd started the evening by showing me where "grandma's number is next to the phone!" while listing all the foods their kid is allergic to. On the one hand, I'm a loser. But on the other? HOW DO WE TRUST ADULT TEENS TO DO THIS? Okay, sure, it's sad for me to rely on burping your infant to pay for my prescriptions. But can a fifteen-year-old really remember the injections your baby gets, and in what order, while simultaneously trying to read all your old *Vanity Fair*s? Okay, fine, the capable ones can and this is probably more an indictment of me than it is a slam on them. I'm just saying that getting a ride home from a dad your age seems sad, but if you justify it enough, it can start to seem like a cool life hack.

On more than one occasion I ran an extension cord from the hallway into my apartment because my electricity had been shut off. This is an undervalued bit of creative genius. Now I can afford to leave the lights on in a room I'm not sitting in (remember when that was the worst child-crime you could ever commit?), but in the old days I was always mindful when choosing a new rat trap in which to live that I ended up in one near a hall outlet in case there was a month that brunch plans with a hot dude > the need to pay for light and heat. It's tricky because sometimes the neighbors are assholes who'll do shit like unplug the extension cord for laughs, knowing your alarm clock won't go off, or tattle to the landlord, but that strategy worked way more often than it didn't. I am also a veritable expert at setting up an emergency payment arrangement plan with the electric company and several popular cell phone providers. I know that talking to a stranger wearing a headset is a terrifying prospect, but if you can summon the courage to call that 1-800 number on the bottom of your bill, it is very easy to get a major corporation to extend you a little bit of credit. This is why I don't, say, bungee jump or do parkour: I have to reserve all my bravery for the days I need to bargain for an extra week of phone call privileges.

Before Obamacare and before there was an urgent care center tucked inconspicuously in the back of every Walgreens, I definitely used the emergency room for routine exams because I couldn't afford to go to the doctor for real, especially since the ER will never turn you away. I've complained about pelvic pain to get a pap smear and claimed "inexplicable tiredness" to get bloodwork done. Now the scam is that having insurance buys you a little time so that you don't have to pay *as much* as you would have without it. I remember once getting a yeast infection, and this witch told me to wrap a piece of uncut garlic in cheesecloth and carefully insert it into my vagina for a couple days. And a few months ago, when the CVS pharmacist told me the actual cost less the handful of change my HMO was going to chip in for my raging candidiasis, I was like, "Oh, I'm sorry, what aisle is the garlic on, ma'am?"

I have never had a school loan, never financed a car, never owned anything worth a damn. I wrote bad checks on an overdrawn account for a month when I was twenty-one, but somehow I never ended up in jail. I did end up in Chex-Systems, which is like poverty jail and meant I couldn't get a real checking account at a recognizable bank for the seven years it took to be removed from my credit history. And because my people are poor people who were masters in the art of robbing Peter to pay Paul, I didn't learn about establishing credit until I was thirty-four. I knew how to write a check to myself and cash it after five at the nearby Currency Exchange, because it wouldn't get deposited at least until the next day, and take another couple of days to clear, and by that time my direct deposit will have gone through and there would be enough in my account to cover it. But I did not know that if you get a store credit card, you have to immediately pay it off; otherwise you risk fucking your credit up for the next *checks watch* thirteen years. When I applied for a Discover card, I got a letter that essentially said, "Wow, are you sure you aren't dead, bye!" because my credit history was so thin. Trying to establish yourself financially late into your thirties is a ridiculous and almost insurmountable undertaking. I'm forty this year. I still don't know shit.

Hence, when Erik, our beloved mailman, delivered the very official letter from the government asking me just where the fuck was their percentage of my money, I hid that letter under a pile of notebooks on my desk in the hopes that it would disappear if I just didn't look at it or think about it.

Am I rich now? Absolutely not. Did I drive away from a toll machine shooting nineteen dollars' worth of quarters at me because I only had a twenty-dollar bill at the Indiana dollar toll, and my card wouldn't swipe, and my rental car was too far away for me to do anything other than fruitlessly claw at them while the seatbelt sliced open my neck skin, and an impatient line formed behind me? Yes, the fuck I did. Because I will melt into a puddle of soft goo if I get violently honked at on the skyway. So that's the kind of money I have. "Drive away rather than be humiliated" money. "I forgot to stop for candy at Walgreens so I'll get my overpriced Red Vines at the theater" money. "This candle is just for decoration" money.

"More than one midweight jacket to choose from this winter" money. "Bitch, you pay for it, I owe the state of Michigan two thousand dollars" money.

hello, 911?

Hello, 911? There's a middle-aged dad standing next to the yogurts in Trader Joe's actively strumming a guitar and trying to make meaningful eye contact with every harried person trying to get a box of Pastry Pups on a dismal Saturday afternoon, and everyone other than me seems to be maintaining a relaxed and happy exterior despite the fact that this is terribly embarrassing and he is singing Bob Marley. Please get me out of here. All I wanted was a bag of reasonably priced shelled nuts sold to me by a relatively attractive retired shoe salesman in a faded Hawaiian shirt. Is that really too much to fucking ask?

Hello, 911? The good guy in this movie has made a lot of dumb mistakes, a lot of miscalculations that I can identify with, because, of course, when you do something in haste under intense pressure, you're bound to make an error or take a misstep. But I can't stop cringing and burrowing into my chair, and I did not watch the trailer all the way through because I didn't want to spoil it for myself, but now I'm not sure if he lives until the end and I'm feeling real stressed out about it. Also, can that woman two rows over hear my nervous popcorn crunching during these excruciatingly quiet scenes?

Hello, 911? Is some invisible force going to push me down this flight of stairs?

Hello, 911? Which line is moving faster, the one I'm in or that other line, and do you think I should switch? Does it matter? It's not like I have anywhere to be, but just standing here makes me feel like my organs are going to burst out of my skin. I can't prove it, but I think this line is moving incrementally slower: Why does that make me feel like I'm losing a race? Should I just stay where I am, or do you think it's okay if I ease over to Lane 8 in a way that silently telegraphs "I'm not mad, just having an inexplicable panic attack, please ignore me" to the checkout girl? If I move to that other line, will the Target gods smite me by throwing a clearance rack shirt with a missing price tag into that lady's cart? Why did I even come here?

Hello, 911? I can see foot shadows beneath the door of this single-service bathroom located in the indie coffee shop I only go to because I really do *want* to care about shopping local even though it's definitely out of my way, and when this person jiggled the doorknob to find it locked why would they not just go sit back down at their table or run out to hide in their car like a normal person? Why stand there, guaranteeing that I will have to confront them with the whoosh of moist air that smells faintly like my dripping undercarriage, when all I wanted to do was piss out this latte I drank too fast and maybe poop a little? What am I supposed to do with my eyes when a stranger and I are trapped in a gentle tornado of my rancid-smelling solid waste? Do I say "oh, hey, good morning" or "wow, please excuse me" or "I'm sorry I ate such a large serving of corn"?

Hello, 911? I am the first person at this party.

Hello, 911? I was watching that show *Greenleaf* on the Oprah network, and these two characters were riding in a car and having a passionate conversation, and dude turned to lady and I was gripped with what can only be described as STOMACH-CURDLING PANIC as my entire body clenched in anticipation of his car jumping the curb and crashing through the plate glass window of a laundromat, because he took his eyes entirely off the road for at least twelve seconds. When was the first movie ever made, 1888? And in all those years of practice people still can't film a realistic conversation in a moving car?! His eyes need to be on the Toyota in front of him, OPRAH WINFREY. I'm going to have a fucking stroke.

Hello, 911? What if I fall asleep on this bus?

· · ·

Hello, 911? I just turned to this guy and said, "I'm so sweaty, right?" to break the tension. Because even though we're both standing still in this air-conditioned bank, I was outside under the August sun five minutes ago and now sweat is just pouring out from under my hair. Good Lord, it's like someone turned a faucet on my scalp, and I am literally squishing around in my shoes, and he has to be noticing, right? He hasn't moved away from me or anything, but it's definitely on his mind. I can tell. He's totally not thinking about his mortgage or anything; his attention is definitely focused on my endocrine system. Oh, man, dude just side-eyed me. Did he just see me swipe my brow sweat into my pants pocket with my forefinger, or am I bugging? Why does he keep suspiciously glancing around like that? Does he think I'm guilty of something or just fat?

Hello, 911? I'm in a parking lot and this brand-new minivan just parked dangerously close to me and I'm afraid of getting out of my car and accidentally banging the door. It's so new it sparkles under the sun, and the reflection of the dirty Honda I haven't washed since last fall in its gleaming passenger-side window is causing me agita every time I glance to my left. Ordinarily I wouldn't be so terrified, but this woman took the only open space in the lot and now she's just sitting there, texting or scrolling through Twitter or reading an in-depth article about the Russia probe, and I know she is going to freak out if I graze her door with mine while she's sitting there, so what do I do? I have things to do after this errand, but it's already been twenty minutes, so should I forget the laundry detergent altogether and just wear dirty clothes until I can get a prescription for this shit or should I just wait here until I die from smiling politely during this self-imposed hostage standoff?

Hello, 911? My doctor asked me to list my symptoms. What if I'm lying without meaning to? What if I forget something? Is my itchy toe worth mentioning? My head hurts, so I either have a brain tumor *or* I haven't had enough caffeine today. How important is it to tell her how many Advil I actually take? Why is she reading my chart so quietly? Was that diarrhea? Is she over there planning an intervention because I went through the Ativan she prescribed me in less than a week? Is she going to watch me climb onto the table, and if so, is there a way I could just die right now instead? Oh mannnn, these are my most dingy underpants. I didn't really think they were going to make me put the gown on! When was my last period? Do I still take—what the fuck did she just say—fluticasone . . . ? That's the green stuff, right? No, wait, it's the spray. I'm here for a sinus infection, but it sounds like she thinks I'm here for obesity? Honestly, why did I even come in? I'm fine.

Hello, 911? Is that Channel 3 News hurricane correspondent safe?

Hello, 911? I have a confirmation e-mail from a hotel in my inbox right now. How come I don't have my room key yet? Is the card I reserved it on expired? Did someone warn them ahead of time that all I'm going to do is drink vending-machine Cokes and mainline whatever marathon the USA network has chosen for me today? I enjoy Mark Harmon! How come the woman at reception isn't talking to me? Is the computer system running slow? Did I accidentally reserve a broom closet? Is it 2:57 p.m. and they're *really* going to make me wait until the official check-in time of three before they let me spread myself diagonally across a king-size bed hundreds of other people have had sex on? Okay, so my card was definitely declined. Or worse, the card of the person who booked this hotel for me was fucking declined. I knew the universe would never allow me to actually be fancy! Is it my responsibility to pay for this now? If it were up to *me*, I'd be at a sixty-two-dollar Comfort Inn next to the highway, not this tony boutique shit. A cheeseburger on the room service menu costs twenty-seven dollars. Bitch, I could franchise my own McDonald's for less than that. Maybe I'm in the wrong hotel. Could I be at the wrong hotel? Dude next to me got his room key thirty seconds after he told them his name! Is this punishment for booking a room on discounthotelsforcheap dot net? Did I accidentally ask her to get me approved for a car loan? Seriously, what is the delay? THEY TYPE SO MUCH. SO MANY THINGS COULD BE WRONG.

Hello, 911? Did I already take my pills?

Hello, 911? How do I step onto the moving walkway? It moves! It's better than a regular floor! But why do I feel like

I'm about to try gymnastics for the first time every time I try to place myself and my suitcase on one? Did all these other people effortlessly gliding through the terminal somehow get lessons on how to step on it without their entire bodies spasming as they try to remain upright?

Hello, 911? It's 11:30 at night and I've got an important meeting (LOL) tomorrow morning at nine thirty. I set my alarm for eight. That should give me plenty of time, right? Google Maps says it's probably going to take seventeen minutes to get there from my hotel barring any major traffic, but what if the Lyft driver is late? Alternately, what if the doorman can't find a cab? I'm planning to go down at nine. Does that leave enough time for me to get eggs from room service? But they run late sometimes, right? Should I risk it? It's midnight now and I think I'll be hungry in the morning, but what if I'm not? Then I'm stuck waiting for eggs I don't want. Maybe I should set my alarm for eight thirty. I definitely want to sleep off this Xanax, but does that give me enough time to take an actual crevice-cleaning, hair-washing shower? Should I be honest about who I really am as a person and factor in twenty minutes of bedside-sitting-and-staring-into-space time? It's 12:30, but to be safe I'm going to set the alarm for seven thirty. Should I attempt to impress these people with eye makeup or do they not care because they are serious businesspersons? Let me just go ahead and set my phone for 6:55, so I have plenty of time to contour and blend (i.e., totally fuck it up and wipe it all off while crying). Since I'm up, it wouldn't hurt to iron my pants, just in case I can't hide my legs under a table. Why does everyone want to "meet" on couches these days? An electric chair would be more relaxing. Wait a minute, it's already 1:00?!

Hello, 911? This takeout spot doesn't have online ordering.

Hello, 911? So I texted this dude and he texted me back, then I texted him back, then he texted me back, then I sent two heart emojis and a cheeseburger, and now those three little "I'm writing something pithy and hilarious, just wait for it" dots are dancing on the left side of my screen, but they disappeared kinda quickly and now no message popped up? Should I just wait five minutes then start obsessively calling him, or just find some train tracks to lie down on?

Hello, 911? I barricaded myself in the bedroom because the cleaning service came before I could think of a reason I needed to leave the house for an hour and forty-five minutes, and, sure, they are very nice and consummate professionals, but it's still weird that I'm here, don't you think? I left the money on the table, including a gigantic tip, but I don't know how to make non-painful small talk with a very cheerful person who is patiently vacuuming the thousands of dead skin cells I've shed all over the couch. And I'm sure they'd prefer that I just stay up here with my phone on vibrate pretending I'm not standing in my dirty shoes on the floor they're trying to clean, but what if they know I'm here and think I'm a rude asshole rather than assuming I just don't want to put on a bra before the sun is even up? Is there any way you can send an officer to make sure that people I know in my rational mind are totally unconcerned with the breakdown I am having over their assumed perceptions of my coarse behavior aren't secretly mad?

Hello, 911? My friend just left me a voice mail.

Hello, 911? I'm watching a live basketball game on television, and I don't really know a lot about audio things, but every time the announcers pause, you can hear individual voices in the crowd, and it is causing me actual physical pain to sit at the edge of the couch with my finger hovering over the mute button in case someone says "FUCK" super loud on national TV and then the commentator has to awkwardly try to joke it off, and is there such a thing as extreme empathy that causes you to literally have a panic attack on behalf of a college sports announcer who may or may not have to cover for athletes yelling, "BULLSHIT, MAN," at the ref, because if that's a real disease, I definitely have it.

Hello, 911? I've been lying awake for an hour each night, reliving a two-second awkward experience I had in front of a casual acquaintance three years ago, for eight months.

Hello, 911? Who decided to get tostadas for this work lunch? I eat like a child, and I don't know what manners class I missed on how not to eat a tostada like a barn animal, but the whole fucking thing collapses in on itself after the first bite, and how is it possible to conduct business this way? Who decided this? Even if I forcibly removed all my teeth, the second I breathe on it, this pile of cabbage and meat on a fragile corn plate would shatter into a dozen pieces, nine of which would end up down the front of this white shirt. Or directly into the perfect U-shaped basin created by this low-cut T-shirt I shouldn't even be wearing. If I don't eat, people will ask why I'm not eating. If I do eat, people will know that I'm actually a giant dog dressed in a human skin suit. Why did I even leave my house this morning?

Hello, 911? I HAVE TO MERGE.

Hello, 911? Why did this woman choose the middle stall in this three-stall public bathroom? I like to give people the benefit of the doubt and maybe both stalls were occupied when she came in, but unless these two phantom poopers evaporated without a trace in the time it took me to walk over here, I think I am dealing with a real live Person Who Intentionally Chooses the Middle Toilet. I'm not sure I've ever been that relaxed and/or confident a day in my life. What must that feel like? I'm the kind of person who has to physically restrain myself from offering a heartfelt apology to everyone in the airport bathroom for farting after a five-hour flight. I cannot imagine having the nerve to force someone to sit next to me while I flush half a dozen times to disguise a totally natural bodily function that no human is exempt from yet somehow fills me with deep, unrelenting shame.

. . .

Hello, 911? I am unwittingly at the mall with my skinny rich friend and she insists that I follow her into Anthropologie, a place I can neither responsibly afford nor comfortably browse because everything is doll-size and expensive, and no one here actually cares about anything I'm doing probably because they can tell by my shoes that I am poor, but I know that if I pull something called a "cropped draped anorak" (color: warm buttermilk; cost: approximately $1,726) off the fucking rack, everyone in here is going to immediately stop whatever it is they're doing (ogling overpriced throw blankets knit from angels' delicate wings, or mentally justifying the purchase of yet another set of whimsical teacups) and their heads will swivel in unison to behold whichever form my shame is going to take today: Will my cheeks blush burning scarlet as I attempt to wedge my human-size arm into the infant-size sleeve only to have it get irreversibly stuck? Or will I ignore all evidence that nothing here is made for my body and confidently stride to the register carrying a breezy wrap skirt that costs roughly the same as my rent past their chiseled, gawking faces, only to have my credit card be declined in a spectacular display of computer-generated shrieks and ominous beeps?! Find out on next week's episode of the endless drama *This Is Why I Rarely Go Outside.*

Hello, 911? BRB, I'm starring in a horror movie called *Crossing the Street at a Stop Sign with an Approaching Car That May or May Not Force Me to Do the "No, You Go First!" Tango.*

. . .

Hello, 911? Tell me why I agreed to a conference call at 11:00 a.m. knowing full well that (1) I hate talking on the phone under 99 percent of circumstances, and (2) that it's going to take me half an hour of giving myself a pep talk just to get out of bed and then another fifteen minutes to four hours to coax myself into the shower to try to find the part of my personality that is charming on the phone, and the reason why I didn't just fake laryngitis or possibly my own death when I had the chance?

Hello, 911? What on Earth am I supposed to say to this bathroom attendant?

Hello, 911? I can't figure out where to wait for my Starbucks. Okay, I know where, but there are a lot of people in here and if I stand where it looks like I should stand, I'll be pressed against the condiment bar and I don't want to start my day with six kinds of milk on my fucking coat. But the corral of hot early-morning bodies vibrating with rage as they wait for gigantic steaming cups of boiling-hot coffee that can spill on me is terrifying to navigate. We are going to do that awkward "you jerk left, I'll stumble right" dance that will spiral into a never-ending chorus of apologies that I won't be able to stop until one of us physically removes ourselves from the premises. I've somehow managed to make it through forty years of having no one around to choreograph these grueling situations for me, but that doesn't mean I won't spend the rest of my life feeling gross when it comes back to haunt me when I can't sleep at two in the morning.

Hello, 911? I put on my jacket and got in my own car and braved the icy parking lot and picked up my own food: AM I SUPPOSED TO TIP?

Hello, 911? Am I going to break this chair? It's happened before and I still have nightmares about it every day, because is there anything more humiliating than that actually happening to you in real life? Definitely not. I've vomited on myself before! And I've had to take a shit in the street! Nothing terrorizes me more than the continuous loop of that creaky chair seconds before it collapsed beneath me. I have the memory of brutal romantic rejections that don't pain me as acutely as remembering the faces of the women gathered around my dining room table as I clawed my way up from the floor. And now I'm here in this unfamiliar place at a thing I didn't even want to be at being offered a chair made of matchsticks and masking tape, and if this thing breaks under me please just shove the largest splinter directly into my heart.

Hello, 911? That lady caught me taking a selfie and walked away before I could convincingly pretend to be holding my phone at this angle for some other reason.

. . .

Hello, 911? Shout-out to targeted Facebook ads for always knowing the exact right moment to show me a cozy knit sweatshirt tunic dress for $17.99 plus shipping, but I just ordered that BS, and after clicking many links and connecting all my social media accounts, now the only page that isn't loading is the one I just clicked "pay" on, so I reloaded and connected to Wi-Fi and closed my other tabs, and now it won't load and I have no idea if it's charged me eight times or not at all.

Hello, 911? I'm on the tollway. I guess I don't have any other choice than to actively have a panic attack while the smoothest dollar in my wallet is somehow not good enough for this finicky machine, and despite the fact that I have opened the door and my actual body is halfway out of the car so I can deposit it at exactly the right angle, it keeps spitting it back out at me and my palms are just getting more and more damp, which definitely isn't making things easier. Oh, look, I'm hyperventilating and starting to cry a little! Wow, what is this, a line forming? And now they're impatiently honking at me over a machine I can't control that doesn't have a working credit card slot and no human attendant anywhere in sight? Great!!!

Hello, 911? I'm on the phone with my cell phone carrier and I actually need to speak to a representative.

Hello, 911? Am I losing it? Sometimes I sit in traffic, and when people are walking their bikes across the street in front of me or crossing with their kids, I just think to myself, "Isn't it wild that you literally can just run over someone?" My conscious self knows it's wrong, but you *really could* just do it, and I know that running people over is wrong so I don't, but the human brain is so strange—what if my brain just decided it was okay to run over people? I'm starting to feel funny and wondering if I actually have a murderer inside just waiting to come out, please help.

Hello, 911? The elevator stopped at my floor and I am on the fourth of the five seconds between when it arrives and when it finally settles and the doors slide open, but should I scream? I'm slippery with perspiration and consumed with how much I have to pee and kicking myself for not stopping at that bathroom I passed in the lobby, and now I'm going to ruin my outfit and be found dead in this elevator with urine-soaked shoes. What if I really am trapped in here and the fire department comes and they have to use the ladder, will it be long enough? What about strong enough? Do I have the wrist strength to heave myself up from the floor of this elevator to the ceiling? How many people will be watching me? If there is a God, he would snap this cable and let me plunge to my death before everyone at this hotel saw me getting wedged out of this metal box in floral cotton briefs. Oh, wait, the doors finally opened, never mind, bye!

Hello, 911? One of the 137 lights on this dashboard just came on, and honestly, I don't know whether it means I need to stop for gas soon or immediately barrel roll out of this motherfucker in the middle of the highway.

Hello, 911? I have to cancel an appointment.

Hello, 911? My brain is a prison, and anxiety is the warden. I am besieged by the undeniable urge to peel off my skin like it's the layers of an onion until death claims me and I find relief in its cool embrace, and I know it took me a long time to finally call and I'm not 100 percent sure that this qualifies as an emergency, but I think I've reached my limit and I might need some help.

Okay, sure, I'll hold.

an extremely specific guide to publishing a book

Here is how I got my books published so far. It is not that helpful!

I started my blog, *bitches gotta eat*, in 2008. Or maybe 2009? I'm not sure. I could look it up, but that's boring! Actually, I first started a blog on MySpace because I wanted to impress this kid I thought wanted to have sex with me. I mean, he did the thing where he was very flirty, and seemed like he wanted to have sex with me, but he wasn't overt about it, so I felt like I had to do something else to win him over. Okay, the truth is that he was very flirty, but not overtly so, and I don't believe that people are honestly attracted to me without my first having to put on some elaborate show. And by "elaborate show," I don't mean "dress nice" or "deal with my seborrhea"; I mean "make them very specific playlists full of songs that prove how interesting I am." From his MySpace, I gleaned that he was dating a poet. I cannot compete with a poet! I feel things very deeply, sure, but instead of making art out of those feelings, I cry inappropriately at commercials for new medicines. So he was dating a poet and she seemed cool and mysterious as poets do, and I immediately was like, "Wow, how did I waste so much time messaging a dude I can't get with?"

I haven't gone to therapy yet because I'm too fucking tired, but if I did my issues would boil down to:

1. Extensive childhood trauma caused by poverty, danger, illness, and grief
2. Callous detachment and fear of intimacy
3. Hours of time wasted on people who pretended to be romantically interested in me but just wanted me to tell them a joke

I don't know that I have the resources to solve this crisis on a national scale, but listen, everyone: you can just ask people to tell you a joke. Leading people on is a hate crime. Especially when you could just say what you want and let them decide whether or not they want to give it to you without getting their romantic feelings involved. This is a careless thing that is probably unintentional sometimes, but, goddamn, just ask for what you want without looking up at me from under your hair (or whatever your chosen flirtation method might be), unless you're truly trying to have clothes-on hand-sex, say what you want in a normal way so I don't have to feel tingly and weird when I say no.

I started writing short stories my sophomore year in high school. I had this amazing teacher, Nancy Kellman, who made us read Shirley Jackson's story "The Lottery" (just, like, wow), and then assigned us to write short stories of our own. Mine was about a teenage girl who kills her mother because (a) I have always been incredibly dark and (b) I was afraid to write the tragicomic love story my heart desired, because what if she read that shit aloud to the class? Mrs. Kellman liked my story, and also sent me to the social worker for being disturbed, and throughout the rest of the year encouraged me to write more and met with me after school to work on all my nightmare fantasies.

Junior year I had a different teacher but I kept sneaking back to Mrs. Kellman's classroom to slide my weird stories under her door, and she would give them back to me with very thoughtful critiques, and sometimes she left me little notes that were like, *Bitch, are you okay?* Not exactly, but you get it. My home life at the time was extremely chaotic, and my grades were definitely a reflection of that. By the time I dragged myself to senior year, my counselor and a couple teachers I actually turned homework in to were determined to help me limp across the finish line no matter what it took so I could graduate and officially become the universe's problem. To do this, they filled up my class load with independent studies, which basically meant I took gym, choir, Spanish, and a few electives, then filled the rest of my gaping schedule with free periods during which I was supposed to be writing, guided one-on-one by a teacher of my choosing. Naturally, I asked Mrs. Kellman to do it, and I set a goal of writing eight short stories per semester. If I completed them all, I would get an A regardless of their quality. I did that, and I won an award at the end of the school year for one of the stories and it came with a four-thousand-dollar cash prize that I spent on Mike and Ikes (probably?), and I stopped writing as soon as I graduated.

When I dropped out of college after the first year, I started working on a novel late at night in the bakery where I worked after we closed for the night. The only sounds were the shuffling and clanking of the bread makers working the night shift drifting up to the office where I was typing on an old computer my boss let me use. I don't know how good the novel was considering I was eighteen and had slept through the only college English course I had taken up to that point, but I liked the book well enough. I didn't do anything with it, just plugged away night after night, because I didn't want to go home to my shitty apartment and eat one of those "10 for $10" Lipton rice mixes while staring at the TV until I fell asleep. When I finished it, I printed the whole thing out, one chapter at a time because I didn't want to conspicuously use up a ream of paper in a day and get my paycheck docked, and I three-hole punched it and put it in a binder and kept that binder in the trunk of my car, because who cares?!

Anyway, dude-I-was-into's poet girlfriend was hot and cool and wrote deep, meaningful stanzas, and by the time I met him, I was just a donkey going on coffee runs at one job and a monkey scheduling cat dentals at the other, falling asleep facedown in sports-bar nachos in between. Needless to say, I was intimidated by her. One day he casually mentioned being ~into writers~ to me, and because everything is a test, I immediately gave up. I knew that if there was a fight, I was absolutely going to lose it, but wait: there was a binder buried under a bunch of "what if I crash my car in the snow?" blankets in the trunk of my car, and my best friend Anna had also stashed a folder in her parents' attic of all the creepy stories I'd written while not learning high school geography. This is writing! I was a writer!! Maybe I could be a writer who had sex!!!

What are some superficial ways you can impress someone handsome in a hurry?

Buy them something luxurious and expensive.

Have the very specific body type of a person they've fantasized about.

Possess an exhaustive knowledge of some obscure thing they care about.

Show off a physical skill, like popping a wheelie on a dirt bike. (Is that a real thing?)

Pretend you need their advice or expertise. (Ha-ha, no!)

Do volunteer work, and go out of your way to tell them about it.

Tap dance??

What is a way you might not?

Hand them a hundred out-of-context pages from a novel you wrote and expect them not only to read it, but to do so and fall hopelessly in love.

I don't have any confidence in myself, so it seemed unlikely to me that I was going to win homeboy over just by saying my normal words to him. I needed a way to get some of my *writer* words into his hands, so he would like me more. In hindsight, don't ever do anything for anyone, but especially not a man who already has a girlfriend, whose relationship terms seem inconsistent at best. Thinking about how much effort I put into this rather than, um, learning anything at all, ever, is extremely embarrassing!

I alluded to being a writer, or at least having written, knowing full well that the response was going to be some combination of "What do you write?" and "When can I read it?" Sure, I could call Anna's mom and ask if I could go digging through her old clothes and lawn furniture to find a story I'd written at fifteen about the scamming children of a traveling tent revival preacher who prey on vulnerable congregants and swindle them (WHAT), or I could try to select the perfect handful of crumbling, moldy pages from the book I refused to retype on a new computer because I misplaced the floppy disk (again, WHAT) I'd saved it on and expect him to read them and return them to me while actively swooning. Isn't that how things work? Absolutely not.

Okay, so let me remind you that this lazy courtship was taking place on MySpace, a website for friends. Facebook was for people with .edu college e-mails and I had no idea it even existed, so my social-media home resided on a rainbow polka-dot background where the song "Shake That" by Spank Rock assaulted your ears every time you clicked on my profile to see what mood I was in. MySpace had a blog feature, and I'm going to be honest with you and tell you that I didn't have the faintest idea what a fucking blog was.

I was born in 1980, and I bought my first computer in 2011. I didn't have the Internet in my home until four or five years ago, because I fucked around and got my cable disconnected in my old apartment and Chicago has that weird thing where you can get Cable Company A on one side of the street and Cable Company B on the other side of the street, and navigating all that when you don't regularly pay your bills is a nightmare. So, when missing the New York Housewives forced me to get cable again, I got DirecTV (excellent customer service, by the way), but they didn't offer Internet, so I just didn't have it. Did you know you can live like that? It's possible!

All that to say that I'm not hyperliterate when it comes to the Internet. I'm not ~extremely online~ even now, you know? I had to google that one SpongeBob meme because I aM oFtEn LaTe To ThE PaRtY. But I'm getting ahead of myself; in 2008, I didn't know what blogs or LiveJournal or any of that really was, because I only had access to the Internet at work. I used the Internet to read Television Without Pity forums about *Project Runway,* and to snicker at Dlisted and What Would Tyler Durden Do? and Go Fug Yourself when the phones at work were slow. Even now, 99 percent of my Internet usage is reading *Vulture* recaps and fancy celebrity profiles and lifestyle blogs. Back then, I was messing around on MySpace one day during a lull and happened upon the blog option, and a tiny cartoon light bulb appeared over my head and blinked to life. At the same time, I exclaimed, "Aha!" and started typing some dumb thing about an art class I once took.

After a few entries that I intentionally spaced out so as not to look super thirsty, I casually alerted him to its existence like, "Oh, hey, I didn't see you lurking online there, but if you've got a couple free minutes to be seduced by this little thing about spoiled milk I just wrote, then here it is, if you want to read it, but I don't, like, actually care if you do, because I'm so cool and aloof." Then I breathlessly refreshed the page and counted the pageviews until I was sure that at least one of them was him.

Let's skip to the end: he read it, and liked it (or pretended to because I was open to anal). Then we had an intense relationship, but not really, because he wasn't entirely honest, and, man, I hate finding out a Thing is just a thing, especially when I had to type all those words to make it happen. I'm nothing if not good-natured, so when it ran its course and blew up, I was like, "Okay, that was something. I learned a lot. Let's move on." Then I thanked my blog for its service and started making preparations to join the rest of the non-college-educated world in a shift over to Facebook, which had finally opened its doors to us plebes and also didn't have a blog feature. Laura, who worked across from me, and to this day serves as my shrewd career adviser and moral compass, was like, "Dude, you can't shut it down! So many people read it!" It was true; so many people other than the intended recipient were reading my nonsensical jokes. But I didn't want to still be on MySpace with all the emo bands and moms. WHAT COULD I DO?

Laura and I went to get cheeseburgers and mai tais after work one night, and she said, "You should try Blogger, it's free," and I said, "Okay, sure," and then when I got home I looked up how to start a blog on the HTC smartphone I'd gotten for free because Sprint, by the way, didn't carry iPhones yet and I couldn't afford to switch cell phone carriers, because have I told you enough times how your credit can get fucked before you're even living a real adult life yet? I still have Sprint, because they were the only ones to offer me a chance to make staticky phone calls while fully operating a dangerous vehicle on the highway back when my credit score was literally 2, and I am loyal to a fault.

I started a blog, and I called it *bitches gotta eat* because of the movie *Boyz n the Hood*. Some people know exactly what I mean when I say that, and other people look at me like I'm speaking Klingon. In case you're in the latter group: there's a scene in the beginning of the movie when the titular Boyz are all at a backyard barbecue celebrating Doughboy's release from prison. Doughboy is played by the rapper Ice Cube, an actual angel. Anyway, Doughboy's mom, Mrs. Baker, comes out with those giant foil pans that let you know the food is FLAMES full of chicken and ribs, and as she's setting it out, all the dudes at the party start shoving their way toward the table, elbowing women and children out of the way. Which I understand, as I, too, love a hot link fresh off the grill. The scene continues as follows, transcribed by me while watching it on my phone in the bathroom, wearing headphones I might have dropped in the bathtub:

Tre, played by a young and passionate Cuba Gooding Jr., is trying to impress his girlfriend, Brandi, as played by Nia Long.

TRE: Hey! Why don't you all act like gentlemen and let these ladies eat first?

Tre motions to Doughboy for backup, and he grudgingly obliges.

DOUGHBOY: Yeah. Y'all act like you ain't never had no barbecue before! Let the ladies eat. Hoes gotta eat too!

SHALIKA (PLAYED BY THE INIMITABLE GODDESS REGINA KING): Wait a minute, nigga, who you callin' a hoe? I ain't no hoe!

DOUGHBOY, FEIGNING CONTRITION: Oh. I'm sorry—bitch.

The first real entry on my blog was about this '90s show called *The Practice*, which I watched religiously, because Dylan McDermott is very handsome, and because I am obsessed with Camryn Manheim, an actual fat woman on TV! I incorporated some of my old MySpace posts that I thought were too funny to lose, but I wasn't 100 percent sure what a blog was supposed to be, or how to maintain it or build it into a thing that might actually be a thing. All I knew was that I didn't want to do anything that felt like a fucking job, because I already had one of those. Also, it couldn't require too much computer knowledge or time, because, like I said before, I hadn't gotten a computer until a few years earlier and I was working eleven hours a day and usually wrote on my lunch breaks on whatever work computer wasn't being used.

My OkCupid handle back then was "FARTTHROB," which probably explains why I never had much romantic success on that website. Although, can I just pause for a minute to interject that having a funny name that is indicative of my entire personality is a detriment only if you're satisfied with attracting people who would never be interested in who you really are. Sure, I could have chosen the screen name "Loves2CookandClean4U" or "MadeForConstantSex," but that is just setting up some unsuspecting person for extreme disappointment, and I don't want to do that. Somehow, despite my true advertising (is that what the opposite of false advertising is called?), I went on a bunch of increasingly unsuccessful dates. Because I wanted a partner and feel like I'm a smart and interesting person, this was devastating to me. Because I try to have a sense of humor about all my devastation, I decided that I should write about it. I don't have good processing skills—at least I don't think I do, because I turn everything into a fucking joke and then bury it in a shallow grave in whatever part of the mind something you never want to think about ever again goes . . . until its decomposing hand emerges from the dirt on a random Tuesday at 3 a.m. to remind you of that embarrassing thing you thought you'd forgotten. But the idea that bad things can't hurt me if I tell everyone about them in a funny way first seemed like a fun way to grieve these tiny deaths. So I put them on my blog.

I wrote about the time I wore a diaper to speed dating because I was in the middle of a Crohn's flare-up, and I pooped in it a little while talking to a gentleman named Terrence. I wrote about the time I started sleeping with this trainer at my gym who was obsessed with watching me eat whole chickens while he jerked off. That kind of shit can really ruin you, you know what I mean? I was having the kinds of dating experiences that, if I'd recounted them on a therapist's couch rather than on a free blog on the utterly terrifying information superhighway, that person would've been like, "Hold up, have you ever heard of self-esteem?" And no, I haven't! Which is why I ate a glazed donut off a dude's dick one time!

There was a freedom in shouting these sordid stories into a faceless Internet void, and the responses I got were positive, so I kept doing it. Turns out a lot of people identified with trying to wring a drop of humor out of the filthy wet mop of dating in the modern era. A lot of my friends wondered, aloud, TO ME, whether I was shooting myself in the foot by writing so candidly about my sex life. *Who wants to fuck the bitch who is immediately going to post a description of your orgasm face online?* First of all, my audience wasn't that big. Second, I wasn't sleeping with the kind of people who did shit like read blogs. Skim the sports pages in a newspaper someone left behind on the train? Maybe. Fire up the old desktop to read some garbage a girl they met on BlackPlanet wrote? Dude, no. Dating online never worked for me in the pre-swipe stone age (I shudder to think about the constant rejection I would suffer if I ever had to get on Tinder or whatever the fuck people have to be on now), because I posted real pictures of my actual torso and answered the prompts in full paragraphs that I'd workshopped with all my coworkers. Remember those days, back when it seemed plausible that someone might actually be curious about your top-five desert island books? Anyway, everything changed when I started performing the shit I'd written onstage.

The first time I ever read some obscene piece of garbage I had scribbled in my diary while crying aloud in front of a crowd of people was late on a Sunday night eightish years ago at this bar in Logan Square called the Burlington. It's a windowless, dimly lit storefront dive dimly lit by dollar-store candles (you for real need *Silence of the Lambs* night-vision goggles to find your way to the bathroom—it's amazing), with taxidermy animal heads mounted behind the bar (many

whiskeys, two-dollar PBR specials, no mixologist concoct-
ing drinks with seven ingredients), and long wooden church
pews running along the east wall. Lots of fixies chained to
the parking meters out front, dudes with slicked-back hair
and hand tattoos in super skinnies rolled halfway up their
calves—you get it.

The Sunday Night Sex Show was a reading series hosted
at the Burlington by my friends Robyn and Allen. It wasn't
like any lit show I'd ever been to before, not that I was ever
a person who would go to things like literary shows, but
it certainly wasn't the type of show I'd anticipated, which
would be filled with earnest middle-aged white people
in cardigans listening to their contemporaries read long-
winded pieces about their stamp collections and artificial
hips while crammed into the back of an indie bookstore.
The Sex Show was an entirely different thing, a show in a
bar featuring unfiltered true confession and creative nonfic-
tion stories about sex and sexuality. Basically, the last Sunday
of the month, the bar would fill up with nerdy writers and
drunk regulars who'd use crayons to write anonymous sex
questions (e.g., *Is there an easy way to make my girlfriend have a
squirting orgasm?*) on blank postcards that had been left around
the bar, which the hosts would answer between stories about
bad dominatrix experiences, public blow jobs, and a predatory personal trainer who liked to seduce fat women at the
gym to eat large amounts of food while he watched and
masturbated. I have no idea who might have written that last
one. *tugs collar nervously*

After I'd read aloud a few times at the Sex Show about the
exploits of my various orifices, Allen retired from nightlife
to teach kindergartners about foot fetishes and roman show-

ers (JK, JK, JK), and I briefly joined Robyn as cohost. I've never done anything more difficult in my life: weeks were spent hassling everyone I knew to pour out their vulnerabilities all over an audience of strangers in a bar full of people who probably weren't paying attention to them anyway. I'd leave my cozy apartment at seven on a Sunday night in the freezing cold, trying to give my rapt attention to boner stories despite many rounds of free bourbon from Mike behind the bar, trying to remain coherent and awake until almost midnight. I had a good time, though, and I was good at it. I made a lot of friends. I grossed out a lot of people.

I know a lot of poets, and poetry is cool, because when you say that's what you do people have at least a general idea of what you're talking about. I have a lot of comic friends, too, and if I say "stand-up," then you think "perform a tight five in front of wasted people who will yell 'fat bitch!' though four of them are in a coma or have an alcohol or drug problem." If I mention "improv," you connote: "worst person in the school play." There's no good way to distill "trying to make tearing open your neuroses interesting and funny in front of six people and a child who wandered over by accident in a darkened corner of the library" into a title that fully encapsulates what it is overly confessional people actually do in live lit storytelling.

One night, I was sitting at the bar drinking whatever well whiskey they gave me for free in exchange for hosting the Sex Show when this dude I knew from ~the scene~, someone who worked for an indie press, asked me if I'd ever thought about publishing a book. Sometimes people don't believe me when I say that I don't have any goals, but seriously, it's the damn truth. No, I'd never thought of publishing a motherfucking book. That sounds like a lot of work. And I already had a job cleaning up cat puke and calming your mom down that time her beagle got stung on its nose by a bee.

Nothing seemed like a bigger nightmare to me than spending a lot of time putting together a thing that people may or may not want, that I would be forced to sell for the rest of my life, that would never make me enough money to solve any of my problems while also creating new ones like one-star reviews and people tweeting me dumb fuckshit, which would literally never go away. WHY DOES ANYONE WANT THAT? Lest you think I'm exaggerating, here is a loose approximation of my first book contract: "You, Samantha Irby, will write us a book that we may or may not edit. When it comes out, we'll give you a box of books you can keep in the trunk of your nonexistent car and sell them to fans at shows, i.e., to your friends who feel bad for you." That was a good fucking deal! It's a better deal than most! I mean, the fact that they had distribution was like, "Wow, this is a real thing." But still, no thanks!

It's one thing to have a useless Internet hobby a handful of people read; it's another to have someone walking around with your fifteen-dollar words in their coat pocket. Also, writing a book feels like it should be an event, a thing that serious people sit down and plan to do. I've never planned anything in my whole life. I still don't. This essay you're reading wasn't in the book I pitched to my editor, and other than some notes I made on a Subway napkin, I didn't map it out or properly outline it or do literally anything else I imagine successful people do. I don't say this to brag—I'm admitting to you that I am an ill-prepared child-person.

I don't do anything hard, because my life has already been hard. You know those people who are always running and jumping and diving into some challenging bullshit to test themselves? That's not me. I have lived without electricity before—no need to thrill seek! While "pragmatic" isn't necessarily an adorable quality I'd list in my dating profile, I'm pretty good at determining the cost-benefit analysis of activities that have the potential to be irritating to me. But I am not immune to constant flattery. And the editors I knew all made it sound so easy. Every time I'd run into someone who worked for or knew of or had read a book put out by Curbside Splendor, the indie press I first published with, they were like, "Have you thought about putting out a book with them?" Finally, outside an open mic night at Cole's, I caved. Of course, I'm a sniveling egomaniac hungry for praise, and I could not resist the idea of an ISBN being forever attached to my name. Plus, they really did make it sound like something I could just wake up and do, which is my main criteria for 99 percent of the things I take on. It seemed almost disrespectful to turn down repeated offers to compile a bunch of swear words and poop jokes and have them be turned into an actual book, so I finally relented and said, "Ugh, fine."

I signed the contract over a couple bottles of sake in a dimly lit Japanese restaurant, a place I dragged myself to reeking of dog saliva and coated in many layers of hand sanitizer at the end of an endless work day. Then I took the train home and immediately regretted the decision, because I hate signing up for things and having people depend on me. I wasn't too keen on exposing my innermost thoughts and feelings to the clogged toilet that is unverified customer reviews and obnoxiously snitch-tagged tweets. Imagine feeling like the nine dollars you spent on a discounted paperback book entitles you to rip the shithole out of the person who wrote it! I know you wouldn't do that, but many people are not graced with your impeccable manners. I didn't have any ideas for a book, or any idea of how to put together a book, and I'm not a perfectionist (clearly), but I still didn't want to spend the rest of my life embarrassed by this dumb thing I made, like when your firstborn somehow grows up to be a studious, responsible attorney instead of a rock star.

That was in the winter, and I basically wrote nothing even though I was inside twenty-three hours a day and spent my time at home watching old episodes of *Grey's Anatomy* on my phone. I'd write something, read it back, curse myself for being an idiot, and not write another word for a week. Which I justified to myself by saying that I had a full-time job and my brain was tired, but I was too invested in Cristina Yang's fictional life for that to actually be true. I think this might be a symptom of a little thing called D E P R E S S I O N, but I'm not a doctor! My friends Cara and Ted are real adults with a guest room and air-conditioning, and when I finally dragged myself out of bed the spring or summer before my book was due, I basically moved into their house and sequestered myself in their back room and wrote down a bunch of stuff that made me laugh plus a couple things that made me cry. Then I sent it all in the day it was due with a very sincere-sounding apology for why it was such a mess. And that became *Meaty*, a gross book about a dumb slut.

One of the things that sucks the most about me, a deeply embarrassing personality flaw that I cannot change, is that I truly don't have any goals. Because of that, I am a terrible person to make things with. No, I'm saying this wrong. I'll do a thing, or make you whatever you want, or show up every day, but I'm never going to humiliate myself by, say, going door to door to sell that thing to people who probably don't want it. I'm never going to haul a box of books across the country and try to convince people to spend money on them, you know? I mean, I already wrote the book, so I'ma just tweet about it and keep doing what I've been doing, and if someone wants to buy it, then great.

I understand how that can be frustrating to a certain kind of person—a hustler, a swindler, a grifter, a snake-oil salesman—but for me it worked. People I didn't know, who weren't related to me, in parts of the country to which I'd never been, were buying my book. Copies were in libraries and in bookstore windows and on end caps in Barnes & Noble. I had written a bunch of butt jokes in my sweltering studio, in an empty exam room at the hospital on my lunch breaks, on a futon with my friend's dog curled up next to me, and somehow it had become a book that you could walk into a store and buy, and that was just fine with me. It was a nice achievement, and I was proud of it. There had been no advance (okay, cool, who cares?), and royalties were a dollar a book and paid out quarterly (also great, it doesn't matter), but that meant I had to keep working my regular-ass job. It's hard to feel like you did a big thing and your life is going to change in any demonstrable way when you're on a packed, sweltering bus after a day of getting screamed at about prescription dog foods.

My little meat book was out in the world, and I immediately retired. The book could serve its purpose of impressing potential love interests whether or not I wrote anything new and, honestly, I didn't want to work that hard ever again. Especially not for free. I wish I had that gene that makes you feel good when you've completed something, but sadly, I do not. What is that called? Ego? Pride? Whatever it is, I ain't got none of it, and that's fine. So I just kept living my best possible life: spending too much on lunch at work every day; reaping the rewards of steady employment, like a working mobile phone and rebated pharmaceuticals; filling out the eHarmony questionnaire with the most clever anecdotes I could come up with between scheduling growth removals for suburban pets; drinking shots of Four Roses and Old Grand-Dad with Melissa at Big Star once a week; fiercely participating in a *Bachelor* contestant fantasy league. Then I got an e-mail from a man named Kent asking if I had an agent.

I had proudly negotiated my one book deal by myself! So I e-mailed him back and told him I did not. Then he e-mailed me back and asked if I wanted one, and the last thing I want to do is disappoint a well-dressed person in a tall, fancy building in New York City, so I told him sure and assumed that meant he now represented me. This was a couple months after *Meaty* came out in the fall of 2013. I received another e-mail from him late in January asking if I'd given it any further consideration, which was a funny thing to ask because I don't, uhhh, *consider* anything. I just say yes if it's a thing that sounds easy enough for me to do, or no if it doesn't. Am I really going to do research? No, I am not. I looked at his Twitter and googled his agency to make sure it existed and just assumed my informal, lowercase, misspelled e-mail response was enough. Turns out I needed to talk to him on the phone first, which I did while watching the Oscars red carpet muted on my TV. Then he sent me a contract I didn't read before signing.

A few weeks after that, he hit me up to let me know that I should start thinking about what my next project was going to be, and I was fucking SHOCKED. I say "I'm dumb" all the time, and people are quick to fight me when they assume it's just my inner saboteur jumping out, but here is a shining example of the ways in which my synapses sometimes do not connect: I thought I would sign with an agent on the off chance that if a new idea ever came to me, I'd have someone to call who would find someone *else* who might want to pay me for it. It never occurred to me not to take this next step without an idea, because he wanted to make some money because this is his job. But I didn't have any ideas. TBH, I still don't. And *of course* this is something I would do. *Of course* I would sign up for a new thing that requires something I wasn't prepared for. Even now, I chastise myself for being such a weird scatterbrain. I don't know if I'm putting a fine enough point on this, but I truly thought he was just my new friend who I might ask to take a look at something I might write several years down the line. What a fucking asshole!

Kent told me to write a detailed outline, and four fleshed-out sample essays that were good and funny enough to convince a person with a marketing budget to buy them. I wrote the outline, and the entire time I was thinking, "Who wants this? Who needs this? What can I do to make someone laugh?" I scraped all my insides out into a notebook and typed it up, then picked the four ideas I thought I could satisfactorily complete the fastest. Then I wrote and sent them to him, and I want to be very clear that I had zero expectations and also that this is the limit of my contribution to the sales process. I didn't ask who he was sending the proposal to (how would I even know?) or what kind of money he thought we could get for it (how much is my pain worth??), I just waited for him to call me and tell me what our next steps were, because I am not interested in the nuts and bolts of anything. I do not want to see how the sausage is made. I just want to eat the sausage, while wearing earmuffs and a blindfold.

We sold my book for what sounded like the equivalent of a good yearly salary, which was an incredible dream. I had unfulfilling sex with a dude, more than once, who gave me a bag of cold tacos and a Pepsi one time, so when it comes to exchanging my goods and services for money, when Kent called me with that offer, I was overcome with joy. But I didn't quit my job, because this is how that shakes out:

1. The book payment is divided into thirds. In my case, it was one-third when they bought it, the next third when it was turned in and edited and finished, and the last third upon publication.
2. Now subtract what my agent gets for his hard work and fierce advocacy, a debt I can never truly repay.
3. Please also keep in mind that I am taxed as a married person with no children, and I can't claim my cats as dependents. I'm no mathematician, so just cut half off what you think I made and that's it. Okay now shave off a little more.

I took a year to write the book. Maybe more, maybe less, but it was definitely late. It wasn't exactly what I'd pitched, but it seemed like that was okay? I wish I had some kind of interesting process that makes it seem like I am doing deep, important work over here, but I mostly just wrote in my apartment and in various hotel rooms and at my cluttered desk in the corner after I moved to Michigan. I wrote a bunch of stuff that made me laugh and a handful of things that didn't. Then I turned it in and crossed my fingers that my editor would like it. And by "editor" I mean "editorial staff, salespeople, marketing people, art directors, and publicists," which I thankfully found out later otherwise I would have crumbled under the pressure. I was stressed out thinking about getting one person's approval; if I had known there was a team of people assigned to my book about diarrhea, I would have gotten diarrhea.

After you turn a book in, your editor goes over it and does all the "Are you serious? This is stupid!" work, and then a copyeditor goes over it with a fine-toothed comb and does all the "Are you stupid? This is serious!" work, and you have to try not to be embarrassed to literal death while getting fact-checked about all the pop culture references you got wrong. On the one hand: murder me without anesthesia, please. But on the other? Thank God this person I will never meet knows that Lifetime movies did not exist in 1987, because I could not be bothered to research that casual reference my nostalgia made me toss in. Luckily, you get to go through all the humiliating shit you fucked up alone at your kitchen table while crying and dreaming about all the things you're going to buy once you get your check, and not across the desk from a person who thinks you don't know how to properly use an Oxford comma.

You fix your mistakes, you send it in *again*, you wait to get paid, you move a bunch of stuff off your Amazon wishlist and into the main cart like a real fucking baller, and eventually you get cover art and an on-sale date, and then the real work begins: telling everyone you've ever met or are connected to online to please order your book while also writing lots of tail-between-your-legs e-mails asking writers you admire if they please wouldn't mind blurbing your book. "Ha-ha, I know you're busy, and I know you've got a lot on your plate, but if you wouldn't mind saying something flattering about this bowl of dog food I'm calling a memoir, I would be so very grateful!" Then there are the follow-up e-mails you have to send a month later, because they're busy and they forgot or they hate your book! By the follow-up to the follow-up, you just want to crawl in a hole and sleep for the rest of your life, because, wow, this is incredibly humbling. Why don't they just let regular people submit blurbs? It would be so much easier. Why did I ever sign up to do this in the first place? I should have just written my dumb blog and worked my old job until I collapsed from old age and emotional exhaustion due to rich-people customer service. Anyway, hope you're ready for my next book! Kenny at the Save A Lot on Elm Street says it's "a layered and nuanced work of simmering genius and unflinching beauty." Just kidding, he said, "Stop trying to hit on me, Sam. I told you I have a wife!"

I wrote all this because I can't figure out how to put an FAQ on my dumb website. You're welcome!

ACKNOWLEDGMENTS

First of all I would like to thank the many adopted families that allow me to call them my own, who let me stay with them and use up all their shit and call them in the middle of the night and put garbage on their credit cards when I need to, and I would also like to thank every single person I have ever met in my entire life. Even the assholes. I mean, fuck it: Why not? I had a weirdly hard time working on this dumb book (who even truly knows why—wait I got it, life is miserable!) and I could not have survived writing it without Jennifer Romolini, Lindy West, and Rainbow Rowell, who all gave me very good and useful notes on my very shitty early drafts.

My north stars: Jessie Martinson, Anna Galland, Cara Brigandi, Ted Beranis, Fernando Meza, Caitlin Pinsof, Melissa Fisher, Brooke Allen, Emily Kastner, Katy Maher, Lauren Hoffman, Megan Stielstra, Sarah Rose Etter, and John Sundholm.

I would like to thank my phone; Forest Whitaker; that one pizza place across town; whoever's Starz subscription I continue to relentlessly abuse; those little cans of La Colombe coffee, but only when they're on sale; Nike sweatshirts; Crissle West; those new blue light–filtering Warby Parker glasses; Ben Affleck in *Gone Girl*; a proper bagel; Roto-Rooter; Evanston, Illinois; quilted toilet paper; Ice Cube; *Who? Weekly*; all those Brené Brown books I read to become a better person when I should've just gone to therapy; Desus and/or Mero; our regular UPS guy; independent bookstores; the makers of Chuckles candy; Tom Cruise; and the entire cast and crew of *Succession*.

More people I owe a giant debt of gratitude: Abbi Jacobson, Mya Seals, Tisha Coats, Laura Munroe, Megan Reynolds, Sarah Hill, Greg Mania, Keila Miranda, Marina Hayes, Michael Arceneaux, Alissa Nutting, Laura Daener, Mary H. K. Choi, Mark de la Vergne, Dan Kastner, Kate Bittman, Anna DeVries, Jared Honn, Vanessa Robinson, Emily Barish, Fawzia Mirza, Jenny Greene, Amy Hagedorn, Joanna Parzakonis, Nick Kreiss, Corey Mifsud, and seriously I will just go on listing people until my fingers go numb so let me stop here and just text everybody else.

Endless thanks and love to Kent D. Wolf, my agent and friend and soulmate; everyone at Vintage Books/Anchor Books who let me continue to expose my private parts in public, especially Angelina Venezia and Maria Goldverg, the kindest editor a person could ask for; and all of the copy editors and fact checkers who make sure I don't look like a fucking moron.

I would also like to thank memes; Wendy Williams clips on YouTube; books; Pat Mahomes; my computer; the bartenders at Principle; every hilarious person I follow on Twitter; James Blake's music; hot water; our new cat, Carrots, who is perfect; slipper socks; Ben Affleck in *The Town*; the ResMed AirCurve 10; every writer alive; Luann de Lesseps; pimiento cheese from Zingerman's; these extra-firm pillows I just got that are a lifesaver; Jia Tolentino; flannel sheets; Spotify playlists; the psychic I saw last summer who WAS NOT WRONG; Feline Pine; Eric and Brian at the Honda dealership; all of my inexpensive dental crowns that are still somehow holding on for dear life; *Judge Mathis*; librarians; Erik the mailman; my lady's kids; and Paul Mooney, Bernie Mac, Robin Harris, Mike Epps, and Tori Amos.

Bless James Hagedorn for spending a decade helping me to become who I am and being the best non-dad a person could ask for. And to Mel Winer for seeing me through some of my worst years.

Thank you to my sisters and their children.

Finally, thanks to my lady, who was patient enough to read all the way to the end of this bullshit just to see her name. Best for last, etc., etc. I love you, Kirsten.